Peru

DREAM TRIP

BEN BOX

CONTENTS

In Peru, I have jumped off the cliffs of Miraflores, flying on a giant kite by the balconies of the tower blocks and over the beaches of Lima. I have crossed the Eyebrow of the Mountains and ridden in an overloaded old car from the Pacific lowlands to Lake Titicaca. I joined a group dancing in an inter-village competition in the Yauyos and, even with me, 'our team' won. I have glided in a canoe along the Tambopata River at dusk, accompanied by a flock of sand-coloured nighthawks, and bobbed in a fishing boat surrounded by pelicans and Inca terns.

The big picture of my travels reveals a country within whose borders you can find almost everything that you would associate with South America: Andean peaks and Amazonian rainforest; pre-Columbian pyramids of adobe and stone, colonial cities and contemporary urban fashion; music, dance and mysticism; adventure sports on mountains and sand dunes, whitewater rivers and Pacific rollers.

On closer inspection, though, you will find so many details that cast a new light on the famous images – a light that comes from way, way back. Machu Picchu and the Inca Trail are just a small part of a network of paths, symbols and politics stemming from the myriad cultures that predate the Incas by many centuries. The Spaniards' opulent cathedrals and the annual round of saints' days are infused with pre-Columbian spirituality. Among the perplexing Nazca Lines are birds and monkeys that have no place in the desert, but which are essential to their hidden meaning. Ceviche and pisco sour may be at the top of the food-loving visitor's wish list, but Peruvian chefs are fusing ancient local ingredients with worldwide cuisines to create one of the most innovative gastronomies of today.

To my mind that is the joy of Peru, its inexhaustible supply of revelations and interconnections. On the one hand, archaeologists and botanists are making new finds every year. On the other, you can make your own discoveries at every turn. However you travel, whatever activities you enjoy, open yourself to the meeting of the familiar and the mysterious. Listen to the distant flutes of long-lost civilizations as well as the new urban beats, and before you sip your Inca Kola, offer a drop to Pachamama/Mother Earth to show your respect for all you have seen and what you are about to uncover.

Ben

Inca Ruins, Moray

FIRST STEPS
PUTTING IT ALL TOGETHER

Peru logically falls into two circuits: the south, with Cuzco and the Sacred Valley of the Incas at its heart, and the north. This book focuses on four 21-day routes, two in the south and two in the north. In the absence of frequent direct flights between the two circuits, Lima is the connecting point as well as the start or end point for any tour of the country. You don't have to stay there, but it is a good place to get your bearings before setting out for the adventures beyond. The four suggested itineraries are separate entities, though there is a certain amount of overlap between the two southern and the two northern routes, and both southern routes include Cuzco. To combine the routes requires some jiggling and the inclusion of 'Going further' suggestions, such as travelling overland through the Central Highlands for those with time to make that journey.

To make the most of Peru in a short time you will need to include some flights in your route planning. For example, you could fly from Lima to Cuzco and spend time in the Sacred Valley, then fly to the southeastern jungle and back to Cuzco. Move on to Lake Titicaca, by road or rail, then back overland to Lima via Arequipa and Colca, Nazca and Paracas. From Lima fly north to Iquitos for the Amazon and Pacaya-Samiria National Reserve; fly on again to Tarapoto and travel overland up into the Andes to Chachapoyas, from where you can go by bus direct to the coast at Chiclayo, or, less speedily, to Trujillo via Cajamarca. From Trujillo you can end your explorations in the Cordillera Blanca, or head straight back to Lima by plane or bus.

With fewer flights: head south from Lima through Paracas, Nazca and Arequipa to Lake Titicaca, from where you can move on to Cuzco, then take the new road to Puerto Maldonado in the southeastern jungle. Return to Cuzco and take a bus to Ayacucho, then overland again to Huancayo. By road, carry on to the Cordillera Blanca and down to Trujillo on the Pacific coast. From Trujillo you can either go back to Lima, or head north to Chiclayo, or to Cajamarca, thence to Chachapoyas and on to Tarapoto. To include Iquitos you will have to fly, or take a boat from Yurimaguas. Fly back to Lima.

The only place on any of these trips that cannot be reached by road is Iquitos. So with limitless time (or several visits), you can cover the country with a smallish carbon footprint. This is easier on the budget, too. However you travel, there are hotels to suit all pockets, from top-of-the-range sophistication through boutiques and family-owned hostales to jungle lodges and hostels for party-loving backpackers.

→ DOING IT ALL

Lima → Paracas → Nazca → Arequipa and Colca → Puno and Lake Titicaca → Cuzco and the Sacred Valley of the Incas → Puerto Maldonado and Tambopata → Cuzco → the Central Highlands route to Ayacucho and Huancayo → Huaraz and the Cordillera Blanca → Trujillo → Cajamarca → Chachapoyas direct, or via Chiclayo → Tarapoto → Iquitos → Lima

1 Blankets at a market 2 Boat going down Amazonian River 3 A deep Andean valley 4 Brown-throated sloth

DREAM TRIP 1
LIMA → CUZCO → SOUTHEASTERN JUNGLE

Best time to visit From May to October, Lima has a sea mist (garúa) and temperatures of 8-15ºC. November to April are sunny with temperatures of 30ºC. From June to September, Cuzco is bursting at the seams. June is also the month of the biggest festivals; Corpus Christi, Qoyllur Rit'i and Inti Raymi. Days are generally clear and sunny, but nights can be very cold. The highlands' wettest months are November to April. The dry season in the jungle is April to October. November to April is oppressively hot (40ºC and above) and it rains for a few hours a day.

The airport for Peru is just outside Lima (page 35), at Callao, and almost every international flight lands there. Flight times will probably dictate that you spend one night in the capital, but with Lima's growing reputation as a tourist destination it's worth staying a few days. The historic centre, with fine religious and civic buildings and elaborate wooden balconies, is one of Peru's ten UNESCO World Heritage Sites and is being regenerated. The residential and commercial districts of San Isidro and Miraflores have places to stay to suit all budgets; they also have the best restaurants, parks and museums, as well as good shopping. Barranco, formerly the artists' district, is now well known for its nightlife and a select few hotels. Museums such as the Museo Larco and Museo de la Nación have world-class pre-Columbian collections. There is a far wider choice of restaurants than anywhere other than Cuzco, with excellent standards of cuisine, and the handicraft markets of Miraflores, even if you don't want to make purchases immediately, at least give an idea of what's available elsewhere. Two archaeological sites make worthwhile excursions: Pachacámac (page 47) is a half-day trip, while Caral (page 49), some 185 km north, is one of the earliest cities ever discovered and needs a full day out.

To minimize the ill effects of altitude, either rest for the first day, or go on immediately to the Sacred Valley, some 1000 m lower.

From Lima you fly to Cuzco (page 52). To minimize the ill effects of a rapid rise from sea level to 3310 m altitude, either rest for the first day, or go on immediately to a hotel or hostel in the Sacred Valley (page 65), which is about 1000 m lower, and move up slowly to the city's heights. A priority is to sort out your combined entry ticket, the Boleto Turístico de Cusco, for many of the city's attractions and others in the Sacred Valley. For Machu Picchu (page 72) you must book in advance online (see www.machupicchu.gob.pe) as visitor numbers are restricted. Tickets for the train to Machu Picchu, or for one of the growing number of alternatives to the train, also have to be booked ahead. Likewise, for the Inca Trail (page 76) you must plan long before you arrive, especially in the June-August high season.

1 View of Cuzco   2 Traditionally dressed Peruvian girls   3 Performer at Cuzco street festival   4 Inca Ruins, Inca Trail

An agency can do all the work for you, of course, so you don't have to spend too much precious time on permits and paperwork. The classic Inca Trail is a commitment in terms of time and effort, but there are many alternatives, some much shorter and less demanding, others equally tough.

Fill your days in the mountains with sightseeing and your evenings with fine dining and nightlife. Find a retreat in the valley and enjoy the magnificent scenery. The Incas built the heart of their empire next to majestic mountains they revered, so many of the citadels and outposts to which tourists flock today are in awe-inspiring locations. After a couple of days' acclimatization you will be ready for one or more of the many activities on offer, such as whitewater rafting, trekking, riding or mountain biking.

The third part of this trip descends from the clear skies and cold nights of the mountains to the heat and humidity of the southeastern jungle (page 84). You can go to either the Manu Biosphere Reserve (page 85) or the Tambopata National Reserve (page 85). Birdwatching is superb – in the forest, on undisturbed lakes and at clay licks – and you can see mammals such as giant otters, tapir, primates and, if you are lucky, big cats. Manu's diversity is unrivalled, with ecosystems ranging from cloudforest to flood plains. Visitor numbers are limited and there are only a few lodges, accessible by small plane or road. Tambopata, on the other hand, has a selection of lodges on the Tambopata and Madre de Dios rivers. These are reached by boat from the town of Puerto Maldonado, which receives regular flights.

→ GOING FURTHER

From Cuzco to the Cordillera Blanca without touching the coast, the **Central Highlands route** passes dramatic scenery and remote Inca sites.
→ page 81

1 Giant river otter **2** Manu National Park **3** Fields of gold, Andes **4** Tambopata River **5** Blue and gold Macaws

1 *Salineras* (salt pans), Salinas

Manu Biosphere◆
Reserve

Puerto
Maldonado

Tambopata
National Reserve◆

⑥
⑦ Sacred Valley Lares ⑨
Urubamba Valley
Machu ⑧ ⑤
Picchu Valley Pisac
Ollantaytambo ⑩
Cuzco
Abancay ④

→ WISH LIST

1 Visit the stately Plaza de Armas and Cathedral in Lima, heart of the Spanish colonial empire. 2 The Museo Larco in Lima has one of the finest collections of pre-Columbian ceramics in the country. 3 Fine dining in Lima is a must; choose somewhere specializing in modern Peruvian cuisine. 4 Highlights in Cuzco include: Sacsayhuaman; the Qoricancha/Santo Domingo complex; the Museo Inka; the Plaza de Armas and Cathedral complex. 5 Pisac market and ruins are also popular, but are closer to Cuzco and make a great day out. 6 The Lares Valley is a good destination for trekking between traditional communities. 7 Machu Picchu is everybody's idea of a 'lost city', but visiting today can be as easy or as energetic as you like. 8 The beautiful, man-made Moray colosseums, together with the nearby Salinas salt pans and village of Chinchero are a great day out. 9 Adventure sports include rafting, mountain biking, trekking; many agencies offer trips of varying length and difficulty. 10 The Manu or Tambopata reserves have some of the best wildlife watching in the country.

DREAM TRIP 2
LIMA → CUZCO → TITICACA → SOUTH COAST

After spending a couple of days in Lima and four nights in Cuzco to see the major sites, this route heads south to Lake Titicaca (page 93). There is a tourist train, luxury tourist buses stopping at the main places of interest en route or regular, cheaper buses, and scheduled flights from Cuzco to Juliaca, from where buses or taxis go to Puno. Juliaca is the commercial hub of the area, but bus and train passengers need not stop there.

The main city on the lake is Puno (page 93), a functional place with a comprehensive range of hotels and some famous festivals, such as La Virgen de la Candelaria in February. Good handicrafts, especially woollen goods, can be found in the markets. From the port, boats make frequent trips to the islands (page 97). Included in just about every trip are the 'floating islands', which the Uros build from

1 Virgen de la Candelaria festival 2 Traditional boats, Lake Titicaca 3 Sillustani funerary towers 4 Arequipa

totora reeds, and on the larger islands of Taquile and Amantaní it is usual to stay a night to experience life among the lake-dwelling communities. Another community-based site is Llachón (page 96) on the Capachica Peninsula, where families welcome visitors to their homes. The burial towers at Sillustani (page 96) and the Andean colonial churches along the southern shore at Juli (page 95) and Pomata (page 96) are worthwhile destinations for day trips.

Arequipa (page 101), at the foot of El Misti and Chachani volcanoes, is the White City, so called because of the distinctive volcanic stone used in its construction. You can take a bus from Puno or a flight from Juliaca. Very much the business heart of southern Peru, Arequipa also has some fine colonial treasures, especially Santa Catalina Convent. The Colca Canyon (page 105), surpassed in depth only by its

neighbour, Cotahuasi, is six hours by bus from Arequipa. Improved roads make it quite easy to get to, but note the extreme altitudes on the way (don't be tempted to try a day trip from Arequipa – far too exhausting). You can stay in hostales in the principal towns of Chivay and Cabanaconde, or at upmarket lodges in the canyon. There are many treks, hot springs and, most famous of all, the Cruz del Cóndor, a viewpoint providing a daily spectacle of these majestic birds rising on the morning thermals.

From Arequipa, the road takes you down to the Pacific, where the next stopping place is Nazca (page 110). The enigmatic lines and drawings in the stony desert have attracted many theories over the years, some of them quite bizarre, but whether you are a champion puzzle-solver or not, they deserve to be seen. The best view is from a small plane, but for those not partial to sharp banks and turns there is a platform at ground level that gives as good a view as that of the people who created the lines. Recent discoveries have been made in the region, throwing more light on this mysterious area.

From Nazca it's a short ride north to Ica (page 113), home of Peru's best producers of wine and pisco, the clear brandy used as a base for pisco sour. The other attraction at Ica and its nearby oasis on a

1 Nazca Lines 2 Andean Condor flying above Colca Canyon 3 Huacachina Oasis 4 Cotahuasi Canyon

lake, Huacachina, is exploring the desert – fossil-hunting, sleeping under the stars, or sandboarding down the dunes.

The last stop before returning to Lima is Paracas (page 113), which has replaced the earthquake-shattered but reviving town of Pisco as the centre for visiting the Islas Ballestas (page 114). These islands in the Pacific are one of the prime sites for seeing marine birds. Thousands of them nest on the rocks, which became the world's main source of fertilizer from bird droppings (guano) before it was overtaken by artificial products. On the Paracas Peninsula itself are pre-Inca archaeological remains from the Paracas culture.

Cruz del Cóndor provides a daily spectacle of these majestic birds rising on the morning thermals.

→ GOING FURTHER

Beyond the Toro Muerto petroglyphs is the deepest canyon in the world, **Cotahuasi**, on the Incas' road to the Pacific. → **page 108**

→ ROUTE PLANNER

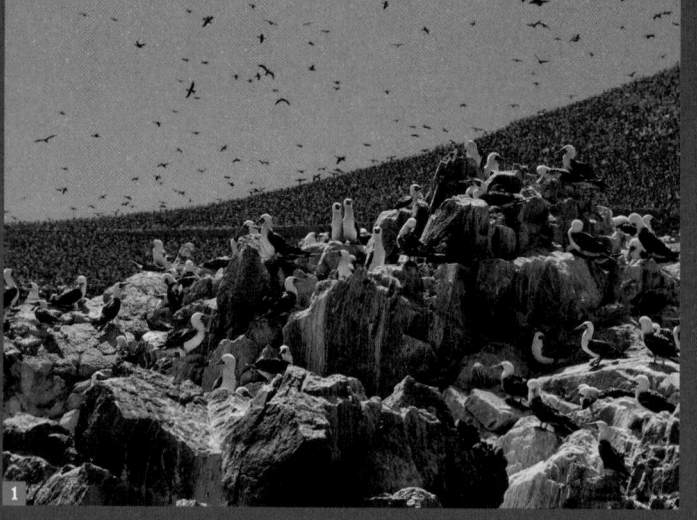

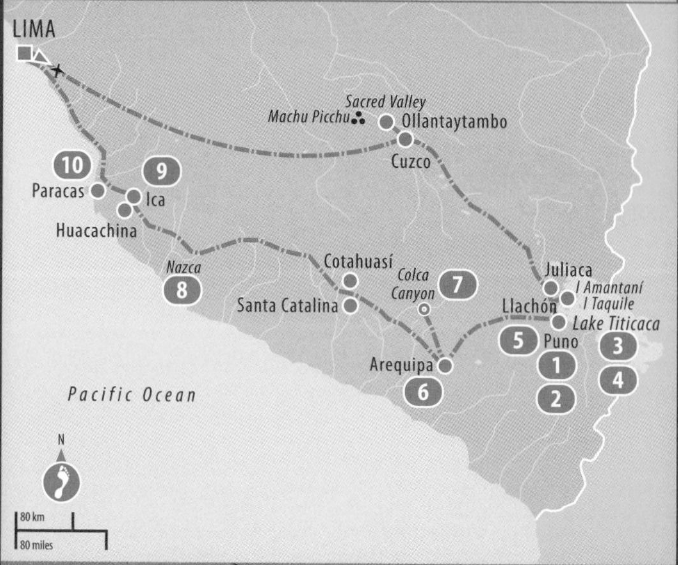
LIMA
Sacred Valley
Machu Picchu
Ollantaytambo
Cuzco
10
9
Paracas
Ica
Huacachina
Nazca
8
Cotahuasí
Colca
Canyon
7
Santa Catalina
Juliaca
I Amantaní
I Taquile
Llachón
Lake Titicaca
5
Puno
3
1
4
2
Arequipa
6
Pacific Ocean
N
80 km
80 miles

1

1 Birds on Islas Ballestas **2** Peruvian woollen hats **3** Vineyards in Ica

→ WISH LIST

1 A festival in Puno, such as La Candelaria in February, is worth catching. **2** Puno's markets are among the best for woollen goods. **3** No trip to Lake Titicaca would be complete without a visit to the communities on the lake's islands of Taquile or Amantaní. **4** *MS Yavari* is a restored lake steamer, now a B&B and museum. **5** The remarkable burial towers at Sillustani are an atmospheric inclusion on a visit to the region. **6** Santa Catalina monastery in Arequipa was for many years a closed community; it is a city in miniature. **7** The Colca Canyon is not only an area of scenic majesty, but also one of the easiest places to see condors. **8** Fly over the Nazca Lines to get the full benefit of these mysterious drawings in the desert. **9** At Ica you can go wine and pisco tasting at one of several bodegas, some traditional, some more modern. **10** The Islas Ballestas are a remarkable sanctuary for marine wildlife.

DREAM TRIP 3 LIMA →
CORDILLERA BLANCA → TRUJILLO → CAJAMARCA

After a four-day visit to Lima you can find a complete change of pace by heading north to the Cordillera Blanca (page 123). This is Peru's main climbing and trekking region in a group of mountain chains, some snowless, others containing some of the highest snow-capped peaks in the Andes. There are several multi-day hikes over high passes, walks to beautiful turquoise lakes and to stands of Puya raimondii (the largest member of the bromeliad family). Two valleys lie beneath the main cordilleras. In the Callejón de Huaylas, between the Cordilleras Blanca and Negra, the main population centres are Huaraz (page 121) and the smaller Caraz (page 127), which serve the tourist trade and many villages the length of the valley. You can limit your stay in the region to the Callejón de Huaylas, or make any number of circuits by road or on foot to the more easterly Cordillera de Conchucos. Here the infrastructure is much less developed, with fewer buses and fewer places to stay. Even though many travellers don't venture far up the eastern flank of the Cordillera Blanca, most do visit Chavín de Huantar (page 125) at its southern end, often as a day trip from Huaraz. Chavín was one of the most significant pre-Inca civilizations in Peru, and the ruins of its dominant city are definitely worth a visit.

There are several multi-day hikes over high passes and walks to beautiful turquoise lakes.

The climbing in the Cordillera Huayhuash is challenging, as massive rock and ice faces rise seemingly sheer out of the green puna.

South of the Cordillera Blanca is the Cordillera Huayhuash (page 121), a mountainous area of great beauty and majesty. The climbing here is challenging, as massive rock and ice faces rise seemingly sheer out of the green puna. Eight to twelve-day treks around the peaks and lakes are testing, but well respected. This is not an expedition to be undertaken lightly, so go with a local agency (or check with one first), find out what conditions are like and be well prepared.

From the highlands, drop back down to the coastal plain and travel north to Trujillo (page 131), one of Peru's best-preserved

1 Rio Santa Valley and Cordillera Huayhuash   **2** The Three Lagoons, Huayhuash trek   **3** Puya raimondii   **4** Trujillo

colonial cities. Many religious and civic buildings can be seen in the centre, which is easy to walk around. Outside the city are some of the most spectacular of Peru's archaeological sites. The Huacas del Sol and de la Luna (page 135), dating from the Moche culture, AD 100-750, reveal new surprises every year and have a brand new site museum. Huaca de la Luna is revealing layer upon layer of polychrome murals and friezes depicting deities and demons, rituals and combat. Between Trujillo and the Pacific stands Chan Chán (page 136), the great adobe city of the Chimú, who were defeated by the Incas in 1450. Only a relatively small portion of this metropolis can be visited, but it is enough to give an idea of the power of the Chimú lords. Another day trip from Trujillo can be made to El Brujo (page 136), 60 km away, with yet more amazing polychrome friezes and the mummy of the tattooed La Señora de Cao (dating from AD 450).

If you have had your fill of ruins, spend a day or two at Huanchaco (page 137), just outside Trujillo, well known for its *caballitos de totora* (reed fishing rafts), surfing and seafood restaurants. Or go further up the coast to Puerto Chicama (page 137), one of Peru's top surfing

1 Reed fishing boats **2** Chan Chán ruins **3** Surfing on the coast **4** Cathedral, Cajamarca **5** Huaca de la Luna

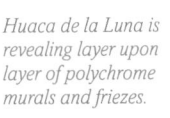

Huaca de la Luna is revealing layer upon layer of polychrome murals and friezes.

beaches. It has a variety of lodges, some of which are open only in season (March-October).

From Trujillo it's an overnight bus ride back to the sierra and the colonial town of Cajamarca (page 141), where the Spaniards inflicted the first major defeat on the Incas. Visitors flock to the room that Inca Atahualpa is supposed to have filled with gold as the ransom to save his life (a pledge Pizarro reneged upon). Good excursions include the Baños del Inca hot springs, several pre-Inca archaeological sites and local dairy farms. From Cajamarca there are direct flights back to Lima, or you can link up with route 4 by taking a bus to Chiclayo.

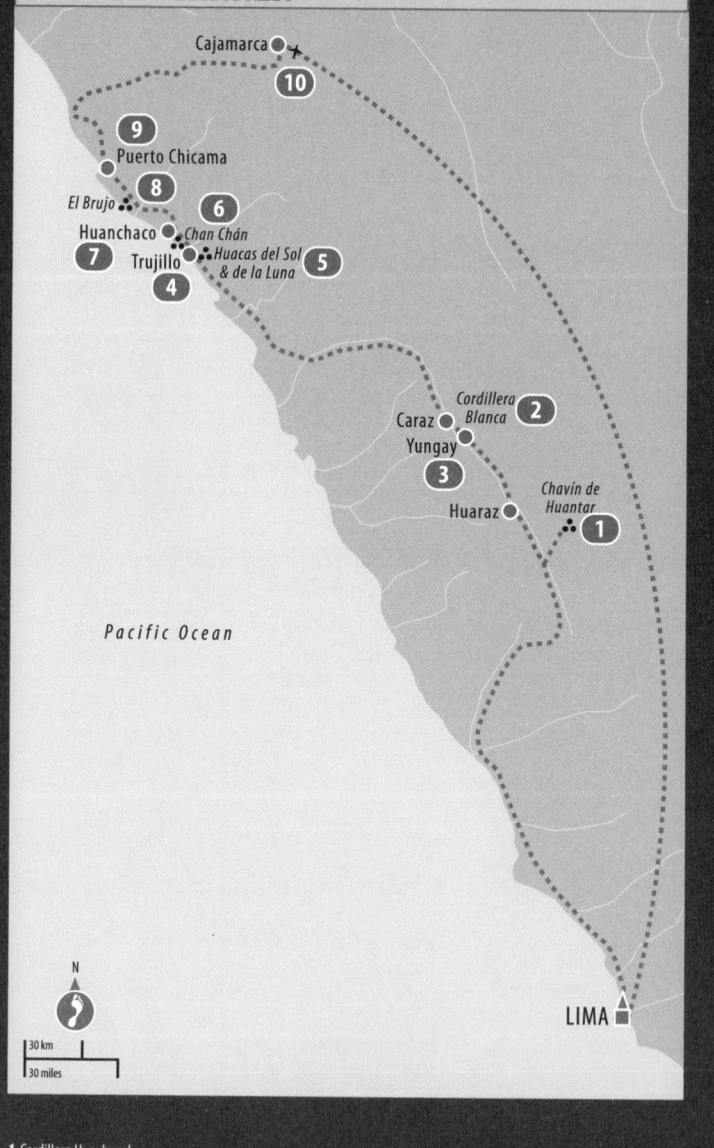

Cajamarca ⑩

⑨ Puerto Chicama

⑧

El Brujo

Huanchaco   Chan Chán   ⑥

⑦   Trujillo   Huacas del Sol   ⑤
          ④   & de la Luna

Cordillera
Caraz   Blanca   ②
Yungay
      ③   Chavín de
Huaraz   Huantar   ①

Pacific Ocean

N

30 km
30 miles

LIMA

1 Cordillera Huayhuash

→ WISH LIST

1 Take a day trip to the ruins of Chavín de Huantar, one of Peru's most important pre-Inca cultures. **2** There are many trekking opportunities in the Cordillera Blanca, some lasting a day, others up to a week. **3** The village of Yungay has been rebuilt after a catastrophic earthquake and avalanche which wiped out almost the entire town. **4** Trujillo has a fine historic centre with some excellent examples of Spanish colonial architecture. **5** The Moche temple of Huaca de la Luna is revealing layer upon layer of polychrome murals and friezes depicting deities and demons, rituals and combat. **6** Chan Chán, the capital of the Chimú Empire, is the largest abode city in the world; it's just outside Trujillo **7** Stop for a seafood lunch and watch the fishermen on their totora-reed rafts at Huanchaco. **8** El Brujo is another archaeological site with remarkable discoveries displayed in a world-class museum. **9** For surfers, the place to go is Puerto Chicama. **10** Outside Cajamarca is the hilltop site of Cumbe Mayo, with a remarkable set of aqueducts.

DREAM TRIP 4 LIMA → CHICLAYO → CHACHAPOYAS → AMAZON JUNGLE

Best time to visit Chiclayo's climate is much the same as Trujillo, if a little hotter, especially from December to April. In Chachapoyas, the dry season is normally May to September. In the wet months roads and trekking trails may become impassable. The dry season in the jungle is April to October and, like the southeast jungle, the wet season, November to April, can be oppressively hot with rain in short, heavy showers. The other feature to note is that the seasons in the Andes affect the Amazon, causing either flooding or significant reductions in water levels. This may bring changes to boat travel.

Whether you are taking this route as a standalone trip from Lima, or carrying on from Cajamarca at the end of route 3, Chiclayo (page 149), the capital of Lambayeque department, makes a good introduction to the far north. While it has few buildings of note, it has a famous traditional medicine section in its municipal market and distinctive cuisine and music. Outside the city, there is yet more evidence of the importance of Peru's coast in the development of pre-Inca culture. In the town of Lambayeque (page 150), 12 km northwest of Chiclayo, are two museums, the Brüning Archaeological Museum and the newer Museo de las Tumbas Reales de Sipán, which give a good overview of the region's archaeological heritage, including collections of some of the sumptuous finds that have been made. The main sites to visit are Sipán (page 152), whose tombs have yielded the undisturbed burial paraphernalia of lords and nobles, Túcume (page 151), with its huge temples, and Sicán (page 151), within the carob forest of Pómac. More cities and pyramids are being excavated all the time, so there is always the possibility of visiting somewhere that has just opened to the public.

As well as the pre-Hispanic attractions, there are coastal towns with long piers and wide beaches where you can watch the fishermen at work, and small towns like Mórrope and Monsefú (page 150), each of which has its own traditions. Chiclayo is also the starting point for the northern birdwatching route, which includes Chaparrí and the white-winged guan centre near Olmos, and which encompasses a wide range of habitats on the road over the Andes to Moyobamba and Tarapoto.

1 A Spectacled bear at Gotca falls   2 Horseriding on Máncora beach   3 Chachapoyan fortress, Kuélap

→ GOING FURTHER

Peruvian holidaymakers head north to **Máncora**, the country's most popular beach resort, with warm waters, safe bathing and good nightlife. → **page 153**

This road climbs up to the Porculla Pass, descends to the Marañón Valley, then rises again to the road junction at Pedro Ruiz. Over the Abra Patricia, the road meanders down to the Amazon lowlands (see below), but a road south from Pedro Ruiz enters the lands of the Chachapoyans, the Cloud People. Here are the remains of a singular culture: huge fortresses of stone like Kuélap (page 158), sarcophagi staring across cloud-covered hillsides, burial chambers perched on ledges and in caves that even modern climbers find difficult to reach. This is also a region of waterfalls, one of which, Gocta (page 160), 771 m high, is rapidly becoming a major tourist attraction. The main town in the area is Chachapoyas (page 156), with a full range of services but no flights. From Chachapoyas you can continue south to Leymebamba (page 158), which has one of the region's most important museums, displaying the finds from Laguna de los Cóndores. If you are travelling slowly there are many more ruins to visit.

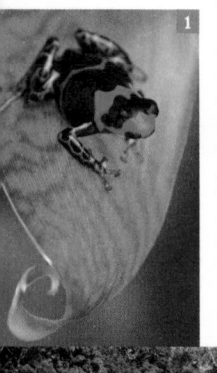

Back at Chachapoyas, retrace your steps to Pedro Ruíz to take the beautiful road that goes over the 'Eyebrow of the Mountain' to the hotter, drier zones of San Martín department. It is best to hop from town to town in shared taxis or minivans. Moyobamba (page 163) is the orchid capital, while Tarapoto (page 164), almost the end of the road, has various nearby attractions. From Tarapoto there are two routes into the Amazon jungle. Either fly to Iquitos (page 166), or carry on by bus to Yurimaguas and catch a river boat to Iquitos. Between Yurimaguas and Iquitos is one of Peru's largest national parks, Pacaya-Samiria (page 164), an area of rivers and forest with abundant wildlife. Tours last from three to seven days (one-day visits are possible) and can be taken from river ports close to the park or from Iquitos. Iquitos itself is the Amazonian river port par excellence, with a riverside malecón (promenade), market and a few buildings dating back to the city's heyday as the centre of the rubber boom. Many lodges offer jungle accommodation for one to four nights; some are close at hand, others more remote.

1 Poison dart frog **2** Floating house on Amazon river **3** Emperor tamarin **4** Buttressed tree in the Amazon

Punta Sal
Máncora

Amazon jungle

9 Iquitos
10

8
Reserva Nacional
Pacaya-Samiria

6
Pedro Ruíz   Moyobamba
3   Revash   *Gocta*
2   *Sicán*   Chachapoyas
Túcume   *Chaparrí*   *Kuélap*   Tarapoto
Lambayeque   *Reserve*   5   Leymebamba
Chiclayo   *Sipán*   4   7
1

Pacific Ocean

N

80 km
80 miles

LIMA

1 Reflection in the Amazon river 2 Cock-on-the-Rock perching 3 Gotca waterfall

→ **WISH LIST**

1 The traditional section of Chiclayo's Mercado Modelo has plenty of surprises. **2** The museums in the colonial town of Lambayeque display the recent sumptuous finds from nearby archaeological sites. **3** Among the pyramid sites of the region, Sicán, in the carob forest of Pómac, is a good place to visit on horseback from Rancho Santana. **4** The Chaparrí ecolodge is a private conservation area with first-class bird and mammal watching in a number of habitats. **5** Kuélap, the massive fortress of the Chachapoyas people, is an awe-inspiring place. **6** Recently opened to tourism, the Gocta waterfall is one of the highest in the world. **7** The Laguna de los Cóndores museum in Leymebamba not only houses a collection of items from a remote burial site, but is also a true artisan construction. **8** Pacaya-Samiria is one of Peru's largest national parks, visited by boat from a number of entry points. **9** Lodges around Iquitos offer a variety of packages for experiencing the Amazonian jungle. **10** Whether in the dry forest around Chiclayo, in the high Andean regions or in the rainforest, birdwatching is truly rewarding in northern Peru.

Machu Picchu

DREAM TRIP 1
Lima→Cuzco→Southeastern Jungle 21 days

Lima 4 nights, page 35

Sacred Valley 2 nights, page 65
Flight from Lima to Cuzco (1 hr 20 mins)
then bus from Cuzco via Pisac (1 hr)
to Sacred Valley (45 mins-1½ hrs
depending on where you are staying)

Cuzco 3 nights, page 52
Car/bus from Pisac or Sacred Valley (1-2 hrs
depending on where you are staying)

Inca Trail (or Lares Valley) 4 nights,
page 76
Transport from Cuzco (3½ hrs to
the start of the classic Inca Trail)

Ollantaytambo en route, page 69
Bus from Cuzco (1½ hrs)

Machu Picchu 2 nights, page 72
Afternoon train from Ollantaytambo (1½ hrs)

Cuzco 1 night, page 52
Train from Aguas Calientes to
Ollantaytambo (1½ hrs) and bus
from Ollantaytambo (1½ hrs)

**Manu OR Tambopata National
Reserve** 4 nights, page 85
Flight from Cuzco to Bocu Manu
or Puerto Maldonado (45-55 mins)

Lima 1 night, page 35
Flight from Bocu Manu to Cuzco (45 mins)
then from Cuzco (1 hr 20 mins) or flight
from Puerto Maldonado (2¾-3 hrs)

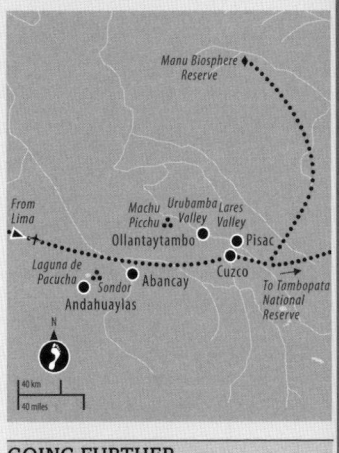

GOING FURTHER

The Central Highlands route page 81
Bus from Cuzco to the Cordillera
Blanca via Abancay and Ayacucho
(48 hrs without stops)

DREAM TRIP 1
Lima→Cuzco→Southeastern Jungle

The centrepiece of this trip is Cuzco and the Sacred Valley of the Incas. It includes the most iconic of 'lost cities', Machu Picchu, the revered landscapes of the greatest of South American civilizations, and the Spanish colonial masterpieces that attempted to rival the Incas' glory. Here you will find not only wonderful historical treasures but also present-day cultural riches, in festivals that combine pre-Hispanic and Christian beliefs and many traditional industries. Cuzco and its surroundings have some of the country's best hotels, shops and restaurants, first-class guides and tour operators. Unsurprisingly, the city is the prime destination for most visitors to Peru.

Don't rush up to the highlands, though. Begin your dream trip in Lima, a vast city spreading over coastal desert and hills. Ruined pyramids are scattered through the city, notably the pre-Inca shrine of Pachacámac. While this is very different from the stone monuments of the Sierra, Lima's museums and private collections can put the archaeology into context. The colonial centre, with its grand Plaza de Armas and wooden balconies, is being regenerated. In thriving Miraflores, the more refined San Isidro and bohemian Barranco, you can seek out Lima's own culture, especially the music and an endless array of restaurants that have earned it the title 'Gastronomic Capital of the Americas'.

To complete this survey of the quintessential Peru, cross the Andes from Cuzco to the rainforests of the southeast. The hot and humid lowlands have always been a source of important trade for the people of the Sierras, but also a region of mystery. Flights, boats, and a new paved road bring the jungles closer to the cosmopolitan world. It is easy to find a lodge to stay at, with nature treks, canopy walkways, river trips and wildlife watching all included.

LIMA

Lima stands between the Pacific Ocean and the dusty ranges that eventually lead up to the Andes. Great efforts are being made to regenerate the historic centre, which is based around the Plaza de Armas and is a reminder of how Lima was in its heyday, the Spaniards' City of Kings. The commercial heart has long gone, moved to suburbs such as San Isidro and Miraflores, but even here you will come across pre-Columbian monuments that are being restored. Lima has some of the finest museums in the country and its food, drink and nightlife are second to none. It is a huge city, ever-developing and fast-paced, in practice often snarled up with traffic. From November to April it is bright and sunny, but for the rest of the year it is shrouded in fog that rolls in from the sea. Affluent suburbs have for neighbours the pueblos jóvenes, which sprawl over the sandy hills overlooking the city. For all its contrasts, though, Lima is the best place to get your bearings and prepare for exploring the rest of the country.

→ ARRIVING IN LIMA

GETTING THERE

All international flights land at Jorge Chávez **Airport**, 16 km northwest of the Plaza de Armas. Transport into town by taxi or bus is easy. If arriving in the city by **bus**, most of the recommended companies have their terminals just south of the centre, many on Avenida Carlos Zavala. This is not a safe area and you should take a taxi to and from there. For further information, see page 182.

MOVING ON

Scheduled flights to **Cuzco** (see page 52) from Lima's Jorge Chávez international airport take one hour 20 minutes.

If you are moving on to **Huaraz**, LC Perú (www.lcperu.pe) has daily one-hour flights from Jorge Chávez Airport. Many bus companies run between Lima and Huaraz, taking seven to eight hours. You could break the journey to visit the ruins at Caral (see page 49) but this would include several changes. Each company has its own terminal in Lima and in Huaraz.

Scheduled flights from Jorge Chávez airport to **Chiclayo** (see page 149) take 1½ hours.

GETTING AROUND

Downtown Lima can be explored on foot by day; at night a taxi is safest. Miraflores is 15 km south of the centre. Many of the better hotels and restaurants are here and in neighbouring San Isidro. Three types of bus provide an extensive public transport system: buses, combis (mid-size) and colectivos (mini-vans or cars). Colectivos run from 0600-0100, and less frequently through the night; they are quicker and stop wherever requested. Buses and combis charge about US$0.40; colectivos a little more. On public holidays, Sunday and from 2400 to 0500 every night, a small charge is added to the fare. None is particularly safe; it is better to take a taxi; all vehicles stop when flagged down. Termini of public transport vehicles are posted above the windscreens, with the route written on the side.

The Metropolitano is a system of articulated buses running on dedicated lanes of the Vía Expresa/Paseo de la República ① *T01-203 9000, www.metropolitano.com.pe*. The Estación Central is in front of the Sheraton hotel in the Paseo de la República. The southern section runs to Matellini in Chorrillos (estimated journey time 32 minutes). For Miraflores take stations between Angamos and 28 de Julio; for Barranco, Bulevar is 170 m from the Plaza. The northern branch runs to Naranjal in Comas, a 34-minute journey. Stations between Estación Central and Ramón Castilla serve the city centre. Tickets are prepaid and rechargeable, from S/.5-100, each journey is S/.2 (US$0.75). Buses run daily from 0600-2150. Monday to Friday 0700-0930, 1700-2030 an express service between Estación Central and Matellini calls at just 10 stations. Buses are packed in rush hour. However good the public transport system or smart your taxi, one thing is unavoidable: Lima's roads are congested almost throughout the whole day. Allow plenty of time to get from A to B and be patient.

There is also an electric railway system, the Metro. The first line, from San Juan de Lurigancha in the north to Villa El Salvador in the south, is in operation. An east-west line, from ATE to Callao, is planned.

In Lima, a *jirón* (often abbreviated to Jr) refers to a long street, made up of several blocks, each with its own name. Street corner signs bear both names, of the *jirón* and of the block.

BEST TIME TO VISIT
Only 12° south of the equator, one would expect a tropical climate, but Lima has two distinct seasons. The winter is May to November, when a *garúa* (Scotch mist) hangs over

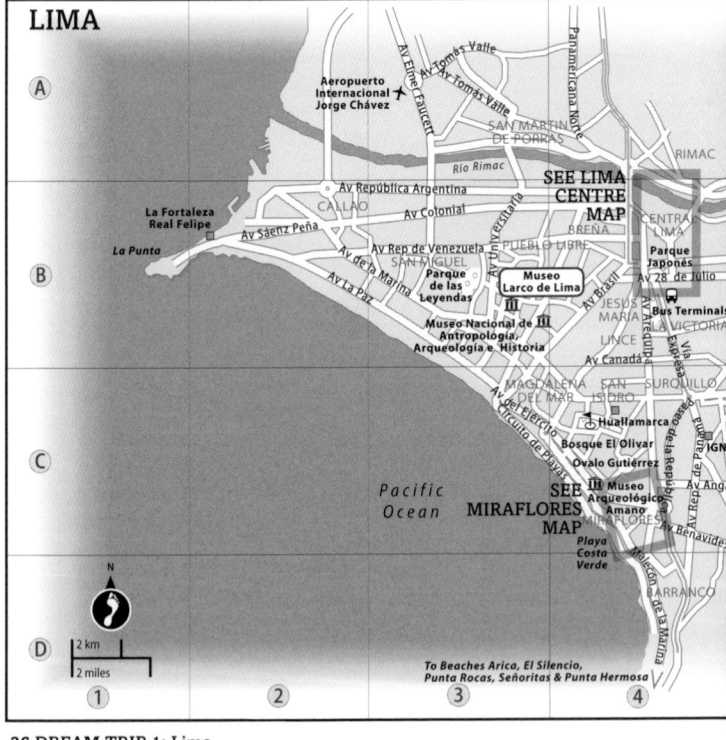

the city, making everything look grey. It is damp and cold, 8-15°C. The sun breaks through around November and temperatures rise to as high as 30°C. Note that the temperature in the coastal suburbs is lower than in the centre because of the sea's influence. Protect against the sun's rays when visiting the beaches around Lima, or elsewhere in Peru.

TOURIST INFORMATION

i perú has offices at **Jorge Chávez International Airport** ⓘ *T01-574 8000, open 24 hrs;* **Casa Basadre** ⓘ *Av Jorge Basadre 610, San Isidro, T01-421 1627, Mon-Fri 0830-1830;* and **Larcomar shopping centre** ⓘ *Módulo 10, Plaza Principal, Miraflores, T01-445 9400, Mon-Fri 1100-1300, 1400-2000.* There is a **Municipal tourist kiosk** on Pasaje Ribera el Viejo, behind the Municipalidad, near the Plaza de Armas, www.munlima.gob.pe. Ask about guided walks in the city centre. There are eight **Miraflores kiosks**: Parque Central; Parque Salazar; Parque del Amor; González Prada y Avenida Petit Thouars; Avenida R Palma y Avenida Petit Thouars; Avenida Larco y Avenida Benivides; Huaca Pucllana; and Ovalo Gutiérrez. **South American Explorers** ⓘ *Enrique Palacios 956 (new address from Aug 2013), Miraflores, write to saelima@gmail.com for details of phone numbers, www.saexplorers.org.* For an English website, see www.limaeasy.com.

HISTORY OF LIMA

Lima, capital of Peru, is built on both sides of the Río Rímac, at the foot of Cerro San Cristóbal. It was originally named *La Ciudad de Los Reyes*, in honour of the Magi, at its founding by conquistador Francisco Pizarro in 1535. From then until the independence of the South American republics in the early 19th century, it was the chief city of Spanish South America. The name Lima, a corruption of the Quechua name *Rimac* (speaker), was not adopted until the end of the 16th century.

The Universidad de San Marcos was founded in 1551, and a printing press in 1595, both among the earliest of their kind in South America. Lima's first theatre opened in 1563, and the Inquisition was introduced in 1569 (it was not abolished until 1820). For some time the Viceroyalty of Peru embraced Colombia, Ecuador, Bolivia, Chile and Argentina. There were few cities in the Old World that could rival Lima's power, wealth and luxury, which was at its height during the 17th and early 18th centuries. The city's wealth attracted many freebooters and in 1670 a protecting wall 11 km long was built round it (demolished in 1869). The earthquake of 1746 destroyed

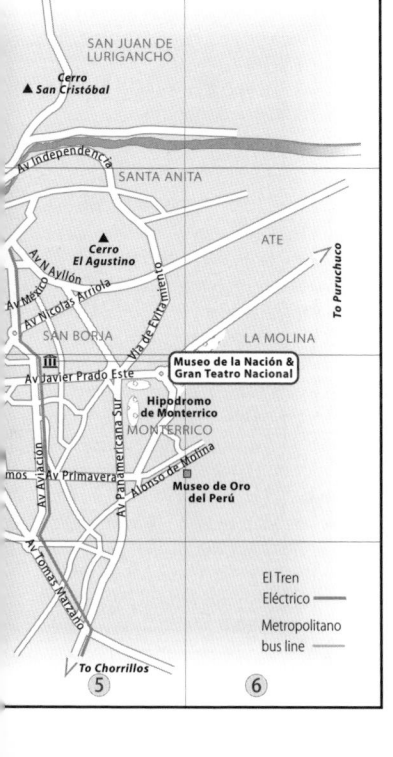

SAN JUAN DE
LURIGANCHO

Cerro
▲ **San Cristóbal**

Av Independencia

SANTA ANITA

▲ **Cerro**
El Agustino

ATE

Av N Ayllón

Av Metro

Av Nicolás Arriola

Vía de Evitamiento

To Puruchuco

SAN BORJA

LA MOLINA

Av Javier Prado Este

Museo de la Nación &
Gran Teatro Nacional

Hipódromo
de Monterrico

MONTERRICO

Panamericana Sur

mos

Av Primavera

Av Aviación

Alonso de Molina

Museo de Oro
del Perú

Av Tomás Marzano

| El Tren Eléctrico | ——— |
| Metropolitano bus line | ——— |

To Chorrillos

5   6

all but 20 houses, killed 4000 inhabitants and ended Lima's pre-eminence. It was only comparatively recently, with the coming of industry, that the city began to change into what it is today.

Modern Lima is seriously affected by smog for much of the year, and is surrounded by *pueblos jóvenes*, 'young towns', or settlements of squatters who have migrated from the Sierra. Villa El Salvador, a few kilometres southeast of Lima, may be the world's biggest 'squatters' camp' with 350,000 people, who have been building up an award-winning self-governing community since 1971.

Over the years the city has changed out of recognition. Many of the hotels and larger business houses have relocated to the fashionable suburbs of Miraflores and San Isidro, thus moving the commercial heart of the city away from the Plaza de Armas.

Half of the town-dwellers of Peru now live in Lima. The metropolitan area contains 8.2 million people, nearly one-third of the country's total population, and two-thirds of its industries. Callao, Peru's major port, runs into Lima; it is a city in its own right, with over one million inhabitants. Within its boundaries is the Jorge Chávez Airport. The docks handle 75% of the nation's imports and some 25% of its exports. Callao has a serious theft problem – avoid being there in the evening.

→ PLACES IN LIMA

The traditional heart of the city, at least in plan, is still what it was in colonial days. An increasing number of buildings in the centre are being restored and the whole area is being given a new lease of life as the architectural beauty and importance of the Cercado (as it is known) is recognized. Most of the tourist attractions are in this area. Some museums are only open 0900-1300 from January-March, and some are closed in January.

PLAZA DE ARMAS

One block south of the Río Rímac lies the Plaza de Armas, which has been declared a World Heritage Site by UNESCO. Running along two sides are arcades with shops: Portal de Escribanos and Portal de Botoneros. In the centre of the plaza is a bronze fountain dating from 1650. The **Palacio de Gobierno**, on the north side of the Plaza, stands on the site of the original palace built by Pizarro. The changing of the guard is at 1200. To take a tour register two days in advance at the Oficina de Turismo (ask guard for directions); the free, 45-minute tours are in Spanish and English Monday-Friday, 0830-1300, 1400-1730. The **Cathedral** ① *T01-427 9647, Mon-Fri 0900-1700, Sat 1000-1300. Entry to cathedral US$3.65, ticket also including Museo Arzobispado US$11*, was reduced to rubble in the earthquake of 1746. The reconstruction, on the lines of the original, was completed in 1755. Note the splendidly carved stalls (mid-17th century), the silver-covered altars surrounded by fine woodwork, mosaic-covered walls bearing the coats of arms of Lima and Pizarro and an allegory of Pizarro's commanders, the 'Thirteen Men of Isla del Gallo'. The remains of Francisco Pizarro, found in the crypt, lie in a small chapel, the first on the right of the entrance. The **Museo de Arte Religioso**, in the cathedral, has sacred paintings, portraits, altarpieces and other items, as well as a café and toilets. Next to the cathedral is the **Archbishop's Palace** and museum ① *Mon-Sat 0900-1700, T01-427 5790, www.palacio arzobispaldelima.com*, rebuilt in 1924, with a superb wooden balcony. Permanent and temporary exhibitions are open to the public.

AROUND THE PLAZA DE ARMAS

Just behind the Municipalidad de Lima is **Pasaje Ribera el Viejo**, which has been restored and is now a pleasant place, with several good cafés with outdoor seating. Nearby is the **Casa Solariega de Aliaga** ① *Unión 224, T01-427 7736, www.casadealiaga.com, Mon-Fri*

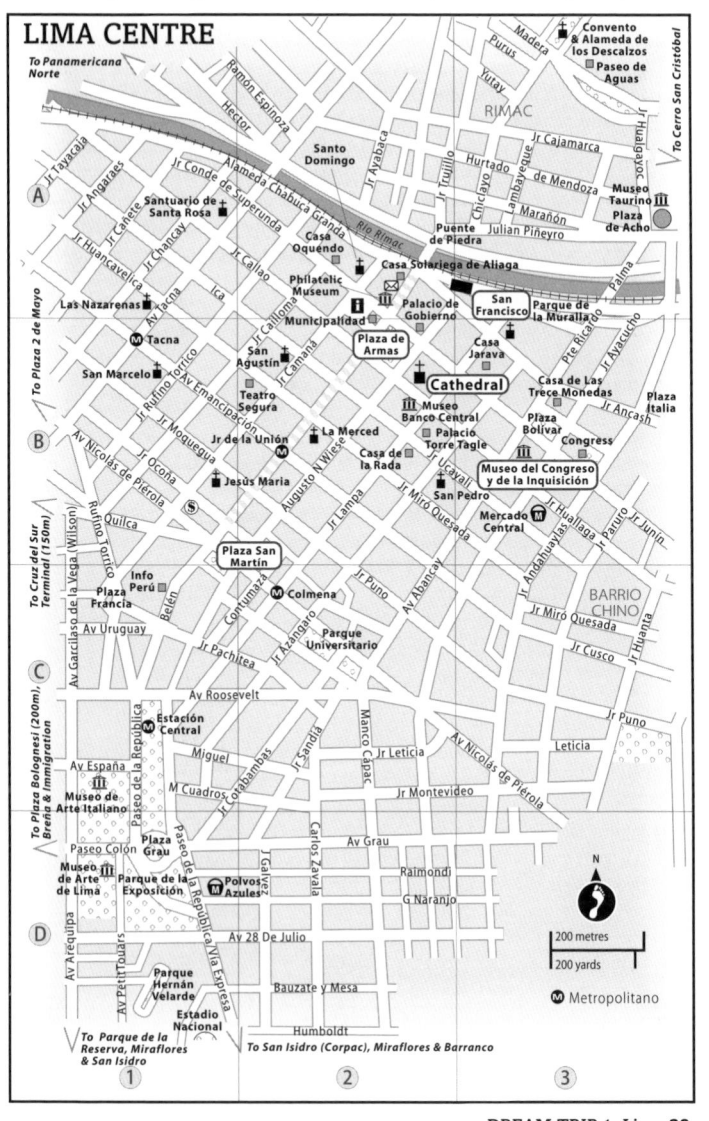

LIMA CENTRE

0930-1300, 1430-1745, US$11, knock on the door and wait to see if anyone will let you in, or contact in advance for tour operators who offer guided visits. It is still occupied by the Aliaga family and is open to the public and for functions. The house contains what is said to be the oldest ceiling in Lima and is furnished entirely in the colonial style.

The baroque church of **San Francisco** ① *on the 1st block of Jr Lampa, corner of Ancash, a few blocks from the Plaza de Armas, T01-427 1381, daily 0930-1645, guided tours only, US$1.65, US$0.50 children,* was finished in 1674 and withstood the 1746 earthquake. The nave and aisles are lavishly decorated in Mudéjar style. The monastery is famous for the Sevillian tilework and panelled ceiling in the cloisters (1620). The Catacombs under the church and part of the monastery are well worth seeing. The late 16th-century **Casa de Jarava** or **Pilatos** ① *Jr Ancash 390,* is opposite San Francisco church. Close by, **Casa de las Trece Monedas** ① *Jr Ancash 536,* still has the original doors and window grilles. **Parque de la Muralla** ① *open 0900-2000,* on the south bank of the Rímac, incorporates a section of the old city wall, and has fountains, stalls and street performers. There is a cycle track, toilets and places to eat both inside and near the entrance on Calle de la Soledad.

The **Palacio Torre Tagle** ① *Jr Ucayali 363, Mon-Fri during working hours,* built in 1735, is the city's best surviving example of secular colonial architecture. Today, it is used by the Foreign Ministry, but visitors are allowed to enter courtyards to inspect the fine, Moorish-influenced wood-carving in balconies and wrought iron work. **Casa de la Rada**, or **Goyoneche** ① *Jr Ucayali 358,* opposite, is a fine mid-18th-century French-style town house which now belongs to a bank. The patio and first reception room are open occasionally to the public. **Museo Banco Central de Reserva** ① *Jr Ucayali at Jr Lampa, T01-613 2000 ext 2655, Tue-Fri 1000-1630, Wed 1000-1900, Sat-Sun 1000-1300, free, photography prohibited,* is a large collection of pottery from the Vicus or Piura culture (AD 500-600) and gold objects from Lambayeque, as well as 19th and 20th-century paintings: both sections highly recommended. **San Pedro** ① *3rd block of Jirón Ucayali, Mon-Sat 0930-1145, 1700-1800,* finished by Jesuits in 1638, has marvellous altars with Moorish-style balconies, rich gilded wood carvings in choir and vestry, and tiles throughout. Several Viceroys are buried here; the bell called La Abuelita, first rung in 1590, sounded the Declaration of Independence in 1821.

Between Avenida Abancay and Jirón Ayacucho is **Plaza Bolívar**, where General José de San Martín proclaimed Peru's independence. The plaza is dominated by the equestrian statue of the Liberator. Behind lies the Congress building, which occupies the former site of the Universidad de San Marcos; visit recommended. Behind the Congress is Barrio Chino, with many *chifas* and small shops selling oriental items. **Museo del Congreso y de la Inquisición** ① *Plaza Bolívar, C Junín 548, near the corner of Av Abancay, T311 7777, ext 5160, www.congreso.gob.pe/museo.htm, daily 0900-1700, free, students offer to show you round for a tip; good explanations in English.* The main hall, with a splendidly carved mahogany ceiling, remains untouched. The Court of Inquisition was held here from 1584; from 1829-1938 it was used by the Senate. In the basement there is a recreation *in situ* of the gruesome tortures. A description in English is available at the desk.

The 16th-century **Santo Domingo church and monastery** ① *T01-427 6793, monastery and tombs open Mon-Sat 0900-1230, 1500-1800; Sun and holidays morning only, US$1.65,* is on the first block of Jirón Camaná. The Cloister, one of the most attractive, dates from 1603. The second Cloister is less elaborate. Beneath the sacristy are the tombs of San Martín de Porres, one of Peru's most revered saints, and Santa Rosa de Lima (see below).

In 1669, Pope Clement presented the alabaster statue of Santa Rosa in front of the altar. Behind Santo Domingo is **Alameda Chabuca Granda**, named after one of Peru's greatest singers. In the evening there are free art and music shows and you can sample foods from all over Peru. A couple of blocks beyond Santo Domingo is **Casa de Osambela** or **Oquendo** ⓘ *Conde de Superunda 298, T01-427 7987. Ask Lizardo Retes Bustamante (lizardo-retes@hotmail.com) if you can visit.* It is said that José de San Martín stayed here after proclaiming independence from Spain. The house is typical of Lima secular architecture with two patios, a broad staircase leading from the lower to the upper floor, fine balconies and an observation tower. It is now the Centro Cultural Inca Garcilaso de la Vega and headquarters of various academies. A few blocks west is **Santuario de Santa Rosa** ⓘ *Av Tacna, 1st block, T01-425 1279, daily 0930-1300, 1500-1800, free to the grounds,* a small but graceful church and pilgrimage centre; here are preserved the hermitage built by Santa Rosa herself, the house in which she was born, a section of the house in which she attended to the sick, her well, and other relics.

San Agustín ⓘ *Jr Ica 251, T01-427 7548, daily 0830-1130, 1630-1900, ring for entry,* is west of the Plaza de Armas: its façade (1720) is a splendid example of churrigueresque architecture. There are carved choir stalls and effigies, and a sculpture of Death, said to have frightened its maker into an early grave. The church has been restored after the last earthquake, but the sculpture of Death is in storage. **Las Nazarenas church** ⓘ *Av Tacna, 4th block, T01-423 5718, daily 0700-1200, 1600-2000,* is built around an image of Christ Crucified painted by a liberated slave in 1655. This, the most venerated image in Lima, and an oil copy of El Señor de los Milagros (Lord of Miracles), encased in a gold frame, are carried on a silver litter, the whole weighing nearly a ton, through the streets on 18, 19, and 28 October and again on 1 November (All Saints' Day). *El Comercio* newspaper and local pamphlets give details of times and routes.

NORTHEAST OF PLAZA DE ARMAS

From the Plaza, passing the Palacio de Gobierno on the left, straight ahead is the **Desamparados** railway station, which now houses fascinating exhibitions on Peruvian themes. **The Puente de Piedra**, behind the Palacio de Gobierno, is a Roman-style stone bridge built in 1610, crossing the Río Rímac to the district of that name. On Jirón Hualgayoc is the bullring in the **Plaza de Acho**, inaugurated on 20 January 1766, with the **Museo Taurino** ⓘ *Hualgayoc 332, T01-482 3360, Mon-Sat 0800-1600, US$1, students US$0.50, photography US$2.* Apart from matador's relics, the museum contains good collections of paintings and engravings, some of the latter by Goya. There are two bullfight seasons: October to first week in December and during July. The **Convento de Los Descalzos** ⓘ *on the Alameda de Los Descalzos in Rímac, T01-481 0441, daily 1000-1300, 1500-1800, except Tue, US$1, guided tour only, 45 mins in Spanish (worth it),* was founded in 1592. It contains over 300 paintings of the Cuzco, Quito and Lima schools, which line the four main cloisters and two ornate chapels. The chapel of El Carmen was constructed in 1730 and is notable for its baroque gold leaf altar. The museum shows the life of the Franciscan friars during colonial and early republican periods. The cellar, infirmary, pharmacy and a typical cell have been restored.

Cerro San Cristóbal dominates downtown Lima and can be visited on a one-hour minibus tour, departing from in front of Santo Domingo (Camaná y Conde Superunda, daily 1000-2100; departures every 15 minutes, US$3). It includes a look at the run-down

Rímac district, passes the Convento de los Descalzos (see above), ascends the hill through one of the city's oldest shanties with its brightly painted houses and spends about 20 minutes at the summit, where there is a small museum and café. Excellent views on a clear day. The second half of the trip is a historical tour. **Urbanito** buses ① *T01-424 3650, www.urbanito.com.pe, 3 hrs, weekends and holidays*, also run from the Plaza de Armas on a tour of central Lima, which includes Cerro San Cristóbal.

BARRIO CHINO

East of the historic centre of Lima in the district of Barrios Altos, next to the Mercado Central, is Lima's Chinatown (*Barrio Chino*). Peru is home to the largest population of first-generation Chinese in all of Latin America. Chinese people born in Peru (referred to as 'Tu-San') number more than a million. Some of the first immigrants arrived at the port of Callao in 1849 from the Chinese provinces of Canton and Fukien to work the coastal fields, replacing the black slaves given their freedom by then-president Ramón Castilla in 1851. More Chinese began to arrive, settling in the north in Chiclayo, Trujillo and the jungle town of Iquitos.

On the seventh block of Jirón Ucayali is the locally famous **Portada China**, the arch that stretches across the street and is the gateway to Chinatown. It was a gift from the Chinese government, officially inaugurated by Lima mayor Alberto Andrade in July 1997.

There are many good Chinese restaurants here, some of which have branches elsewhere in the city.

SOUTH OF PLAZA DE ARMAS

The Jirón de la Unión, the main shopping street, runs to the Plaza de Armas. It has been converted into a pedestrian precinct, which teems with life in the evening. In the two blocks south of Jirón de la Unión, known as Calle Belén, several shops sell souvenirs and curios. **La Merced** ① *Unión y Miró Quesada, T01-427 8199, 0800-1245, 1600-2000 (Sun 0700-1300, 1600-2000); monastery daily 0800-1200 and 1500-1730*, is in Plazuela de la Merced. The first Mass in Lima was said here on the site of the first church to be built. The restored façade is a fine example of colonial Baroque. Inside are some magnificent altars and the tilework on some of the walls is noteworthy. A door from the right of the nave leads into the Monastery. The cloister dates from 1546. Jirón de la Unión leads to **Plaza San Martín**, which has a statue of San Martín in the centre. The plaza has been restored and is now a nice place to sit and relax.

Museo de Arte Italiano ① *Paseo de la República 250, T01-423 9932, Tue-Fri 0900-1900, Sat-Sun 1100-1700, US$1*, is in a wonderful neoclassical building, given by the Italian colony to Peru on the centenary of its independence. Note the remarkable mosaic murals on the outside. It consists of a large collection of Italian and other European works of art and houses the Instituto de Arte Contemporáneo, which has many exhibitions.

Museo de Arte de Lima ① *Paseo Colón 125, T204 0000, www.mali.pe, Tue-Sun 1000-2000, Sat 1000-1700, US$2.25 minimum, US$4.50 suggested, children, students and over-65s US$1.50, guides US$1.15, bilingual guides available 1030-1600, signs in English*, is in the Palacio de la Exposición, built in 1868 in Parque de la Exposición (designed by Gustave Eiffel). There are more than 7000 exhibits, giving a chronological history of Peruvian cultures and art from the Paracas civilization up to today. It includes excellent examples of 17th- and 18th-century Cuzco paintings, a beautiful display of carved furniture, heavy silver and jewelled stirrups and also pre-Columbian pottery. The Filmoteca (movie club) is on the premises and shows films just about every night. See the local paper for details, or look in the museum itself. The **Gran Parque Cultural de Lima** ⓘ *0800-2030,* is in the grounds. Inaugurated in January 2000, this large park has an amphitheatre, Japanese garden, food court and children's activities. Relaxing strolls through this green, peaceful and safe oasis in the centre of Lima are recommended.

In **Parque de la Reserva** is the **Circuito Mágico del Agua** ⓘ *block 8 of Av Arequipa and going up towards the centre, Santa Beatriz, www.munlima.gob.pe/lugares-de-recreacion/, Wed-Sun and holidays 1600-2200, US$1.50,* a display of 13 fountains, the highest reaching 80 m, enhanced by impressive light and music shows four times a night, great fun and very popular.

SAN BORJA AND SURCO

Museo de la Nación ⓘ *Javier Prado Este 2465, T01-476 9875, Tue-Sun 0900-1700, closed major public holidays, US$2.50. 50% discount with ISIC card,* in the huge Banco de la Nación building, is the museum for the exhibition and study of the art and history of the aboriginal races of Peru. There are good explanations in Spanish and English on Peruvian history, with ceramics, textiles and displays of many ruins in Peru. It is arranged so that you can follow the development of Peruvian precolonial history through to the time of the Incas. A visit is recommended before you go to see the archaeological sites themselves. There are displays of the tomb of the Señor de Sipán, artefacts from Batán Grande near Chiclayo (Sicán culture), reconstructions of the friezes found at Huaca La Luna and Huaca El Brujo, near Trujillo, and of Sechín and other sites. Temporary exhibitions are held in the basement, where there is also a Ministerio de Cultura bookshop. The museum has a cafeteria. To get there, take a taxi from downtown Lima or Miraflores, US$3.20. From Av Garcilaso de la Vega in downtown Lima take a combi with a "Javier Prado/Aviación" window sticker. Get off at the 21st block of Javier Prado at Av Aviación. From Miraflores take a bus down Av Arequipa to Av Javier Prado (27th block), then take a bus with a "Todo Javier Prado" or "Aviación" window sticker.

The **Museo de Oro del Perú** ⓘ *Alonso de Molina 1100, Monterrico, Surco (between blocks 18 and 19 of Av Primavera), Lima 33, T01-345 1292, www.museoroperu.com.pe, daily 1030-1800, US$11.55, children under 11 US$5.60, multilingual audioguides,* houses an enormous collection of Peruvian gold, silver and bronze objects, together with an impressive array of international arms and military uniforms from Spanish colonial times to the present day and textiles from Peru and elsewhere. Allow plenty of time to appreciate all that is on view. It is directed by the **Fundación Miguel Mujica Gallo**, which also exhibits 167 of its pieces in the **Sala Museo Oro del Perú**, in Larcomar (see Miraflores, below).

PUEBLO LIBRE

The original museum of anthropology and archaeology is **Museo Nacional de Antropología, Arqueología e Historia** ⓘ *Plaza Bolívar in Pueblo Libre, not to be confused with Plaza Bolívar in the centre, T01-463 5070, Tue-Sat 0900-1700, Sun and holidays 0900-1600, US$4, students US$1.20, guides available for groups.* On display are ceramics of the Chimú, Nazca, Mochica and Pachacámac cultures, various Inca curiosities and works of art, and interesting textiles. **Museo Nacional de Historia** ⓘ *T01-463 2009, Tue-Sat 0900-1700, Sun and holidays 0900-1600, US$3.65,* in a mansion occupied by San Martín (1821-1822) and Bolívar (1823-1826) is next door. It exhibits colonial and early republican paintings, manuscripts and uniforms. Take any public transport on Avenida Brasil with a window sticker saying "Todo Brasil." Get off at the 21st block called Avenida Vivanco. Walk about five blocks down Vivanco. The museum will be on your left. From Miraflores take bus SM 18 Carabayllo-Chorrillos, marked "Bolívar, Arequipa, Larcomar", get out at block 8 of Bolívar by the Hospital Santa Rosa, and walk down Av San Martín five blocks until you see the 'blue line'; turn left. The 'blue line' marked on the pavement, very faded, links the Museo Nacional de Antropología, Arqueología e Historia to the Museo Larco (see below), 15 minutes' walk. Taxi from downtown US$3; from Miraflores US$4.

Museo Larco de Lima ① *Av Bolívar 1515, T01-461 1312, www.museolarco.org, 0900-2200, 0900-1800 24 Dec-1 Jan; texts in Spanish, English and French, US$11.25 (half price for students), disabled access, photography not permitted.* Located in an 18th-century mansion, itself built on a seventh-century pre-Columbian pyramid, this museum has a collection that gives an excellent overview on the development of Peruvian cultures through their pottery. It has the world's largest collection of Moche, Sicán and Chimú pieces. There is a Gold and Silver of Ancient Peru exhibition, a magnificent textile collection and a fascinating erotica section. Don't miss the storeroom with its vast array of pottery, unlike anything you'll see elsewhere. There is a library and computer room for your own research and a good café open during museum hours. It is surrounded by beautiful gardens, and has a new entrance and park outside. Take any bus to the 15th block of Avenida Brasil. Then take a bus down Avenida Bolívar. From Miraflores, take the SM 18 Carabayllo-Chorrillos (see above) to block 15 of Bolívar. Taxi from downtown, Miraflores or San Isidro, 15 minutes, US$4. Follow the 'blue line' marked on the pavement to the Museo Nacional de Antropología, Arqueología e Historia (see above), 15 minutes' walk.

SAN ISIDRO
To the east of Avenida La República, down Calle Pancho Fierro, is **El Olivar**, an olive grove planted by the first Spaniards, which has been turned into a park. Some 32 species of birds have been recorded there. Between San Isidro and Miraflores, is **Huallamarca** ① *C Nicolás de Rivera 201 and Av Rosario, 0900-1700, closed Mon, US$1.75. Take bus 1 from Av Tacna, or minibus 13 or 73 to Choquechaca, then walk.* An adobe pyramid of the Maranga culture, it dates from about AD 100-500. There is a small site museum. There are many good hotels and restaurants in San Isidro.

MIRAFLORES
Avenida Arequipa continues to the coast, to the most important suburb of Lima. Together with San Isidro and Barranco this is the social centre of Lima.

Parque Kennedy, the Parque Central de Miraflores, is located between Avenida Larco and Avenida Mcal Oscar Benavides (locally known as Avenida Diagonal). This extremely well-kept park has a small open-air theatre with performances Thursday-Sunday and an arts and crafts market most evenings of the week. The house of the author **Ricardo Palma** ① *Gral Suárez 189, T01-445 5836, Mon-Fri 1000-1300, 1500-1700, US$2.20,* is now a museum. At the end of Avenida Larco and running along the Malecón de la Reserva is the renovated **Parque Salazar** and the very modern shopping centre called **Centro Comercial Larcomar**. Here you will find expensive shops, hip cafés and discos and a wide range of restaurants, all with a beautiful ocean view. There is a bowling alley, and the 12-screen cinema is one of the best in Lima, with a 'cine-bar' in the 12th theatre. A few hundred metres to the north is the famous **Parque del Amor** where on just about any night you'll see at least one wedding party taking photos of the newlyweds. These cliff-top parks are also where parapenting takes place. You can book a tandem ride with several agencies that advertise in hostels.

Museo Arqueológico Amano ⓘ *Retiro 160, 11th block of Av Angamos Oeste, Miraflores, T01-441 2909, www.fundacionmuseoamano.org.pe, open by appointment only Mon-Fri 1500-1700, donations (photography prohibited)* houses a collection of artefacts from the Chancay, Chimú and Nazca periods, owned by the late Mr Yoshitaro Amano. It has one of the most complete exhibits of Chancay weaving, and is particularly interesting for pottery and pre-Columbian textiles, all superbly displayed and lit. Take a bus or colectivo to the corner of Avenida Arequipa y Avenida Angamos and another one to the 11th block of Avenida Angamos Oeste. Taxi from downtown US$3.20; from Parque Kennedy US$2.25.

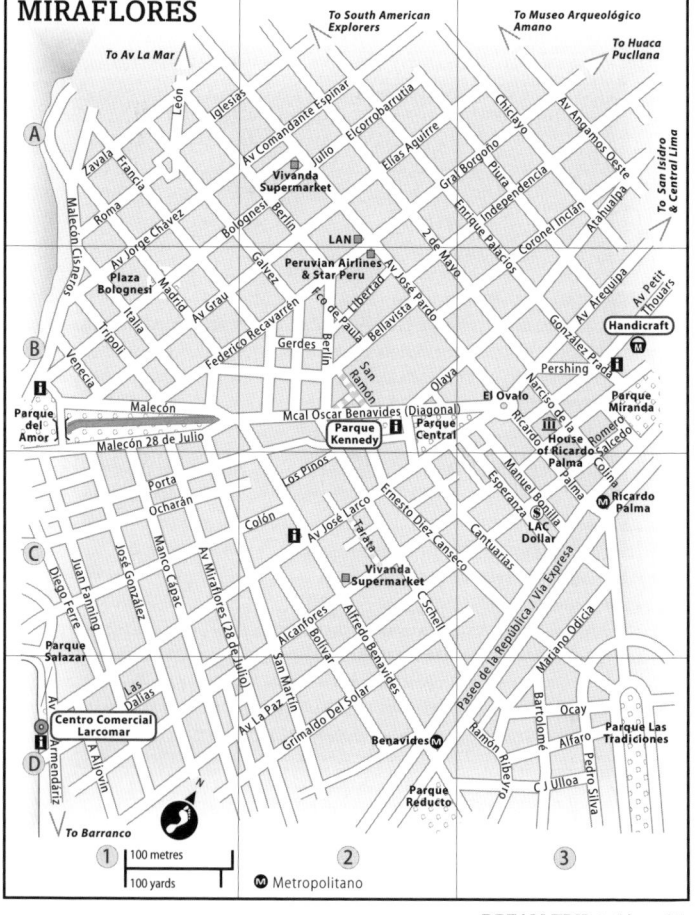

Museo Enrico Poli ① *Almte Cochrane 466, T01-422 2437, tours cost US$15 per person irrespective of the size of the group, allow 2 hrs, call in advance to arrange tours*, one of the best private collections of colonial and pre-Columbian artefacts in Peru, including material from Sipán. At General Borgoño, eighth block s/n, turn off Avenida Arequipa at 45th block, is **Huaca Pucllana** ① *T01-445 8695, www.mirafloresperu.com/huacapucllana, US$2.50, includes 45-min tour in Spanish or English, 0900-1600, closed Tue*, a fifth- to eighth-century AD, pre-Inca site which is under excavation. It has a small site museum with some objects from the site itself, and a souvenir shop.

BARRANCO

This suburb further south was already a seaside resort by the end of the 17th century. Nowadays, a number of artists have their workshops here and there are several chic galleries. The attractive public library, formerly the town hall, stands on the plaza. Nearby is the interesting *bajada*, a steep path leading down to the beach. The **Puente de los Suspiros** (Bridge of Sighs) leads towards the Malecón, with fine views of the bay. Barranco is quiet by day but comes alive at night. The 45-minute walk from Miraflores to Barranco along the Malecón is nice in summer. **Museo de Arte Colonial Pedro de Osma** ① *Av Pedro de Osma 423, T01-467 0141, www.museopedrodeosma.org, Tue-Sun 1000-1800, US$6.75, students half price, guided tours in English or Spanish*, is a private collection of colonial art of the Cuzco, Ayacucho and Arequipa schools. **MATE (Asociación Mario Testino)** ① *Av Pedro de Osma 409, T01-251 7755, www.mate.pe, Tue-Sat 1100-2000, Sun 1100-1800*, is a museum and cultural centre dedicated primarily to the work of photographer Mario Testino. It holds exhibitions, concerts and other events and has a café.

The district of **Chorrillos**, beyond Barranco, has a redesigned Malecón and fashionable beachfront with mosaics and parks. It has always been a popular resort and is a good place to go to find fish restaurants. Playa Herradura is a little further on and is well known for surfing. From Chorrillos you can get to some of the sites such as Pachacámac and Pántanos de Villa, which are south of the city.

LIMA BEACHES

In summer (December-April) the city's beaches get very crowded at weekends and lots of activities are organized. Even though the water of the whole bay has been declared unsuitable for swimming, Limeños see the beach more as part of their culture than as a health risk. Do not camp on the beaches as robbery is a serious threat and, for the same reason, take care on the walkways down. Don't take any belongings with you to the beach, only what is really necessary.

The beaches of Miraflores, Barranco and Chorrillos are very popular, and sand and sea get dirty. It's much better to take a safe taxi 40 km south to Punta Rocas, Señoritas or Silencio along Punta Hermosa which has frequent surfing and volleyball tournaments. The *Circuito de Playas*, which begins with Playa Arica (30 km from Lima) and ends with San Bartolo (45 km), has many great beaches for all tastes.

PANTANOS DE VILLA

① *Daily 0830-1630. US$3, guides available for US$7 (maximum 20 people), boat trip US$4.25, bicycle tour US$3.50, www.prohvilla.munlima.gob.pe.*
In the district of Chorrillos is the 396-ha wildlife sanctuary, Pántanos de Villa, an ecological wetland reserve with brackish water and abundant emergent vegetation. It provides the

habitat for waterfowl typical of coastal Peru, including 17 species of migratory shorebirds. There are several species of fish, four types of reptile and over 50 species of waterplant. The visitor centre has lots of information in Spanish. Allow up to two hours for a visit and take binoculars if you have them. Access is by the road that goes to the seaside district of La Villa; the nearest public transport stops about 1 km away, so it's best to take a taxi from Barranco, US$4.

PACHACAMAC

ⓘ *T01-430 0168, www.ulb.ac.be/philo/ychsma, Tue-Sun 0900-1700; closed public holidays except by appointment. US$2.10, includes the museum, students US$0.70, guide US$6.*

When the Spaniards arrived, Pachacámac in the Lurín Valley was the largest city and ceremonial centre on the coast. A wooden statue of the creator-god, after whom the site is named, is in the site museum. Hernando Pizarro was sent here by his brother in 1533 in search of gold for Inca emperor Atahualpa's ransom. In their fruitless quest, the Spaniards destroyed images and killed the priests. The ruins encircle the top of a low hill, whose crest was crowned with a **Temple of the Sun**, now partially restored. Slightly apart is the reconstructed **House of the Mamaconas**, where the 'chosen women' spun fine cloth for the Inca and his court. An impression of the scale of the site can be gained from the top of the Temple of the Sun, or from walking or driving the 3-km circuit, which is covered by an unmade road for cars and tour buses. The site is large and it is expected that tourists will be visiting by vehicle. There are six parking areas.

→CALLAO

There is no separation between Lima and Callao; the two cities run into each other and the road between the two is lined with factories. But Callao is a city in its own right, the second largest in Peru with over one million inhabitants (many more if you include shanty town dwellers). Callao (not Lima) is the location of **Jorge Chávez International Airport** and is the most important Peruvian port, handling 75% of the nation's imports and some 25% of its exports. Shipyards far from sea load newly built fishing vessels on to huge lorries to be launched into the ocean here. Most parts of the city are ugly, unkempt, poor and dangerous. However, if you are willing to use some imagination, and if you like ports, Callao is worth visiting. Some attempts are being made to restore the historic centre and port area.

BACKGROUND

Founded in 1537, Callao used to be one of the most important cities in South America, the only seaport on the continent authorized to trade with Spain during the 16th and 17th centuries. During much of the 16th century Spanish merchants were plagued by threats from English pirates such as Sir Francis Drake and Richard Hawkins, who were all too willing to relieve the Spanish armada of its colonial spoils. The harbour was fortified in 1639 in order to prevent such attacks. In 1746, the port was completely destroyed by a massive wave, triggered by the terrible earthquake of that year. According to some sources, all 6000 of Callao's inhabitants were drowned. The watermark is still visible on the outside of the 18th-century church of **Nuestra Señora del Carmen de la Legua**, which stands near the corner of Avenida Oscar Benavides and the airport road, Avenida Elmer Faucett. In 1850, the first railway in South America was opened between Lima and Callao. It was used not only as a passenger service but also, more importantly, for the growing import-export trade, transporting ore from the mines in the Central Highlands and manufactured goods from incoming ships.

PLACES IN CALLAO

The most elegant area of Callao proper is **Plaza Grau**. It is well maintained and from here you can see a large part of the port and the **Palomino Islands** (inhabited by birds, seals and other marine species), including **Isla San Lorenzo**. This island has an underwater military bunker, where two famous prisoners were incarcerated, Abimael Guzmán, founder of Sendero Luminoso, and Víctor Polay, leader of MRTA. Trips to the islands by **Vientosur** and other agencies can be arranged from the pier next to Plaza Grau; ask around, as departures are mostly unscheduled. **Museo Naval del Perú** ① *Av Jorge Chávez 121, Plaza Grau, T01-429 4793, Tue-Sat 0900-1600, Sun 0900-1700, US$1,* has models of Peruvian and foreign ships, weapons, uniforms, torpedoes and other relics. There are also interesting photographs. It's recommended if you are in the area.

Several houses surrounding the **Iglesia Matriz** have been restored, but generally the centre is in a state of permanent decay. **La Fortaleza del Real Felipe** and **Museo del Ejército** ① *T01-429 0532, www.regioncallao.gob.pe, Tue-Sun 0930-1600, US$2.20, students half price, no cameras allowed,* is an enormous Spanish castle in the heart of the city. It is still used by the Peruvian armed forces, but the parts open to the public include various areas and buildings within the fort, the museum itself, the fortifications and plenty of cannons.

LA PUNTA

Founded in 1555, La Punta is a green peninsula next to Callao. It has only 6800 permanent residents and enjoys the relaxed, nostalgic atmosphere of a beach resort, good local seafood restaurants, pleasant walks, friendly people and great views. It's an interesting place to come for lunch, but the ride back to Lima, even in a taxi, can be dangerous at night, as you have to drive through Callao proper.

La Punta's main artery, **Avenida Coronel Bolognesi**, is lined with impressive old villas. There is a well-maintained Malecón parallel to Bolognesi, a lovely walk and great views of the islands, sailing boats and Callao port. On the corner of El Malecón and Jirón García y García is the **Club de Regatas Lima**, with a nice café and view from the second floor (open sporadically). Nearby is the **Club de Regatas Unión**. Along El Malecón is a pebble beach, but the water is not very clean, due to the proximity of Callao port. **Plaza Grau** has been well restored, with a library inside the municipality building. It has no tourist pamphlets, but you can get information about the past and the present of La Punta there. At Plaza Grau bright pleasure boats, complete with life jackets, take trippers out to the end of La Punta beach and back. The journey takes about 25 minutes and costs US$1.50. See also Ecocruceros, page 51.

CARAL

ⓘ *0900-1600, US$4; all visitors must be accompanied by an official guide, US$7 per group, in the car park is the ticket office, toilets, handicrafts stalls; for details, Proyecto Especial Caral, Av Las Lomas de la Molina 327, Urb Las Lomas, Lima 12, T205 2500, www.caralperu.gob.pe.*

North of Lima and a few kilometres before Barranca (by-passed by the Highway) a turning to the right (east) at Km 184 leads to the UNESCO World Heritage Site Caral. This ancient city, 26 km from the coast, dates from about 2600 BC. Many of the accepted theories of Peruvian archaeology have been overturned by Caral's age and monumental construction. It appears to be easily the oldest city in South America. The dry, desert site lies on the southern fringes of the Supe valley, along whose flanks there are more ruins, 19 out of 32 of which have been explored. Caral covers 66 ha and contains eight significant pyramidal structures. To date seven have been excavated by archaeologists from the University of San Marcos, Lima. They are undertaking careful restoration on the existing foundations to re-establish the pyramidal tiers. It is possible to walk around the pyramids. A viewpoint provides a panorama across the whole site. The site is well organized, criss-crossed by marked paths which must be adhered to. Allow at least two hours to visit the site. You can stay or camp at the **Casa del Arqueólogo**.

LIMA LISTINGS

WHERE TO STAY

$$$$ Hotel B, San Martín 301, Barranco, T01-700 5106, www.hotelb.pe. New boutique hotel in an early 20th-century mansion. Redesigned as a luxury hotel with period and modern design features, convenient for galleries, etc, restaurant and bar, plunge pool, all up-to-date services.

$$$$ Country Club, Los Eucaliptos 590, San Isidro, T01-611 9000, www.hotel country.com. Excellent, fine service, luxurious rooms, safes in rooms, good bar and restaurant, classically stylish.

$$$$ Sonesta El Olivar, Pancho Fierro 194, San Isidro, T01-712 6000, www.sonesta. com/Lima/. Excellent, one of the top 5-star hotels in Lima overlooking El Olivar park, modern, many superb eating options, bar, garden, swimming pool, quiet, very attentive, popular. Sonesta have other hotels in the city and around the country.

$$$ San Antonio Abad, Ramón Ribeyro 301, Miraflores, T01-447 6766, www.hotel sanantonioabad.com. Secure, quiet, helpful, tasty breakfasts, justifiably popular, good value.

$$$-$$ Casa de Baraybar, Toribio Pacheco 216, Miraflores, T01-652 2260, www.casadebaraybar.com. 1 block from the ocean, extra long beds, a/c or fan, colourful decor, high ceilings, 24-hr room service, laundry. Bilingual staff. Recommended.

$$$-$$ Hostal El Patio, Diez Canseco 341, Miraflores, T01-444 2107, www. hostalelpatio.net. Very nice suites and rooms, comfortable, English and French spoken, convenient, *comedor*, gay friendly. Very popular, reservations are essential.

$$ Chez Elizabeth, Av del Parque Norte 265, San Isidro, T01-9980 07557, http://chezelizabeth.typepad.fr. Family house in residential area 7 mins' walk from Cruz del Sur bus station. Shared or private bathrooms, TV room, laundry, airport transfers.

$$ Mami Panchita, Av Federico Gallessi 198 (ex-Av San Miguel), San Miguel, T01-263 7203, www.mamipanchita.com. Dutch/Peruvian-owned, English, Dutch and Spanish spoken, includes breakfast and welcome drink, comfortable rooms with bath, hot water, living room and bar, patio, email service, book exchange, airport transfers, 15 mins from airport, 15 mins from Miraflores, 20 mins from historical centre. Frequently recommended.

$$-$ Condor's House, Martín Napanga 137, Miraflores, T01-446 7267, www. condorshouse.com. Award-winning, quiet hostel, two categories of dorm rooms with lockers, good bathrooms, also doubles, good meeting place, TV room with films, book exchange, *almuerzo criollo* and *parrillada* prepared once a week, bar. Helpful manager, Arturo Luna, and staff.

$$-$ The Lighthouse, Cesareo Chacaltana 162, Miraflores, T01-446 8397, www.the lighthouseperu.com. Near Plaza Morales Barros, British/Peruvian-run, relaxed, small dorm or private rooms with private or shared bath. Good services, small indoor patio.

RESTAURANTS

$$$ Astrid & Gastón, Cantuarias 175, Miraflores, T01-242 5387, www.astridy gaston.com. Exceptional local/Novo Andino and international cuisine, one of the best in Lima. The flagship of internationally famous chef, Gastón Acurio's restaurants, all of which are recommended. Their 11-course tasting menu takes 3 hrs, US$95.

$$ Segundo Muelle, Av Conquistadores 490, San Isidro, T01-717 9998, and other branches, www.segundomuelle.com. Excellent ceviche and other very good seafood dishes from responsibly sourced produce, popular at all times.

$$$ Huaca Pucllana, Gral Borgoño cuadra 8 s/n, alt cuadra 45 Av Arequipa, Miraflores, T01-445 4042, www.resthuacapucllana.com. Facing the archaeological site of the same name, contemporary Peruvian fusion cooking, very good food in an unusual setting, ideal for a special occasion, popular with groups.

$$$ Saqra, Av La Paz 646, Miraflores, T01-650 8884, www.saqra.pe. Mon-Thu 1200-2400, Fri and Sat 1200-0100. Colourful and casual, indoor or outdoor seating, popular with Peruvians and visitors for its interesting use of ingredients from all over Peru, classic flavours with an innovative twist, vegetarian options, many organic products. Also good cocktail bar.

$$$-$$ AlmaZen, Federico Recavarrén 298 y Galvez, Miraflores, T01-243 0474. Organic slow-food, reportedly one of the best in Latin America, Mon-Fri 1300-1600, 1930-2230, Sat 1930-2230.

$$ El Huarike, Enrique Palacios 140, Miraflores, T01-241 6086, www.el huarike.com. Fashionable, delicious combinations of ceviche and sushi.

WHAT TO DO

Las Brisas de Titicaca, Pasaje Walkuski 168, at 1st block of Av Brasil near Plaza Bolognesi, T01-332 1901, www.brisasdeltiticaca.com. A cultural association and Lima institution offering folkloric shows and dinner.

Dédalo, Paseo Sáenz Peña 295, Barranco, T01-477 0562, http://dedaloarte.blogspot.co.uk. A labyrinthine shop selling furniture, jewellery and other items, as good as a gallery. It also has a nice coffee shop and has cinema shows.

Ecocruceros, Av Arequipa 4964, oficina 202, Miraflores, T01-226 8530, www.islas palomino.com or www.ecocruceros.com. Daily departures at 1000 from Plaza Grau in Callao to see the sealions at Islas Palomino, 30-40 minutes wet-suit swimming with guide, snack lunch, US$45 (take ID).

Lima Mentor, T01-624 9360, www.lima mentor.com. Contact through web, phone or through hotels. An agency offering cultural tours of Lima using freelance guides in specialist areas (eg gastronomy, art, archaeology, Lima at night), entertaining, finding different angles from regular tours. Half-day or full day tours.

CUZCO

The ancient Inca capital is said to have been founded around AD 1100, and since then has developed into a major commercial and tourism centre of 326,000 inhabitants, most of whom are Quechua. Today, colonial churches, monasteries and convents and extensive pre-Columbian ruins are interspersed with countless hotels, bars and restaurants that cater for the hundreds of thousands of visitors. Almost every central street has remains of Inca walls, arches and doorways; the perfect Inca stonework now serves as the foundations for more modern dwellings. This stonework is tapered upwards (battered); every wall has a perfect line of inclination towards the centre, from bottom to top. The curved stonework of the Temple of the Sun, for example, is probably unequalled in the world. The Spaniards transformed the centre of the magnificent Inca civilization into a jewel of colonial achievement. Yet the city today is not some dead monument; its history breathes through the stones. The Quechua people bring the city to life, with a combination of pre-Hispanic and Christian beliefs, and every visitor is made welcome.

→ ARRIVING IN CUZCO

GETTING THERE

Flights from Lima (one hour 20 minutes) arrive from early morning to mid-afternoon. There are no night flights. The **airport** is 1.6 km to the southeast of the city and the road into the centre goes close to Wanchac train station. The **bus terminal** is near the Pachacútec statue in Ttio district. Transport to your hotel is not a problem from any of these places by taxi or in transport arranged by hotel representatives.

MOVING ON

Buses and colectivos run from various bus stops and termini in Cuzco to towns in the Sacred Valley; they have no fixed schedule, but leave when full. To **Pisac** (see page 65) they go from Calle Puputi on the outskirts of the city, near the Clorindo Matto de Turner school and Avenida de la Cultura. To **Urubamba** (page 68), **Chinchero** (page 68) and **Ollantaytambo** (page 69) they go from 300 block of Avenida Grau, one block before crossing the bridge. A direct taxi-colectivo service to **Ollantaytambo** runs from Calle Pavitos. You can also take a tour, or hire a taxi to the Sacred Valley.

  Machu Picchu (see page 72) cannot be reached directly by road from Cuzco. The most leisurely way is by train to the town of Aguas Calientes. Services run from Poroy, Urubamba or Ollantaytambo, all reached by bus from Cuzco. Buses run from Aguas Calientes to the ruins. There are other options, some involving combinations of road, rail and walking, others, like the Inca Trail (page 76) and its variations, involving extended treks.

  Following 12 days visiting Cuzco, Machu Picchu and the Sacred Valley, Dream Trip 1 moves on to the Southeastern jungle for a four-night tour in either **Manu National Park** (see page 85) or **Tambopata National Reserve** (see page 87). Flights to Manu National Park can only be arranged as part of a tour. There are, however, scheduled 45- to 55-minute flights to **Puerto Maldonado** (see page 86) for Tambopata. To return to Lima by plane from Puerto Maldonado takes 2¾ to three hours. It is also possible to travel overland to the Southeastern Jungle. The route to Manu is long and slow, part by road, part by river, but it gives opportunities to see the various ranges of habitat in the national park. Puerto Maldonado and Cuzco are now connected by the new Interoceánica highway and buses take 10-11 hours.

From Cuzco you can get to **Puno** (see page 93) on Lake Titicaca by aeroplane, train or bus. A 55-minute flight from Cuzco goes to Juliaca, from where a bus or taxi will take about an hour to Puno. **PerúRail** runs a luxury service three times a week to Puno, four in high season, taking 10 hours. Tourist buses from Cuzco to Puno also take 10 hours, stopping at five sites of interest en route. Normal buses take six to seven hours; it is not advisable to take night buses on this route (besides, if you did, you would miss the scenery).

GETTING AROUND

The centre of Cuzco is quite small and possible to explore on foot. Taxis in Cuzco are cheap and recommended when arriving by air, train or bus and especially when returning to your hotel at night. On arrival in Cuzco, respect the altitude: two or three hours' rest after arriving makes a great difference; avoid meat and smoking, eat lots of carbohydrates and drink plenty of clear, non-alcoholic liquid; remember to walk slowly.

TOURIST INFORMATION

Official tourist information ① *Portal Mantas 117-A, next to La Merced church, T084-263176, open 0800-1830*. There is also an **i perú** tourist information desk at the airport ① *T084-237364, open daily for flights*, and another at ① *Av Sol 103, of 102, Galerías Turísticas, T084-252974, iperucusco@promperu.gob.pe, daily 0830-1930*. **Dircetur** ① *Plaza Túpac Amaru Mz 1 Lte 2, Wanchac, T084-223761, open Mon-Fri 0800-1300*, gives out good maps. Other information sources include **South American Explorers** ① *Atocsaycuchi 670, T084-245484, www.saexplorers.org, Mon-Fri 0930-1700, Sat 0930-1300*. It's worth making the climb up the steps to the large new clubhouse, which has a garden. It sells a good city map, members get many local discounts and there is a comprehensive recycling centre. As

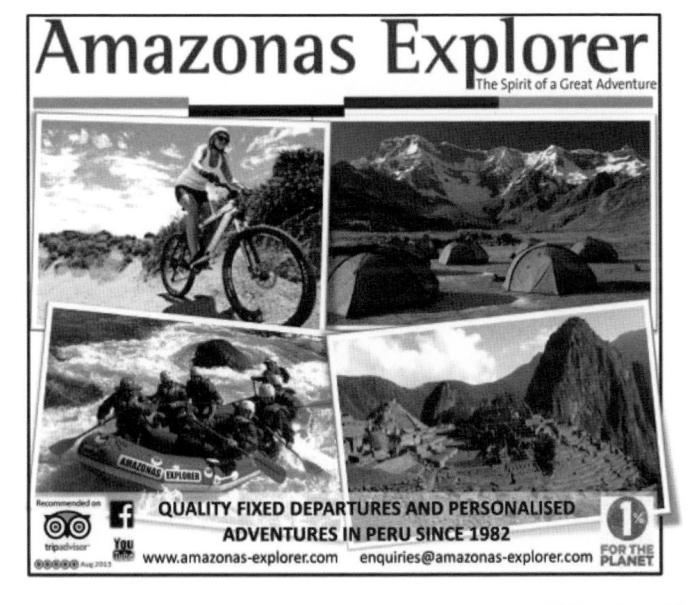

with SAE's other clubhouses, this is the place to go for specialized information, member-written trip reports and maps. It also has rooms for rent. Many churches close to visitors on Sunday. See also www.aboutcusco.com and www.cuscoonline.com.

Visitors' tickets A combined entrance ticket, called *Boleto Turístico de Cusco* (BTC), is available to most of the sites of main historical and cultural interest in and around the city, and costs as follows: 130 soles (US$46/€35) for all the sites and valid for 10 days; or 70 soles (US$25/€19) for either the museums in the city, or Sacsayhuaman, Qenqo, Puka

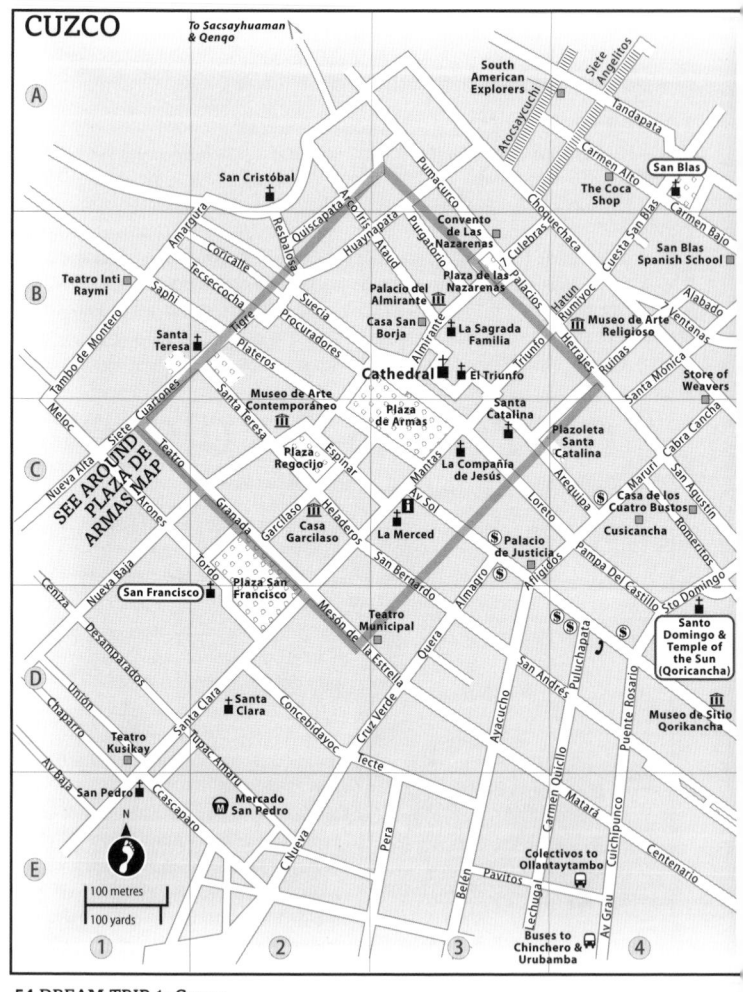

Pukara and Tambo Machay, or Pisac, Ollantaytambo, Chinchero and Moray; the 70 soles ticket are valid for one day. The BTC can be bought at the offices of **Cosituc** ① *Av Sol 103, Of. 102, Galerías Turísticas, T084-261465, Mon-Sat 0800-1800, Sun 0800-1300, or Yuracpunku 79-A (east of centre, go along Recoleta), www.cosituc.gob.pe or www.boletoturisticocusco. net*, or at any of the sites included in the ticket. For students with an ISIC card the general BTC costs 70 soles (US$25), that is only available at the Cosituc office upon presentation of the ISIC card. Take your ISIC card when visiting the sites, as some may ask to see it. Photography is not allowed in the churches, nor in museums.

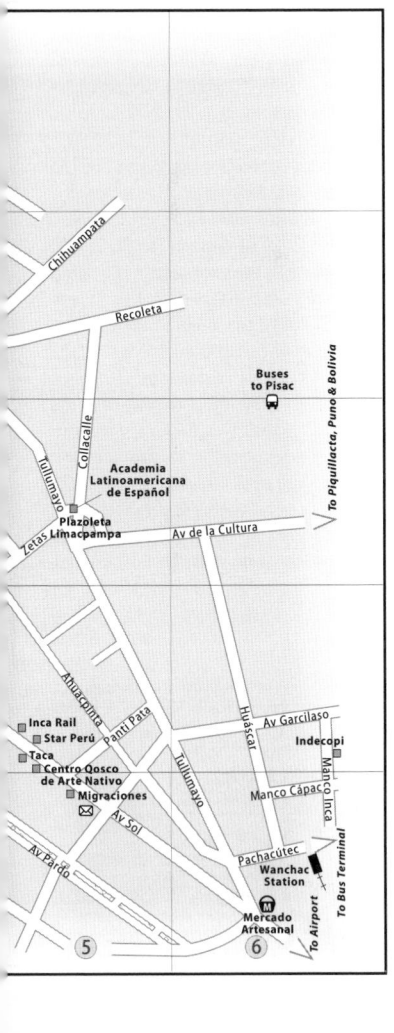

Entrance tickets for the Santo Domingo/ Qoricancha, the Inka Museum (El Palacio del Almirante) and La Merced are sold separately, while the Cathedral (including El Triunfo and La Sagrada Familia), La Compañía, San Blas and the Museo de Arte Religioso del Arzobispado are included on a religious buildings ticket, which costs 50 soles (US$17.75) and is valid for 10 days. Each of these sites may be visited individually. Entrance tickets for the Machu Picchu ruins and Inca trail are sold electronically at www.machupicchu.gob.pe, at the **Dirección Regional de Cultura Cusco** ① *Av de la Cultura 238, Condominio Huáscar, T084-236061, www.drc-cusco.gob.pe, Mon-Fri 0715-1600*, and other outlets listed on the *machupicchu.gob.pe* website.

Security Police patrol the streets and stations, but still be vigilant. On no account walk back to your hotel after dark from a bar or club, as strangle muggings and rape do occur. Pay for a taxi called by the club's doorman and make sure the taxi is licensed. Other areas in which to take care include San Pedro market (otherwise recommended), the San Cristóbal area, and at out-of-the-way ruins. Also take special care during Inti Raymi. If you need a *denuncia* (report for insurance purposes), which is available from the Banco de la Nación, go to the **Tourist Police (POLTUR)** ① *Plaza Túpac Amaru, Wanchac, T084-249665/084-221961*, where they will type it out. Always go to the police if you are robbed, even though it will cost you some time. There is also a **Consumer Protection**

Bureau (Indecopi) ① *Av Manco Inca 209, Wanchac, T084-252987, mmarroquin@indecopi. gob.pe; toll free 0800-44040 (24-hr hotline, not available from payphones).*

→ PLACES IN CUZCO

The heart of the city in Inca days consisted of *Huacaypata* (the place of tears) and *Cusipata* (the place of happiness), divided by a channel of the Saphi River. Today, Cusipata is Plaza Regocijo and Huacaypata is the Plaza de Armas, around which are colonial arcades and four churches. To the northeast is the early 17th-century baroque **Cathedral** ① *US$9, open daily 1000-1800, Quechua mass is held 0500-0600.* It is built on the site of the Palace of Inca Wiracocha (*Kiswarcancha*). The high altar is solid silver and the original altar *retablo* behind it is a masterpiece of Andean wood carving. The earliest surviving painting of the city can be seen, depicting Cuzco during the 1650 earthquake. In the far right hand end of the church is an interesting local painting of the Last Supper replete with *cuy*, *chicha*, etc. In the sacristy are paintings of all the bishops of Cuzco. The choir stalls, by a 17th-century Spanish priest, are a magnificent example of colonial baroque art. The elaborate pulpit and the sacristy are also notable. Much venerated is the crucifix of El Señor de los Temblores, the object of many pilgrimages and viewed all over Peru as a guardian against earthquakes. The tourist entrance to the Cathedral is through the church of **La Sagrada Familia** (1733), which stands to its left as you face it. Its gilt main altar has been renovated. **El Triunfo** (1536), on the right of the Cathedral, is the first Christian church in Cuzco, built on the site of the Inca Roundhouse (the *Suntur Huasi*). It has a statue of the Virgin of the Descent, reputed to have helped the Spaniards repel Manco Inca when he besieged the city in 1536.

On the southeast side of the plaza is the beautiful **La Compañía de Jesús** ① *US$3.55, or by religious buildings ticket, open daily 0900-1750,* built on the site of the Palace of the Serpents (*Amarucancha*, residence of Inca Huayna Capac) in the late 17th century. Its twin-towered exterior is extremely graceful, and the interior rich in fine murals, paintings and carved altars. Nearby is **Santa Catalina** ① *Arequipa at Santa Catalina Angosta, daily 0900-1200, 1300-1700, except Fri 0900-1200, 1300-1600, joint ticket with Santo Domingo US$5.35,* a church, convent and museum, built upon the foundations of the *Acllahuasi* (House of the Chosen Women). There are guided tours by English-speaking students; tip expected. **Museo Machupicchu** (**Casa Concha**) ① *Santa Catalina Ancha 320, T084-255535, Mon-Sat 0900-1700, US$7,* is a new museum that features objects found by Hiram Bingham during

his initial excavations of Machu Picchu in 1912, returned by Yale University to the Peruvian government in 2010.

If you continue down Arequipa from Santa Catalina you come to Calle Maruri. Between this street and Santo Domingo is **Cusicancha** ① *US$1.75, Mon-Fri 0730-1600, sometimes open at weekends*, an open space showing the layout of the buildings as they would have been in Inca times.

The church of **La Merced** ① *on C Márquez, church Mon-Fri 0800-1700, Sat 0900-1600; monastery and museum 1430-1700, except Sun, US$1*, was first built in 1534 and rebuilt in the late 17th century. Attached is a very fine monastery with an exquisite cloister. Inside the church are buried Gonzalo Pizarro, half-brother of Francisco, and the two Almagros, father and son. The church is most famous for its jewelled monstrance, which is on view in the monastery's museum during visiting hours.

Much **Inca stonework** can be seen in the streets and most particularly in the Callejón Loreto, running southeast past La Compañía de Jesús from the main plaza. The walls of the **Acllahuasi** are on one side, and of the **Amarucancha** on the other. There are also Inca remains in Calle San Agustín, to the east of the plaza. The stone of 12 angles is in Calle Hatun Rumiyoc, halfway along its second block, on the right-hand side going away from the Plaza. The **Palacio Arzobispal** stands on Hatun Rumiyoc y Herrajes, two blocks northeast of Plaza de Armas. It was built on the site of the palace of Inca Roca, occupied in 1400. It contains the **Museo de Arte Religioso** ① *0800-1800, included on the religious buildings ticket, or US$5.35*, a collection of colonial paintings and furniture. The collection includes the paintings by the indigenous master, Diego Quispe Tito, of a 17th-century Corpus Christi procession that used to hang in the church of Santa Ana.

The **Palacio del Almirante**, just north of the Plaza de Armas, is impressive. It houses the **Museo Inka** ① *Cuesta del Almirante 103, T084-237380, Mon-Fri 0800-1900, Sat 0900-1600, US$3*, which is run by the Universidad San Antonio de Abad. The museum exhibits the development of culture in the region from pre-Inca, through Inca times to the present day: textiles, ceramics, metalwork, jewellery, architecture, technology. See the collection of miniature turquoise figures and other offerings to the gods. Weaving demonstrations are given in the courtyard. On the northwest side of the Plaza de las Nazarenas, No 231, is **Museo de Arte Precolombino** ① *www.map.org.pe, 0900-2200, US$7, US$3.50 with student card; under same auspices as the Larco Museum in Lima*, housed in the **Casa Cabrera**. This beautiful museum is set around a spacious courtyard and contains many superb examples of pottery, metalwork (largely in

gold and silver), wood carvings and shells from the Moche, Chimú, Paracas, Nazca and Inca cultures. There are some vividly rendered animistic designs, giving an insight into the way Peru's ancient peoples viewed their world and the creatures that inhabited it. Every exhibit carries explanations in English and Spanish. Highly recommended. It also has the MAP Café, which serves first-class international and Peruvian-Andean cuisine. The **Convento de las Nazarenas**, also on Plaza de las Nazarenas, is now an annex of Orient Express' **Monasterio** hotel. You can see the Inca-colonial doorway with a mermaid motif, but ask permission to view the lovely 18th-century frescos inside. In the San Blas district, now firmly on the tourist map, the small church of **San Blas** ① *Carmen Bajo, 0800-1800, on the religious buildings ticket or US$5.35*, has a beautiful carved *mestizo* cedar pulpit, which is well worth seeing.

Santo Domingo, southeast of the main Plaza, was built in the 17th century on the walls of the **Qoricancha, Temple of the Sun** ① *Mon-Sat 0830-1730, Sun 1400-1700 (closed holidays), US$3.55, or joint ticket with Santa Catalina US$5.35, English-speaking guides, tip of US$2-3 expected*, and from its stones. Excavation has revealed more of the five chambers of the Temple of the Sun, which shows the best Inca stonework to be seen in Cuzco. The Temple of the Sun was awarded to Juan Pizarro, the younger brother of Francisco, who

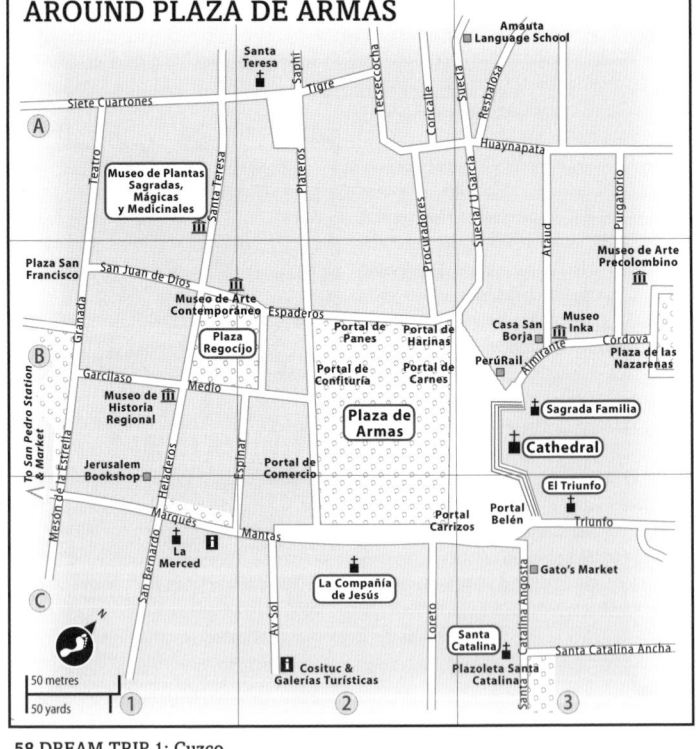

willed it to the Dominicans after he had been fatally wounded in the Sacsayhuaman siege. The baroque cloister has been gutted to reveal four of the original chambers of the great Inca temple – two on the west have been partly reconstructed in a good imitation of Inca masonry. The finest stonework is in the celebrated curved wall beneath the west end of Santo Domingo. This was rebuilt after the 1950 earthquake, at which time a niche that once contained a shrine was found at the inner top of the wall. Below the curved wall was a garden of gold and silver replicas of animals, maize and other plants. Excavations have revealed Inca baths below here, and more Inca retaining walls. The other superb stretch of late Inca stonework is in C Ahuacpinta outside the temple, to the east or left as you enter.

Museo de Sitio Qoricancha ① *Av Sol, Mon-Sat 0900-1200, 1300-1700, Sun 0800-1400, entrance by BTC*, (formerly Museo Arqueológico) is under the garden below Santo Domingo. It contains a limited collection of pre-Columbian items, Spanish paintings of imitation Inca royalty dating from the 18th century, and photos of the excavation of Qoricancha. The palace called **Casa de los Cuatro Bustos**, whose colonial doorway is at San Agustín 400, is now the **Hotel Libertador**. The general public can enter the Hotel from Plazoleta Santo Domingo, opposite the Temple of the Sun/Qoricancha.

Museo de Historia Regional ① *in the Casa Garcilaso, Jr Garcilaso y Heladeros, 0730-1700, entrance by BTC*, tries to show the evolution of the Cuzqueño school of painting. It also contains Inca agricultural implements, colonial furniture and paintings. **San Francisco** ① *on Plaza San Francisco, 3 blocks southwest of the Plaza de Armas, 0600-0800, 1800-2000*, is an austere church reflecting many indigenous influences. Its monastery is being rebuilt and may be closed. **San Pedro** ① *in front of the San Pedro market, Mon-Sat 1000-1200, 1400-1700*, was built in 1688. Its two towers were made from stones brought from an Inca ruin.

Museo de Plantas Sagradas, Mágicas y Medicinales ① *Santa Teresa 351, T084-222214, www.museoplantascusco.org, Mon-Sat 0800-2100, Sun 0800-1800, US$5.50*, has nine exhibition rooms detailing the history and uses of plants such as coca, Ayahuasca and San Pedro.

Above Cuzco, on the road up to Sacsayhuamán, is **San Cristóbal**, built to his patron saint by Cristóbal Paullu Inca. The church's atrium has been restored and there is a sidewalk access to the Sacsayhuamán Archaeological Park. North of San Cristóbal, you can see the 11 doorway-sized niches of the great Inca wall of the **Palacio de Colcampata**, which was the residence of Manco Inca before he rebelled against the Spanish and fled to Vilcabamba.

→ SACSAYHUAMAN

① *The site is about a 30-min walk up Pumacurco from Plaza de las Nazarenas. Daily 0700-1730; free student guides, give them a tip.*

There are some magnificent Inca walls in this ruined ceremonial centre, on a hill in the northern outskirts. The Incaic stones are hugely impressive. The massive rocks weighing up to 130 tons are fitted together with absolute perfection. Three walls run parallel for over 360 m and there are 21 bastions. Sacsayhuaman was thought for centuries to be a fortress, but the layout and architecture suggest a great sanctuary and temple to the Sun, which rises exactly opposite the place previously believed to be the Inca's throne – which was probably an altar, carved out of the solid rock. Broad steps lead to the altar from either side. The hieratic, rather than the military, hypothesis was supported by the discovery in 1982 of

FESTIVALS
The festival of Inti Raymi

The sun was the principal object of Inca worship and at their winter solstice, in June, the Incas honoured the solar deity with a great celebration known as Inti Raymi, the sun festival. The Spanish suppressed the Inca religion, and the last royal Inti Raymi was celebrated in 1535.

However, in 1944, a group of Cuzco intellectuals, inspired by the 'indigenist' movement, revived the ceremony in the form of a pageant, putting it together from chronicles and historical documents. The event caught the public imagination, and it has been celebrated every year since then on 24 Jun, now a Cuzco public holiday. Hundreds of local men and women play the parts of Inca priests, nobles, chosen women, soldiers (played by the local army garrison), runners, and the like. The coveted part of the Inca emperor Pachacuti is won by audition, and the event is organized by the municipal authorities.

It begins around 1000 at the Qoricancha (page 58) – the former sun temple of Cuzco – and winds its way up the main avenue into the Plaza de Armas, accompanied by songs, ringing declarations and the occasional drink of *chicha*. At the main plaza, Cuzco's presiding mayor is whisked back to Inca times, to receive Pachacuti's blessing and a stern lecture on good government. Climbing through Plaza Nazarenas and up Pumacurcu, the procession reaches the ruins of Sacsayhuaman at about 1400.

Before Pachacuti arrives the *Sinchi* (Pachacuti's chief general) ushers in contingents from the four *Suyus* (regions) of the Inca empire. Much of the ceremony is based around alternating action between these four groups of players. A *Chaski* (messenger) enters to announce the imminent arrival of the Inca and his *Coya* (queen). Men sweep the ground before him and women scatter flowers. The Inka takes the stage alone and has a dialogue with the sun. Then he receives reports from the governors of the four *Suyus*. This is followed by a drink of the sacred *chicha*, the re-lighting of the sacred fire of the empire, the sacrifice (faked) of a llama and the reading of auguries in its entrails. Finally the ritual eating of *sankhu* (corn paste mixed with the victim's blood) ends the ceremonies. The Inca gives a last message to his assembled children, and departs. The music and dancing continue until nightfall.

the graves of priests, who would have been unlikely to be buried in a fortress. The precise functions of the site, however, will probably continue to be a matter of dispute as very few clues remain, owing to its steady destruction.

The site survived the first years of the conquest. Pizarro's troops had entered Cuzco unopposed in 1533 and lived safely at Sacsayhuaman, until the rebellion of Manco Inca, in 1536, caught them off guard. The bitter struggle that ensued became the decisive military action of the conquest, for Manco's failure to hold Sacsayhuaman cost him the war, and the empire. The destruction of the hilltop site began after the defeat of Manco's rebellion. The outer walls still stand, but the complex of towers and buildings was razed to the ground. From then until the 1930s, Sacsayhuaman served as a kind of unofficial quarry of pre-cut stone for the inhabitants of Cuzco.

Along the road from Sacsayhuaman to Pisac, past a radio station, is the temple and amphitheatre of **Qenqo** with some of the finest examples of Inca stone carving *in situ*, especially inside the large hollowed-out stone that houses an altar. On the same road are **Puka Pukara** (Red Fort, but more likely to have been a *tambo*, or post-house), wonderful views; and the spring shrine of **Tambo Machay**, which is in excellent condition. Water still flows by a hidden channel out of the masonry wall, straight into a little rock pool traditionally known as the Inca's bath. Take a guide to the sites and visit in the morning for the best photographs. Carry your multi-site ticket, as there are roving ticket inspectors. You can visit the sites on foot, a pleasant walk of at least half a day through the countryside; take water, sun protection, and watch out for dogs. Alternatively, take the Pisac bus up to Tambo Machay (US$0.70) and walk back, or arrange a horseback tour with an agency.

CUZCO LISTINGS

WHERE TO STAY

$$$$ Andean Wings, Siete Cuartones 225, T084-243166, www.andeanwingshotel.com. In a restored 17th-century house, in the same group as **Casa de la Gringa** backpacker hostel (www.casadelagringa.com) and Another Planet tour operator (http://anotherplanetperu.org), 5-star, intimate, suites, some with jacuzzi, are individually designed (one is accessible for the disabled), spa, restaurant and bar.

$$$$ La Casona Inkaterra, Plazoleta Las Nazarenas 113, T084-223010, www.inka terra.com. A private, colonial-style boutique hotel in a converted 16th-century mansion, built on the site of Manco Cápac's palace. 11 exclusive suites, all facilities, concierge service with activities and excursions, highly regarded and the height of luxury.

$$$$ Casa Andina Private Collection Cusco, Plazoleta de Limacpampa Chico 473, T084-232610, www.casa-andina.com. The most upmarket and comfortable in this group of hotels' properties in the city (they have others around the country), in a 16th-century mansion with 4 courtyards, enriched oxygen available in the rooms, plus a gourmet restaurant serving local cuisine and a bar with an extensive pisco collection.

$$$$ El Monasterio, C Palacios 136, Plazoleta Nazarenas, T084-604000, www.monasteriohotel.com. 5-star, beautifully restored Seminary of San Antonio Abad (a Peruvian National Historical Landmark), including the Baroque chapel, spacious comfortable rooms with all facilities (some rooms offer an oxygen-enriched atmosphere to help clients acclimatize), very helpful staff, good restaurants (buffet breakfast, open to non-residents, will fill you up for the rest of the day), lunch and dinner à la carte, business centre with internet for guests.

$$$$-$$$ Casa San Blas, Tocuyeros 566, just off Cuesta San Blas, T084-237900, www.casasanblas.com. An international-standard boutique hotel with bright, airy rooms decorated with traditional textiles. Pleasant balcony with good views, attentive service. Breakfast served in the **Tika Bistro** next door, which specializes in a fusion of Peruvian and Thai/Vietnamese food (www.casasanblas.com/tikabistro).

$$$ El Arqueólogo, Pumacurco 408, T084-232522, www.hotelarqueologo.com. Includes breakfast, hot water, heating extra, helpful, French and English spoken, will store luggage, garden, cafeteria and kitchen.

$$$ Rumi Punku, Choquechaca 339, T084-221102, www.rumipunku.com. An Inca doorway leading to a sunny courtyard, comfortable rooms, helpful staff, safe, sauna, jacuzzi, gym.

$$$-$ Hostal Amaru, Cuesta San Blas 541, T084-225933, www.amaruhostal.com. Rooms around a pretty colonial courtyard, some with no windows, good beds, pleasant, relaxing, some Inca walls. Private or shared bath. Price includes airport/train/bus pick-up. Oxygen, kitchen for use in the evenings, laundry, book exchange. Also has **$$ Hostal Amaru II**, Chihuampata 642, San Blas, T084-223521, www.amaruhostal 2.com, and **$$-$ Hostería de Anita**, Alabado 525-5, T084-225933, www.amaru hostal.com/hosteria_de_ anita, with rooms or dorm beds, safe, quiet, good breakfast. **$$ Niños/Hotel Meloc**, Meloc 442, T084-231424, www.ninoshotel.com. Modern decor in colonial building. Hot water, excellent breakfast extra, restaurant, laundry service, luggage store, English spoken, run as part of the Dutch foundation **Niños Unidos Peruanos** and all profits are invested in projects to help street children. Also has **Niños 2/Hotel Fierro**, on C Fierro 476, T084-254611, with all the same features.

$$-$ Hostal Qorichaska, Nueva Alta 458, some distance from centre, T084-228974, www.qorichaskaperu.com. Rooms are clean and sunny, the older ones have traditional balconies. Also has dorms, mixed and men or women only. Includes breakfast, use of well-equipped kitchen, safe, laundry service.

RESTAURANTS

$$$ Chicha, Plaza Regocijo 261, p 2 (above **El Truco**), T084-240520, www.chicha.com. pe. Daily 1200-2400. Specializes in regional dishes created by restaurateur Gastón Acurio (see page 51), Peruvian cuisine of the highest standards in a renovated colonial house, at one time the royal mint, tastefully decorated, open-to-view kitchen, bar with a variety of pisco sours, good service.

$$$ Inka Grill, Portal de Panes 115, Plaza de Armas, T084-262992, www.cusco restaurants.com. Specializing in Novo Andino cuisine, also home-made pastas, wide vegetarian selection, live music, excellent coffee and home-made pastries 'to go'. The first of group of good, varied eating places including **$$$ Limo**, Portal de Carnes 236, T084-240668, with strong emphasis on fish and seafood, fine pisco bar,

$$$ Pachapapa, Plazoleta San Blas 120, opposite church of San Blas, T084-241318, good Cusqueña and other dishes, and

$$ Greens Organic, Santa Catalina Angosta 135, upstairs, T084-243379, exclusively organic, but not wholly vegetarian.

$$$-$$ Divina Comedia, Pumacurco 406, T084-437640, www.restaurantcusco.com. Daily 1230-1500, 1830-2300. An elegant restaurant just 1 block from the Monasterio hotel. Diners are entertained by classical piano and singing, friendly atmosphere with comfortable seating, perfect for a special night out, reasonable prices.

$$ Jack's Café, Choquechaca 509, T084-254606, www.jackscafecusco.com, Open 0730-2230. Excellent varied menu, generous portions, relaxed atmosphere, can get very busy at lunchtime, expect a queue in high season.

$$-$ Aldea Yanapay, Ruinas 415, upstairs. Good café serving breakfast, lunch and dinner. Run by a charity that supports children's homes (www.aldeayanapay.org).

$ El Encuentro, Santa Catalina Ancha 384, T084-247977, and Choquechaca 136, T084-225496. One of the best-value eateries in Cuzco, 3 courses of good healthy vegan food and a drink for US$2, very busy at lunchtime.

Café El Ayllu, Almagro 133, T084-232357, and Marqués 263, T084-255078, www.cafe ayllu.com. Classical/folk music, good atmosphere, superb range of milk products, wonderful apple pastries, good selection for breakfast, great juices, quick service.

BARS AND CLUBS

Cross Keys Pub, Triunfo 350 (upstairs), T084-229227, www.cross-keys-pub-cusco-peru.com. Open 0800-2400, run by Barry Walker of **Manu Expeditions**, a Mancunian and ornithologist, cosy, darts, cable sports, pool, bar meals, plus daily half-price specials, very popular, great atmosphere, free Wi-Fi.
Norton Rat's Tavern, Santa Catalina Angosta 116, http://nortonratspub.com. On the corner of the Plaza de Armas, fine balcony, open 0700-0200, also serves meals, cable TV, popular, English spoken, pool, darts, motorcycle theme with information for motorcyclists from owner, Jeffrey Powers.
Ukuku's, Plateros 316, T084-254911, www.ukukusbar.com. Nightspots come and nightspots go, but Ukuku's is well-established, very popular, good atmosphere, good mix of music including live shows nightly.
Centro Qosqo de Arte Nativo, Av Sol 604, T084-227901, www.cusco.net/centroqosqo. Presents a regular nightly folklore show from 1900 to 2030, entrance on BTC ticket.

SHOPPING

In the **Plaza San Blas** and the surrounding area, authentic Cuzco crafts still survive. A market is held on Sat. Many leading artisans welcome visitors. Among fine objects made are Biblical figures from plaster, wheatflour and potatoes, reproductions of pre-Columbian ceramics and colonial sculptures, pious paintings, earthenware figurines, festive dolls and wood carvings.

Store of Weavers (Asociación Central de Artesanos y Artesanas del Sur Andino Inka-kunaq Ruwaynin), Av Tullumayo 274, T084-260942, www.tejidosandinos.com. Store run by 5 local weaving communities, some of whose residents you can see working on site. All profits go to the weavers themselves.

SACRED VALLEY OF THE INCAS

The name conjures up images of ancient rulers and their god-like status, with the landscape itself as their temple. And so it was, but the Incas also built their own tribute to this dramatic land in monuments such as Machu Picchu, Ollantaytambo, Pisac and countless others. For the tourist, the famous sights are now within easy reach of Cuzco, but the demand for adventure, to see lost cities in a less 21st-century context, means that there is ample scope for exploring. But if archaeology is not your thing, there are markets to enjoy, birds to watch, trails for mountain-biking and a whole range of hotels to relax in. The best time to visit is April to May or October to November. The high season is June-September, but the rainy season, from December to March, is cheaper and pleasant enough.

→ PISAC

Pisac, 30 km north of Cuzco, is known for its **market**, which contains sections for the tourist and for the local community. Traditionally, Sunday is the day when the people of the highlands come down to sell their produce (potatoes, corn, beans, vegetables, weavings and pottery). These are traded for essentials such as salt, sugar, rice, noodles, fruit, medicines, plastic goods and tools. The market comes to life after the arrival of tourist buses around 1000, and is usually over by 1700. However, there is also an important ceremony every Sunday, in which the *Varayocs* (village mayors) from the surrounding and highland villages participate in a Quechua Catholic Mass in **Pisac church**. It is a good example of the merging of, and respect for, different religious cultures. This aspect of the traditional Pisac Sunday market is still celebrated at 1100 sharp. Pisac has other, somewhat less crowded, less expensive markets on Tuesday and Thursday morning; in each case, it's best to get there before 0900.

On the plaza are the church and a small, interesting folklore museum. The **Museo Comunitario Pisac** ⓘ *Av Amazonas y Retamayoc K'asa, museopisac@gmail.com, daily 1000-1700, free but donations welcome* has a display of village life, created by the people of Pisac. There are many souvenir shops on Bolognesi. The local fiesta is on 15 July.

High above the town on the mountainside is a superb **Inca fortress** ⓘ *0700-1730, guides charge about US$5, you must show your BTC multi-site ticket to enter*. The walk up to the ruins begins from the plaza (but see below), past the Centro de Salud and a control post. The path goes through working terraces, giving the ruins a context. The first group of buildings is Pisaqa, with a fine curving wall. Climb then to the central part of the ruins, the Intihuatana group of temples and rock outcrops in the most magnificent Inca masonry. Here are the *Reloj Solar* ('Hitching Post of the Sun') – now closed because thieves stole a piece from it, palaces of the moon and stars, solstice markers, baths and water channels. From Intihuatana, a path leads around the hillside through a tunnel to Q'Allaqasa, the military area. Across the valley at this point, a large area of Inca tombs in holes in the hillside can be seen. The end of the site is Kanchiracay, where the agricultural workers were housed. Road transport approaches from this end. The descent takes 30 minutes. At dusk you will hear, if not see, the *pisaca* (partridges), after which the place is named. Even if going by car, do not rush as there is a lot to see and a lot of walking to do. Road transport approaches from the Kanchiracay end. The drive up from town takes about 20 minutes.

Walking up, although tiring, is recommended for the views and location. It's at least one hour uphill all the way. The descent takes 30 minutes on foot. Combis charge US$0.75 per person and taxis US$7 one way up to the ruins from near the bridge. Then you can walk back down (if you want the taxi to take you back down, usually from a lower level, it will be another US$7).

→ PISAC TO URUBAMBA

Calca, 2900 m, is 18 km beyond Pisac. There are basic hotels and eating places, and buses stop on the other side of the divided plaza. The **Fiesta de la Virgen Asunta** is on 15-16 August. The ruins of a small Inca town, **Huchuy Cuzco** ① *US$7.15 for trek and entry*, are dramatically located on a flat esplanade almost 600 m above Calca, from where a road has been built to the ruins. Alternatively, a steep trail goes to the site from behind the village of Lamay, across the river. A magnificent one- or two-day trek leads to Huchuy Cuzco from Tambo Machay, the route once taken by the Inca from his capital to his country estate.

VALLE DE LARES

To the north of Urubamba and Calca, beyond the great peaks that tower above the Sacred Valley, lies the valley of **Lares**, an area famed for its traditional Quechua communities and strong weaving traditions. The mountainous territory that lies between these two valleys and, indeed, the valleys themselves offer a great deal for the ambitious trekker. The entire Urubamba range is threaded with tracks and the remains of ancient Inca trails and, as

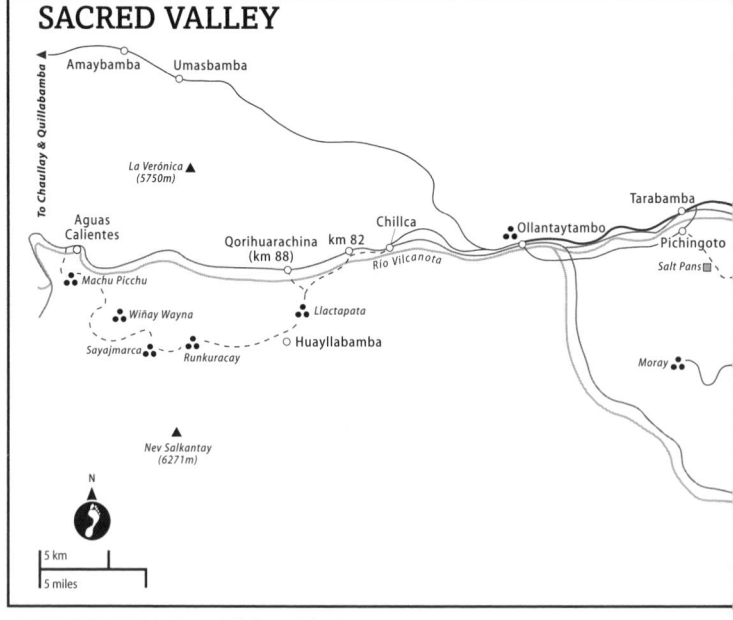

SACRED VALLEY

To Chaullay & Quillabamba

Amaybamba
Umasbamba
La Verónica ▲ (5750m)
Tarabamba
Aguas Calientes
Chillca
Ollantaytambo
Qorihuarachina (km 88)
km 82
Pichingoto
Río Vilcanota
Salt Pans ▥
Machu Picchu
Wiñay Wayna
Llactapata
Sayajmarca
Runkuracay
Huayllabamba
Moray
▲ Nev Salkantay (6271m)

N

5 km
5 miles

you might expect, the variety of trekking routes is almost endless. One of these options is presented below.

The four-day trek from **Huarán** (6 km west of Calca) to **Yanahuara** (beyond Urubamba on the road to Ollantaytambo) goes via the village of Lares through ancient native forests and past some of the Cordillera Urubamba's greatest snow peaks, their waters feeding jewelled lakes and cascades below. It provides an insight into the communities that inhabit this rugged and challenging land. Halfway you can have a good soak in the hot springs at Lares. Many of the locals may offer to sell weavings or *mantas* along the route, at prices a fraction of those in Cuzco. Remember if you bargain that many of these works take weeks, or perhaps a month or more to complete, so always give a fair price; at least here all the money goes to the weavers themselves.

Lares is also a perfect example of Peru's fabulous mountain-biking opportunities and it has something for everyone, suiting all levels of daring and technical ability. In two days you can freewheel from chilly mountain passes, past llamas and traditional Quechua communities, on unpaved but drivable roads, or down technical single-track routes following old Inca trails and through precipitous canyons alongside rushing mountain torrents. The area is firmly established with Cuzco agencies for trekking and cycling tours, often as an alternative or add-on to the Inca Trail.

YUCAY

About 3 km east of Urubamba, Yucay has two grassy plazas divided by the restored colonial church of Santiago Apóstol, with its oil paintings and fine altars. On the opposite

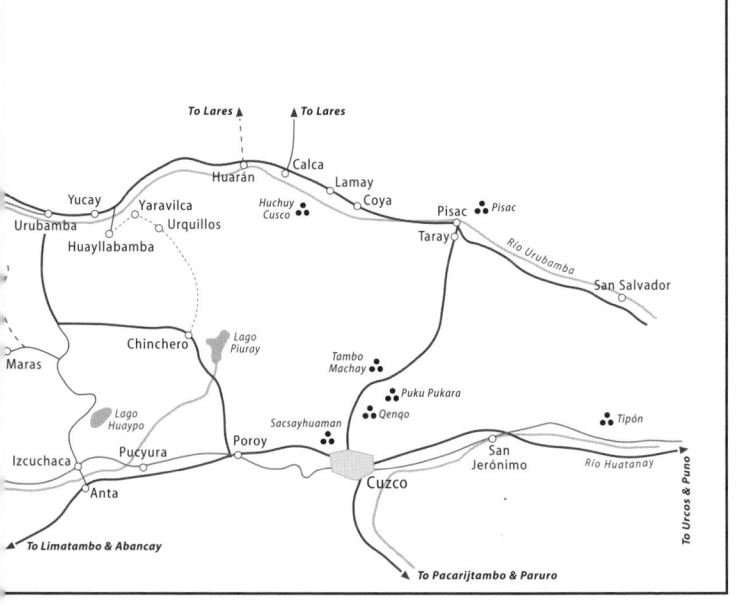

side from Plaza Manco II is the adobe palace built for Sayri Túpac (Manco's son) when he emerged from Vilcabamba in 1558. In Yucay monks sell milk, ham and eggs from their farm on the hillside.

→ URUBAMBA

Like many places along the valley, Urubamba is in a fine setting with snow-capped peaks in view. Calle Berriózabal, on the west edge of town, is lined with scarlet-flowered pisonay trees. The large market square is one block west of the main plaza. The main road skirts the town, and the bridge for the road to Chinchero is just to the east of town. Visit **Seminario-Bejar Ceramic Studio** ① *Berriózabal 111, T084-201002, www.ceramicaseminario.com*, where Pablo Seminario and his workshop have investigated and use pre-Columbian techniques and designs, highly recommended. For local festivals, May and June are the harvest months, with many processions following ancient schedules. Urubamba's main festival, El Señor de Torrechayoc, occupies the first week of June.

About 6 km west of Urubamba is **Tarabamba**, where a bridge crosses the Río Urubamba. Turn right after crossing the bridge to **Pichingoto**, a tumbled-down village built under an overhanging cliff. Also, just over the bridge and before the town to the left of a small, walled cemetery is a salt stream. Follow the footpath beside the stream to Salineras, a small village below which is a mass of terraced **pre-Inca salt pans** that are still in operation (entry US\$1.80) after thousands of years; there are over 5000 of them. The walk to the salt pans takes about 30 minutes. Take water as this side of the valley can be very hot and dry.

→ CHINCHERO AND MORAY

At 3762 m, **Chinchero** ① *site 0700-1730, entrance by BTC (see page 54)*, is just off a direct road to Urubamba from Cuzco. It has an attractive church built upon an Inca temple. The church has been restored to reveal in all their glory the interior paintings. The ceiling, beams and walls are covered in beautiful floral and religious designs. The church is open on Sunday for mass and at festivals; ask in the tourist office in Cuzco for other times. Recent excavations there have revealed many Inca walls and terraces. The food market and the handicraft market are separate. The former is held every day, on your left as you come into town. The latter, on Sunday only, is up by the church, small but attractive. On any day but Sunday there are few tourists. The local fiesta is the Day of the Virgin, on 8 September. Much of the area's character will change if a plan to build a new airport for Cuzco on nearby agricultural land goes ahead.

At **Moray** ① *US\$3, or by BTC*, there are three 'colosseums', used by the Incas, according to some theories, as a sort of open-air crop nursery, and known locally as the laboratory of the Incas. The great depressions contain no ruined buildings, but are lined with fine terracing. Each level is said to have its own microclimate. It is a very atmospheric place which, many claim, has mystical power, and the scenery is absolutely stunning. The most interesting way to get to Moray is from Urubamba via the Pichingoto bridge (see above). The climb up from the bridge is fairly steep but easy. The path passes by the spectacular salt pans (see above), taking 1½ to two hours to the top. The village of Maras is about 45 minutes further on, then it's 9 km by road or 5 km through the fields to Moray. There is a paved road from the main road between Chinchero and Urubamba to Maras from where an unmade road leads to Moray. Ask in Maras for the best route to walk, other than on the main road. Any bus between Urubamba and Cuzco via Chinchero passes the clearly marked turning to Maras. From the junction taxi colectivos charge US$2.50 per person to Maras, or you can walk (30 minutes). There is public transport from Chinchero to Maras; it stops running between 1700 and 1800. A taxi to Moray, with a one-hour wait, can then take you to the salt pans, from where you can walk back to the Urubamba–Ollantaytambo road, US$25. Tour companies in Cuzco offer cycle trips to Moray. There are no hotels at all in the area, so take care not to get stranded.

→ OLLANTAYTAMBO

ⓘ *Inca ruins open 0700-1730. If possible arrive very early, 0700, before most of the tourists. Admission by BTC (see page 54). Guides at the entrance.*

The Inca town, or *llacta*, on which the present-day town is based is clearly seen in the fine examples of Inca *canchas* (blocks), which are almost entirely intact and still occupied behind the main plaza. Entering Ollantaytambo from Pisac, the road is built along the long wall of 100 niches. Note the inclination of the wall: it leans towards the road. Since it was the Incas' practice to build with the walls leaning towards the interiors of the buildings, it has been deduced that the road, much narrower then, was built inside a succession of buildings. The road out of the plaza leads across a bridge, down to the colonial church with its enclosed *recinto*. Beyond is Plaza Araccama (and car park) with the entrance to the archaeological site.

The so-called **Baño de la Ñusta** (bath of the princess) is of grey granite, and is in a small area between the town and the temple fortress. Some 200 m behind the Baño de la Ñusta along the face of the mountain are some small ruins known as **Inca Misanca**, believed to have been a small temple or observatory. A series of steps, seats and niches have been carved out of the cliff. There is a complete irrigation system, including a canal at shoulder level, some 15 cm deep, cut out of the sheer rock face. The flights of **terraces** leading up above the town are superb, and so are the curving terraces following the contours of the rocks overlooking the Urubamba. These terraces were successfully defended by Manco Inca's warriors against Hernando Pizarro in 1536. Manco Inca built the wall above the site and another wall closing the Yucay Valley against attack from Cuzco. These are visible on either side of the valley.

The **temple** itself was started by Pachacútec, using Colla Indians from Lake Titicaca – hence the similarities of the monoliths facing the central platform with the Tiwanaku remains on the lake's southeastern shore.. The massive, highly finished granite blocks at the top are worth the climb to see. The Colla are said to have deserted halfway through the work, which explains the many unfinished blocks lying about the site.

The **Bio Museo** ⓘ *K'uychipunku y Calle La Convención, T084-204181, T984-962607, www.biomuseo.org, Tue-Sun 0930-2030, US$1.80 requested as a donation*, houses a comprehensive collection of native herbs, potatoes and grains and holds workshops and evening storytelling sessions.

On the west side of the main ruins, a two-dimensional 'pyramid' has been identified in the layout of the fields and walls of the valley. A fine 750 m wall aligns with the rays of the winter solstice on 21 June. It can be appreciated from a high point about 3.5 km from Ollantaytambo.

SACRED VALLEY OF THE INCAS LISTINGS

WHERE TO STAY

$$$$ Pakaritampu, C Ferrocarril s/n, Ollantaytambo, T084-204020, www. pakaritampu.com. Modern, TV room, restaurant and bar, laundry, safe and room service. Adventure sports can be arranged. Lunch and dinner are extra. Excellent quality and service.

$$$$ Sol y Luna, Fundo Huincho, west of Urubamba, T084-201620, www.hotelsoly luna.com. Award-winning bungalows and suites set off the main road in lovely gardens, pool, excellent gourmet restaurant, wine tastings, spa, handicrafts shop. Also has **Wayra** lounge bar and dining room, open to non-guests, for freshly cooked, informal lunches, and arranges adventure and cultural activities and traditional tours. Profits go to **Sol y Luna** educational association, www.colegiosolyluna.com.

$$$$ Sonesta Posadas del Inca Sacred Valley, Plaza Manco II de Yucay 123, Yukay, T084-201107, www.sonesta.com. Converted 300-year-old monastery, like a little village with plazas, chapel, 69 comfortable, heated rooms, price includes buffet breakfast. Lots of activities can be arranged, canoeing, horse riding, mountain biking, etc. Inkafe restaurant is open to all, serving Peruvian, fusion and traditional cuisine with a buffet.

$$$ El Albergue Ollantaytambo, within the railway station gates, Ollantaytambo, T084-204014, www.elalbergue.com. Owned by North American artist Wendy Weeks. Also has **Café Mayu** on the station and a good restaurant. Characterful rooms, rustic elegance, some larger than others, some with safe, lovely gardens, great showers and a eucalyptus steam sauna. Books for sale and exchange, also handicrafts. Private transport can be arranged to nearby attractions, also mountain-biking, rafting and taxi transfers to the airport. Expect to hear the movements of the trains.

$$$ The Green House, Km 60.2 Huaran, T084-115375, www.thegreenhouseperu. com. A charming, Wi-Fi-free retreat, only 4 rooms, breakfast included, comfortable lounge, restaurant, small kitchen for guests, beautiful garden, restricted internet. No children under 10. Information on walks and day trips in the area. Activities include hiking, biking, horse riding and rafting. Intimate, beautiful and relaxing.

$$ Apu Lodge, Calle Lari, Ollantaytambo, T084-797162, www.apulodge.com. On the edge of town, great views of the ruins and surrounding mountains. Good service, can help organize tours and treks. They work with **Leap Local** (www.leaplocal.org) guides project.

$$ Las Chullpas, Querocancha s/n, 3 km from Urubamba, T084-201568, www.chullpas.pe. Very peaceful, excellent breakfast, vegetarian meals, English and German spoken, natural medicine, treks, riding, mountain biking. Mototaxi from town US$1, taxi (ask for Querocancha) US$3.

$$ Pisac Inn, at the corner of Pardo on the Plaza, Pisac, T084-203062, www. pisacinn.com. Bright and charming local decor, pleasant atmosphere, private and shared bathrooms, hot water, sauna and massage. Good breakfast, the **Cuchara de Palo** restaurant serves meals using local ingredients, plus pizza and pasta, café.

RESTAURANTS

$$$-$$ El Huacatay, Arica 620, Urubamba, T084-201790, www.elhuacatay.com. Open Mon-Sat. A small restaurant with a reputation for fine, creative fusion cuisine (local, Mediterranean, Asian).

$$ Heart's Café, Plaza de Armas, Ollantaytambo, T084-204013, www.livingheartperu.org. Open 0700-2100. Mainly wholefood restaurant serving international and Peruvian dishes, including vegetarian, box lunch and takeaway available, good coffee. All profits to education and self-help projects in the Sacred Valley. Deservedly popular.

$$-$ Mullu, Plaza de Armas 352 and Mcal Castilla 375, Pisac, T084-208182. Open Tue-Sun 0900-1900. Café/restaurant related to the **Mullu** store in Cuzco, also has a gallery promoting local artists.

$ Pizza Wasi, Av Mcal Castilla 857, Urubamba, T084-434751 for delivery. Good pizzas and pastas. Mulled wine served in a small restaurant with nice decor, good value. Has another branch on Plaza Araccama in Ollantaytambo.

Ulrike's Café, Plaza de Armas 828, Pisac, T084-203195. Has possibly the best apple crumble with ice cream, excellent coffee, smoothies and a wide range of international dishes. Good value 3-course daily menu. A good place to chill out.

MACHU PICCHU AND THE INCA TRAIL

There is a tremendous feeling of awe on first witnessing Machu Picchu. The ancient citadel straddles the saddle of a high mountain (2380 m) with steep terraced slopes falling away to the fast-flowing Río Urubamba snaking its hairpin course far below in the valley floor. Towering overhead is Huayna Picchu, and green jungle peaks provide the backdrop for the whole majestic scene. Machu Picchu is a complete Inca city. For centuries it was buried in jungle, until Hiram Bingham stumbled upon it in 1911. It was then explored by an archaeological expedition sent by Yale University. The ruins – staircases, terraces, temples, palaces, towers, fountains and the famous Intihuatana (the so-called 'Hitching Post of the Sun') – require at least a day to visit. Take time to appreciate not only the masonry, but also the selection of large rocks for foundations, the use of water in the channels below the Temple of the Sun, and the surrounding mountains.

→MACHU PICCHU

ARRIVING AT MACHU PICCHU

Getting there The most leisurely way to get to Machu Picchu is by train to the town of Aguas Calientes. Services run from Poroy, Urubamba or Ollantaytambo, all reached by bus from Cuzco. **PerúRail** (www.perurail.com) runs from all three, **Inca Rail** (www.incarail. com) runs only from Ollantaytambo. Buses run from Aguas Calientes to the ruins every 30 minutes from 0530, 25 minutes, US$18.50 return, US$9.25 single, children US$10, valid 48 hours. The bus stop in Aguas Calientes is 50 m from the railway station, with the ticket office opposite. Tickets can also be bought in advance at **Consetur**, Santa Catalina Ancha, Cuzco, which saves queuing when you arrive in Aguas Calientes.

Another option is to take a Machu Picchu By Car tour, which agencies in Cuzco run over one or two nights. Passengers are taken to the Hidroeléctrica train station via Ollantaytambo and Abra Málaga, with an overnight stay in Aguas Calientes or Santa Teresa before visiting the site. The tour includes transport, lodging, Machu Picchu entry, some meals and guide, US$115-160 per person.

Tourist information The site is open from 0600 to 1730. Only 2500 visitors are allowed entry each day and tickets must be purchased in advance. Entrance fee to Machu Picchu only is 128 soles (US$45.50), 65 soles (US$23) for Peruvians, 63 soles (US$22.40) with ISIC card. To climb Huayna Picchu you have to buy a ticket for site entry plus the climb and specify whether you are going to go 0700-0800 or 1000-1100 (only 400 people are allowed up at one time), 152 soles (US$54). There is also a combined Machu Picchu and Museum ticket, 150 soles (US$53.30) and a Machu Picchu + Montaña ticket (also limited to 400 per day) for 142 soles (US$50.50). Because of the limit on numbers it is wise to reserve your ticket online well in advance at www.machupicchu.gob.pe. You can pay online with Visa or at a number of outlets given on the website. These include branches of Banco de la Nación, **Centro Cultural de Machu Picchu** in Aguas Calientes ① *Av Pachacútec cuadra 1, 0500-2200 (also i perú here, of 4, T084-211104, iperumachupicchu@ promperu.gob.pe, daily 0900-1300, 1400-2000)*, **Dirección Regional de Cultura** in Cuzco

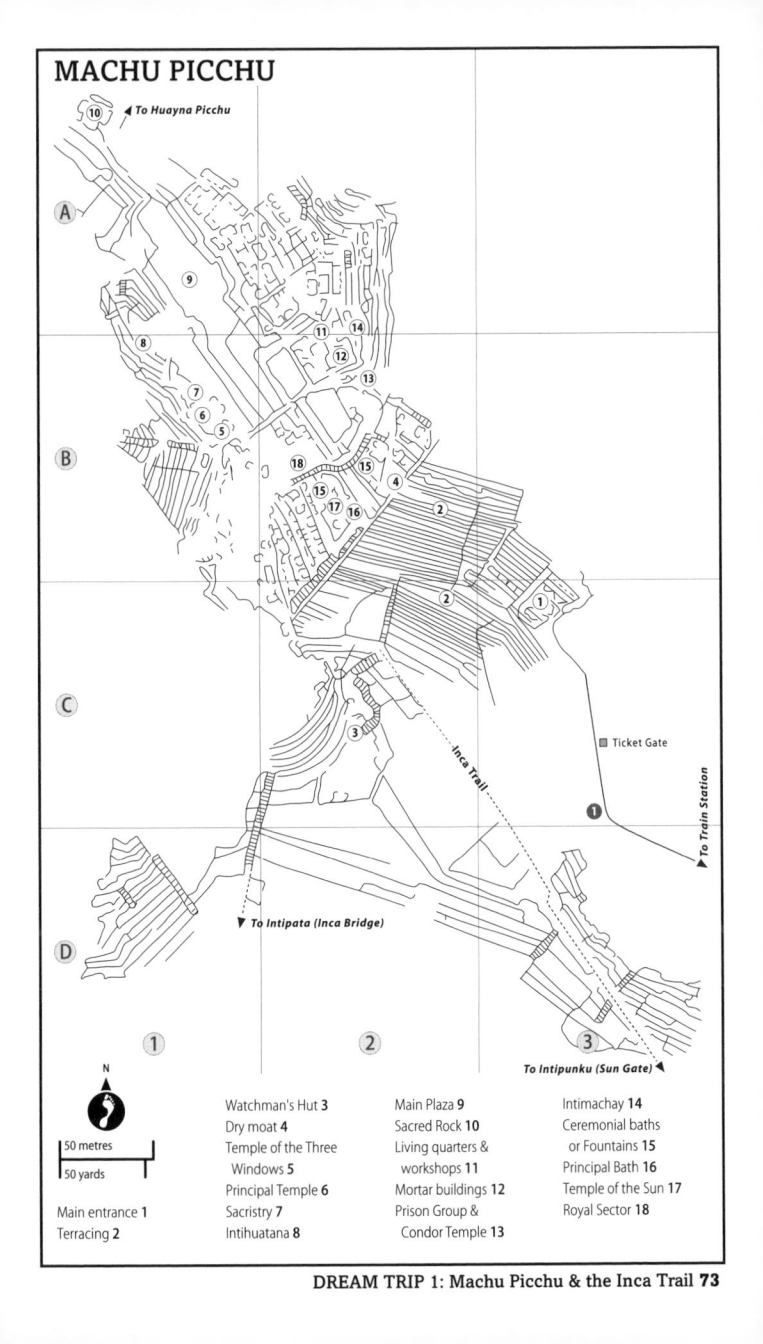

MACHU PICCHU

To Huayna Picchu

⑩

Ⓐ

⑨

⑧

⑪ ⑭
⑫
⑬

⑦
⑥
⑤

Ⓑ
⑱
⑮ ④
⑮ ②
⑰ ⑯

② ①

Ⓒ
③

Inca Trail

☐ Ticket Gate

①

To Train Station ►

Ⓓ

▼ To Intipata (Inca Bridge)

③

To Intipunku (Sun Gate) ◄

Ⓝ

N

50 metres
50 yards

① ② ③

Main entrance **1**
Terracing **2**

Watchman's Hut **3**
Dry moat **4**
Temple of the Three
  Windows **5**
Principal Temple **6**
Sacristry **7**
Intihuatana **8**

Main Plaza **9**
Sacred Rock **10**
Living quarters &
  workshops **11**
Mortar buildings **12**
Prison Group &
  Condor Temple **13**

Intimachay **14**
Ceremonial baths
  or Fountains **15**
Principal Bath **16**
Temple of the Sun **17**
Royal Sector **18**

(see page 55), AATC, C Nueva Baja 424, Cuzco, offices of PerúRail and Inca Rail in Cuzco, Hotel Monasterio. Other websites offer tickets for sale, at an inflated price. Do not buy (fake) tickets on the street in Cuzco.

You can deposit your luggage at the entrance for a small fee. Guides are available at the site, and they are often very knowledgeable and worthwhile. The official price for a guide is US$80 for a full tour for one to 10 people. Site wardens are also informative, in Spanish only. A guarded gate by the river in Aguas Calientes opens only at 0530, so it is not possible to walk up to the ruins to be there before the first buses. After 1530 the ruins are quieter, but note that the last bus down leaves at 1730. Monday and Friday are bad days in high season because there is usually a crowd of people on guided tours who are going or have been to Pisac market on Sunday. One hotel is located next to the entrance, with a self-service restaurant. Take your own food and drink if you don't want to pay hotel prices, and take plenty of drinking water. Note that food is not officially allowed into the site and drink can only be carried in canteens/water bottles. In the dry season sandflies can be a problem, so take insect repellent and wear long clothes.

AGUAS CALIENTES

It's advisable to should spend the night at Aguas Calientes (also known as Machu Picchu Pueblo) so that you can visit the ruins early in the morning, when fewer people are around. Most hotels and restaurants are near the railway station, on the plaza, or on Avenida Pachacútec, which leads from the plaza to the **thermal baths** ① *0500-2030, US$3.15, 10 mins' walk from the town*, a communal pool, smelling of sulphur, with a good bar for cocktails in the pool. You can rent towels and bathing costumes (US$3) at several places on the road to the baths; basic toilets and changing facilities and showers for washing *before* entering the baths; take soap and shampoo, and keep an eye on valuables. The **Museo Manuel Chávez Ballón** ① *Carretera Hiram Bingham, Wed-Sun 0900-1600, see above for tickets*, displays objects found at Machu Picchu.

AROUND THE SITE

Once you have passed through the ticket gate you follow a path to a small complex of buildings that now acts as the **main entrance** (1) to the ruins. It is set at the eastern end of the extensive **terracing** (2) that must have supplied the crops for the city. Above this point, turning back on yourself, you can see the final stretch of the Inca Trail leading down from **Intipunku** (Sun Gate), see page 80. From a promontory here, on which stands the building called the **Watchman's Hut** (3), you get the perfect view of the city (the one you've seen on all the postcards), laid out before you with Huayna Picchu rising above the furthest extremity. Go round the promontory and head south for the **Intipata** (Inca bridge), see page 75. The main path into the ruins comes to a **dry moat** (4) that cuts right across the site. At the moat you can either climb the long staircase that goes to the upper reaches of the city, or you can enter the city by the baths and the Temple of the Sun.

The more strenuous way into the city is by the former route, which takes you past quarries on your left as you look down to the Urubamba on the west flank of the mountain. To your right are roofless buildings where you can see in close-up the general construction methods used in the city. Proceeding along this level, above the main plazas, you reach the **Temple of the Three Windows** (5) and the **Principal Temple** (6), which has a smaller building called the **Sacristy** (7). The two main buildings are three-sided and were clearly of great importance, given the fine stonework involved. The wall with the three windows is built onto a single rock, one of the many instances in the city where the architects did not merely put their construction on a convenient piece of land. They used and fashioned its features to suit their concept of how the city should be tied to the mountain, its forces and the alignment of its stones to the surrounding peaks. In the Principal Temple, a diamond-shaped stone in the floor is said to depict the constellation of the Southern Cross.

Continue on the path behind the Sacristy to reach the **Intihuatana** (8), the 'Hitching-Post of the Sun'. The name comes from the theory that such carved rocks (*gnomons*), found at all major Inca sites, were the point to which the sun was symbolically 'tied' at the winter solstice, before being freed to rise again on its annual ascent towards the summer solstice. The steps, angles and planes of this sculpted block appear to indicate a purpose beyond simple decoration, and researchers have sought the trajectory of each alignment. Whatever the motivation behind this magnificent carving, it is undoubtedly one of the highlights of Machu Picchu.

Climb down from the Intihuatana's mound to the **Main Plaza** (9). Beyond its northern end is a small plaza with open-sided buildings on two sides and on the third, the **Sacred Rock** (10). The outline of this gigantic, flat stone echoes that of the mountains behind it. From here you can proceed to the entrance to the trail to Huayna Picchu (see below). Returning to the Main Plaza and heading southeast, you pass, on your left, several groups of closely packed buildings that have been taken to be **living quarters** and **workshops** (11), **mortar buildings** (12; look for the house with two discs let into the floor) and the **Prison Group** (13), one of whose constructions is known as the **Condor Temple**. Also in this area is a cave called **Intimachay** (14).

A short distance from the Condor Temple is the lower end of a series of **ceremonial baths** (15) or fountains. They were probably used for ritual bathing, and the water still flows down them today. The uppermost, **Principal Bath** (16), is the most elaborate. Next to it is the **Temple of the Sun** (17), or Torreón. This singular building has one straight wall from which another wall curves around and back to meet the straight one, but for the doorway. From above it looks like an incomplete letter P. It is another example of the architecture being at one with its environment, as the interior is taken up by the partly worked summit of the outcrop onto which the building is placed. All indications are that this temple was used for astronomical purposes. Underneath the Torreón a cave-like opening has been formed by an oblique gash in the rock. Fine masonry has been added to the opposing wall, making a second side of a triangle, which contrasts with the rough edge of the split rock. But the blocks of masonry appear to have been slotted behind another sculpted piece of natural stone, which has been cut into a four-stepped buttress. Immediately behind this is a two-stepped buttress. This strange combination of the natural and the man-made has been called the Tomb or Palace of the Princess. Across the stairway from the complex that includes the Torreón is the group of buildings known as the **Royal Sector** (18).

The famous Inca bridge – **Intipata** – is about 30 minutes along a well-marked trail south of the Royal Sector. The bridge, which is actually a couple of logs, is spectacularly sited, carved into a vertiginous cliff-face. The walk is well worth it for the fine views, but the bridge itself is closed to visitors.

Huayna Picchu, the mountain overlooking the site (on which there are also ruins), has steps to the top for a superlative view of the whole site, but it is not for those who are afraid of heights and you shouldn't leave the path. The climb takes up to 90 minutes but the steps are dangerous after bad weather. Visitors are given access to the main path at

0700 and 1000 daily, latest return time 1500 (maximum 200 people per departure). Check with the Ministerio de Cultura in Aguas Calientes or Cuzco for current departure times and to sign up for a place. Another trail to Huayna Picchu, down near the Urubamba, is via the Temple of the Moon, in two caves, one above the other, with superb Inca niches inside. For the trail to the Temple of the Moon: from the path to Huayna Picchu, take the marked trail to the left. It is in good shape, although it descends further than you think it should. After the Temple you may proceed to Huayna Picchu, but this path is overgrown, slippery in the wet and has a crooked ladder on an exposed part about 10 minutes before reaching the top (not for the faint-hearted). It is safer to return to the main trail to Huayna Picchu, although this adds about 30 minutes to the climb. The round trip takes about four hours. Before doing any trekking around Machu Picchu, check with an official which paths may be used, or which are one-way.

→ THE INCA TRAIL

The most impressive way to reach Machu Picchu is via the centuries-old Inca Trail that winds its way from the Sacred Valley near Ollantaytambo, taking three to five days. The spectacular hike runs from Km 88 (from Cuzco along the Urubamba), Qorihuayrachina (2600 m), a point immediately after the first tunnel 22 km beyond Ollantaytambo station. A sturdy suspension bridge has now been built over the Río Urubamba. Guided tours often start at Km 82, Piscacucho, reached by road. Rules for hiking the trail are detailed below. What makes this hike so special is the stunning combination of Inca ruins, unforgettable views, magnificent mountains, exotic vegetation and extraordinary ecological variety.

ARRIVING AT THE INCA TRAIL

Equipment The Inca Trail is rugged and steep, but the magnificent views compensate for any weariness that may be felt. It is cold at night, however, and weather conditions change rapidly, so it is important to take not only strong footwear, rain gear and warm clothing but also food, water, water purification for when you fill bottles from streams, insect repellent, a supply of plastic bags, coverings, a good sleeping bag, a torch/flashlight and a stove for preparing hot food and drink to ward off the cold at night. A stove using paraffin (kerosene) is preferable, as fuel can be bought in small quantities in markets. A tent is essential, but if you're hiring one in Cuzco, check carefully for leaks. Walkers who have not taken adequate equipment have died of exposure.

All the necessary equipment can be rented in Cuzco from specialist shops if the agency organizing your trek is not providing the gear. A deposit will be asked for. Check the equipment for missing parts or faults. If you have any doubts about carrying your own pack, reasonably priced porters/guides are available. Carry a day-pack for your water, snacks, etc in case you walk faster than the porters and you have to wait for them to catch you up.

Tours Travel Agencies in Cuzco arrange transport to the start, equipment, food, etc, for an all-in price for all treks that lead to Machu Picchu. Prices start at about US$540-620 per person for a four-day/three-night trek on the Classic Inca Trail and rise according to the level of service given. If the price is significantly lower, you should be concerned as the company will be cutting corners and may not be paying the environment the respect the regulations were designed to instil. All are subject to strict rules and must be licensed. Tour

ON THE ROAD
Inca society

Cuzco was the capital of the Inca Empire – one of the greatest planned societies the world has known – from its rise during the 11th century to its fall in the early 16th century. (See John Hemming's *Conquest of the Incas* and B C Brundage's *Lords of Cuzco* and *Empire of the Inca*.) It was solidly based on other Peruvian civilizations, which had attained great skill in textiles, building, ceramics and working in metal. Immemorially, the political structure of the Andean *indígena* had been the *ayllu*, the village community; it had its divine ancestor, worshipped household gods, was closely knit by ties of blood to the family and by economic necessity to the land, which was held in common. Submission to the *ayllu* was absolute, because it was only by such discipline that food could be obtained in an unsympathetic environment. All the domestic animals, the llama and alpaca and the dog, had long been tamed, and the great staple crops, maize and potatoes, established. What the Incas did – and it was a magnificent feat – was to conquer enormous territories and impose upon the variety of *ayllus*, through an unchallengeable central government, a willing spiritual and economic submission to the state. The common religion, already developed by the classical Tiwanaku culture, was worship of the Sun, whose vice-regent on earth was the absolute Sapa Inca. Around him, in the capital, was a religious and secular elite, which never froze into a caste because it was open to talent. The elite was often recruited from chieftains defeated by the Incas; an effective way of reconciling local opposition. The mass of the people were subjected to rigorous planning. They were allotted land to work, for their group and for the state; set various tasks (the making of textiles, pottery, weapons, ropes, etc) from primary materials supplied by the functionaries, or used in enlarging the area of cultivation by building terraces on the hillsides. Their political organization was simple but effective. The family, and not the individual, was the unit. Families were grouped in units of 10, 100, 500, 1000, 10,000 and 40,000, each group with a leader responsible to the next largest group. The Sapa Inca crowned the political edifice; his four immediate counsellors were those to whom he allotted responsibility for the northern, southern, eastern and western regions (*suyos*) of the empire.

Equilibrium between production and consumption, in the absence of a free price mechanism and good transport facilities, must depend heavily upon statistical information. This the Incas raised to a high degree of efficiency by means of their *quipus*: a decimal system of recording numbers by knots in cords. Seasonal variations were guarded against by creating a system of state barns in which provender could be stored during years of plenty, to be used in years of scarcity. Statistical efficiency alone required that no one should be permitted to leave his home or his work. The loss of personal liberty was the price paid by the masses for economic security. In order to obtain information and to transmit orders quickly, the Incas built fine paved pathways along which couriers sped on foot. The whole system of rigorous control was completed by the greatest of all their monarchs, Pachacuti, who also imposed a common language, Quechua, as a further cementing force.

operators taking clients on any of the Inca Trails leading to Machu Picchu have to pay an annual fee. Groups of up to seven independent travellers who do not wish to use a tour operator are allowed to hike the trails if they contact an independent, licensed guide to accompany them, as long as they do not contact any other persons such as porters or cooks. A maximum 500 visitors per day are allowed on the Classic Inca Trail. Operators pay US$15 for each porter and other trail staff; porters are not permitted to carry more than 20 kg. Littering is banned, as is carrying plastic water bottles (canteens only may be carried). Pets and pack animals are prohibited, but llamas are allowed as far as the first pass. Groups have to use approved campsites only.

Trail tickets On all hiking trails (Km 82 or Km 88 to Machu Picchu, Salkantay to Machu Picchu, and Km 82 or Km 88 to Machu Picchu via Km 104) adults must pay US$95, students and children under 15 US$47. On the Camino Real de los Inkas from Km 104 to Wiñay-Wayna and Machu Picchu the fee is US$55 per adult, US$31 for students and children, and Salkantay to Huayllabamba and Km 88, US$55. The Salkantay trek is subject to a trekking charge of US$45. All tickets must be bought at the Dirección de Cultura office in Cuzco (see page 55); tickets are only sold on presentation of a letter from a licensed tour operator on behalf of the visitor, including full passport details. Tickets are non-refundable and cannot be changed, so make sure you provide accurate passport details to your tour operator. None is sold at the entrance to any of the routes. Depending on the time of year you want to hike the Trail, you should reserve your ticket anything from two months to a year in advance. You can save a bit of money by arranging your own transport back to Ollantaytambo in advance, either for the last day of your tour, or by staying an extra night in Aguas Calientes and taking the early morning train, then take a bus back to Cuzco. If you take your own tent and sleeping gear, some agencies give a discount. Make sure your return train ticket to Cuzco has your name on it (spelt absolutely correctly) for the tourist train, otherwise you have to pay for any changes.

    The Trail is closed each February for cleaning and repair. The Annual Inca Trail Clean-up takes place usually in September. Many agencies and organizations are involved and volunteers should contact South American Explorers in Cuzco for full details of ways to help.

Advice Four days would make a comfortable trip (though much depends on the weather). Allow a further day to see Machu Picchu when you have recovered from the hike. You cannot take backpacks into Machu Picchu; leave them at the ticket office. The first two days of the Trail involve the stiffest climbing, so do not attempt it if you're feeling unwell. Leave all your valuables in Cuzco and keep everything inside your tent, even your shoes. Security has, however, improved in recent years. Always take sufficient cash in soles to tip porters and guides at the end (each trekker, at his or her discretion, should provide about 100 soles, which will be put into a pot to be distributed among the staff). Avoid the July-August high season and check the conditions in the rainy season from November to April (note that this can vary). In the wet it is cloudy and the paths are very muddy and difficult. Also watch out for coral snakes in this area (black, red, yellow bands).

THE TRAIL
The trek to the sacred site begins either at Km 82, **Piscacucho**, or at Km 88, **Qorihuayrachina**, at 2600 m. In order to reach Km 82 hikers are transported by their tour operator in a minibus on the road that goes to Quillabamba. From Piri onward the road follows the riverbank and ends at Km 82, where there is a bridge. The Inca Trail equipment, food, fuel and field personnel reach Km 82 (depending on the tour operator's logistics) for the SERNANP staff to weigh each bundle before the group arrives. When several groups are

ON THE ROAD

The **Camino Real de los Inkas** starts at Km 104, where a footbridge gives access to the ruins of Chachabamba and the trail, which ascends, passing above the ruins of Choquesuysuy, to connect with the main trail at Wiñay-Wayna. This first part is a steady, continuous ascent of three hours (take water) and the trail is narrow and exposed in parts. Many people recommend this short Inca Trail. Good hiking trails from Aguas Calientes have been opened along the left bank of the Urubamba, for day hikes crossing the bridge of the hydroelectric plant to Choquesuysuy. A three-night trek goes from Km 82 to Km 88, then along the Río Urubamba to Pacaymayo Bajo and Km 104, from where you take the Camino Real de los Inkas.

Two treks involve routes from **Salkantay**: one, known as the **High Inca Trail**, joins the Classic Trail at Huayllabamba, then proceeds as before on the main Trail through Wiñay Wayna to Machu Picchu. To get to Salkantay, you have to start the trek in **Mollepata**, northwest of Cuzco in the Apurímac valley. Ampay buses run from Arcopata on the Chinchero road, or you can take private transport to Mollepata (three hours from Cuzco). Salkantay to Machu Picchu this way takes three nights. The second Salkantay route, known as the **Santa Teresa Trek**, takes four days and crosses the 4500-m Huamantay Pass to reach the Santa Teresa Valley, which you follow to its confluence with the Urubamba. The goal is the town of Santa Teresa from where you can go to the Hidroeléctrica station for the local train to Aguas Calientes. On this trek, **Machu Picchu Lodge to Lodge** ① Mountain Lodges of Peru, T084-243636 (in Lima T01-421 6952, in North America T1-510-525 8846, in Europe 43-664-434 3340), www.mountainlodgesofperu.com, conducts fully guided tours of seven days, going from lodge to lodge, set up at Soraypampa (**Salkantay Lodge and Adventure Resort**), Huayraccmachay (**Wayra Lodge**), Collpapampa (**Colpa Lodge**) and Lucmabamba (**Lucma Lodge**). Contact **Mountain Lodges of Peru** for rates, departure dates and all other details, also for their new lodge-to-lodge route from Lamay to Ollantaytambo.

Inca Jungle Trail This is offered by several tour operators in Cuzco: on the first day you cycle downhill from Abra Málaga to Santa María: four or five hours of riding on the main Quillabamba–Cuzco highway with speeding vehicles inattentive to cyclists on the road. It's best to pay for good bikes and back-up on this section. The second day is a hard seven-hour trek from Santa María to Santa Teresa. It involves crossing three adventurous bridges and bathing in the hot springs at Santa Teresa (US$1.65 entry). The third day is a six-hour trek from Santa Teresa to Aguas Calientes and the final day is a guided tour of Machu Picchu.

leaving on the same day, it is more convenient to arrive early. Km 88 can only be reached by train, subject to schedule and baggage limitations. The train goes more slowly than a bus, but you start your walk nearer to Llaqtapata and Huayllabamba. (See box, above, for variations in starting points for the Inca Trail.)

The walk to **Huayllabamba**, following the Cusichaca River, needs about three hours and isn't too arduous. Beyond Huayllabamba, a popular camping spot for tour groups, there is a camping place about an hour ahead, at **Llulluchayoc** (3200 m). A punishing 1½-hour climb further is **Llulluchapampa**, an ideal meadow for camping. If you have the energy to reach this point, it will make the second day easier because the next stage, the ascent to the first pass, **Warmiwañuska** (Dead Woman's Pass) at 4200 m, is tough; 2½ hours.

Afterwards take the steep path downhill to the Pacamayo Valley. Beware of slipping on the Inca steps after rain. Tour groups usually camp by a stream at the bottom (1½ hours from the first pass). It is no longer permitted to camp at **Runkuracay**, on the way up to the second pass (a much easier climb, 3850 m). These are magnificent views near the summit in clear weather. A good overnight place is about 30 minutes past the Inca ruins at **Sayacmarca** (3500 m), about an hour on after the top of the second pass.

A gentle two-hour climb on a fine stone highway leads through an Inca tunnel to the third pass. Near the top there's a spectacular view of the entire Vilcabamba range. You descend to Inca ruins at **Phuyopatamarca** (3650 m), well worth a long visit, even camping overnight. There is a 'tourist bathroom' here where water can be collected (but purify it before drinking).

From there steps go downhill to the impressive ruins of **Wiñay-Wayna** (2700 m, entry US$5.75), with views of the recently cleared terraces of Intipata. Access is possible, but the trail is not easily visible. There is a basic hostel with bunk beds, **$**, showers and a small restaurant. There is a small campsite in front of the hostel. After Wiñay-Wayna there is no water and no camping till Machu Picchu. The path from this point goes more or less level through jungle until the steep staircase up to the **Intipunku** (two hours), where there's a magnificent view of Machu Picchu, especially at dawn, with the sun alternately in and out, clouds sometimes obscuring the ruins, sometimes leaving them clear.

Get to Machu Picchu as early as possible, preferably before 0830 for best views but in any case before the tourist trains in high season. **Note** Camping is not allowed at Intipunku; guards may confiscate your tent. You may only camp in the field by the river below Puente Ruinas station.

GOING FURTHER
The Central Highlands route

It is possible to travel north from Cuzco to the Cordillera Blanca (see Dream Trip 3) through the Andes, without descending to the Pacific coast. It involves lots of changes of bus, but it does provide an insight into a different side of Peru, that of the highland communities and the harsh but beautiful landscape in which they live.

The main road out of Cuzco heads northwest, passing the Inca ruins of **Tarahuasi** (76 km), and in about 120 km it makes the exciting descent into the deep Apurímac canyon. The road crosses the river by a modern bridge and climbs again to give access to other important Inca sites for those with time to make a detour: the city of **Choquequirao**, comparable to Machu Picchu (allow four days for the hike in and out – no other way to get there) and the stone of **Saywite**, a large carved rock (one to two hours). The first town of any size is **Abancay** (195 km, at 2378 m), growing in importance as a commercial centre since it is at the junction of the main Cuzco–Nazca–Lima highway and the highland road to Ayacucho.

From Abancay the road makes a rough, tortuous climb to the high Sierra and after 138 km reaches **Andahuaylas** (2980 m), which has a good Sunday market and is surrounded by beautiful scenery. There are excursions to the Laguna de Pacucha and the Inca site of Sóndor. From Andahuaylas the road goes through Uripa (80 km) and Chincheros before descending to Río Pampas. It then climbs through Ocros to a wide stretch of treeless *páramo* that leads to Ayacucho (158 km from Chincheros). Both Abancay and Andahuaylas have reasonable hotels for breaking the journey.

Ayacucho *(population: 106,000, altitude 2748 m) is 240 km from Andahuaylas*. The climate is lovely, with warm, sunny days and pleasant balmy evenings. It was founded on 29 January 1539 and is famous for its Semana Santa (Holy Week) celebrations, with nightly candle-lit processions, floral paintings on the streets and daily fairs (accommodation is booked up months in advance). The city is built round the Plaza Mayor, the main plaza. Here is the **Cathedral** (1612) ① *daily 1700-1900, Sun 0900-1700*, which has superb gold-leaf altars. It is beautifully lit at night. On the north side of the Plaza, at Portal de la Unión 37, are the **Casonas de los Marqueses de Mozobamba y del Pozo**, now the Centro Cultural de la Universidad Nacional de San Cristóbal de Huamanga (UNSCH), with frequent artistic and cultural exhibitions. There's a **tourist office** ① *Portal Municipal 45, T066-318305, iperuayacucho@promperu.gob.pe, daily 0830-1930, Sun 0830-1430*.

North of the Plaza are the churches of **Santo Domingo** (1548) and **San Francisco de Asís** (1552), opposite which is the **Mercado de Abastos Carlos F Vivanco**, the packed central market. As well as all the household items and local produce, look for the cheese sellers, the breads and the section dedicated to fruit juices. Of the city's 33 churches, **San Cristóbal** (rarely open) was the first church to be founded in the city (1540), one of the oldest in South America. It is opposite, and dwarfed by **Santa Teresa** (1683). In the 16th-century Casona Vivanco is the **Museo Andrés A Cáceres** ① *Jr 28 de Julio 508, T066-812360, Mon-Sat 0900-1300, 1400-1800. US$1.25*, displaying baroque painting, colonial furniture, republican and contemporary art, and exhibits on Mariscal Cáceres' battles in the War of the Pacific. Another museum worth seeing is **Museo de Anfasep (Asociación Nacional de Familiares de Secuestrados Detenidos y Desaparecidos del Perú)** ① *Prol Libertad 1226, 15 mins' walk from Mercado Artesanal Shosake Nagase, or mototaxi, entry free but give a donation*, providing an insight into the recent history of this region during the violence surrounding the Sendero Luminoso (Shining Path) campaign and the government's attempts to counter it.

For a fascinating insight into Inca and pre-Inca art and culture, a visit to **Barrio Santa Ana** is a must. The district is full of *artesanía* shops, galleries and workshops (eg of textiles and sculptures in alabaster – *piedra de huamanga*). Galleries are closed on Sunday.

EXCURSIONS

The Inca ruins of **Vilcashuamán**, 120 km to the south, were an important provincial capital, the crossroads where the road from Cuzco to the Pacific met the empire's north–south highway. Tours can be arranged with Travel Agencies in Ayacucho, including **Intihuatana Inca baths**, about two hours from Vilcashuamán, five from Ayacucho. A good road going 22 km north from Ayacucho leads to **Huari**, dating from the 'Middle Horizon' (AD 600-1000), when the Huari culture spread across most of Peru. This was the first urban walled centre in the Andes. The huge irregular stone walls are up to 3-4 m high, and rectangular houses and streets can be made out. The ruins now lie in an extensive *tuna* cactus forest. **Quinua** village, 37 km northeast of Ayacucho, has a charming cobbled main plaza, and many of the buildings have been restored. There is a small market on Sunday. Nearby, on the Pampa de Quinua, a 44 m-high obelisk commemorates the decisive battle of Ayacucho, fought on 9 December 1824, bringing an end to Spanish rule in Peru. The village's handicrafts are recommended, especially ceramics. Tours can be arranged from Ayacucho to Huari, Quinua village and the battlefield.

From Ayacucho the Libertadores highway goes to the coast, meeting the Pan-American Highway just outside Pisco. To stay in the Sierra, though, take a bus to Huancayo, 9-10 hours mostly on unpaved roads through breathtaking scenery.

Huancayo is in the Mantaro Valley. It is the capital of Junín Department and the main commercial centre for inland Peru. All the villages in the valley produce their own original crafts, such as the famous *mate burilado*, or gourd carving, hats, wooden chairs, textiles and silver filigree jewellery. At the important festivals in Huancayo, people flock in from far and wide with an incredible range of food, crafts, dancing and music. The city's Sunday market gives a little taste of this every week (it gets going after 0900). Jirón Huancavelica, 3 km long and four stalls wide, still sells clothes, fruit, vegetables, hardware, handicrafts and traditional medicines and goods for witchcraft. There is a small **tourist information booth** ⓘ *Plaza Huamanmarca, Real 481, T064-238480/233251; see also www.huancayoperu.com*. The **museum** ⓘ *at the Salesian school, north of the river on Pasaje Santa Rosa, Mon-Fri 0900-1800, Sun 1000-1200*, is a fascinating cabinet of curiosities with everything ranging from two-headed beasts to a collection of all the coins of the United States of America. The **Parque de Identidad Wanka** ⓘ *on Jr San Jorge in the Barrio San Carlos northeast of the city, entry free, but contributions are appreciated*, is a mixture of surrealistic construction interwoven with native plants and trees and the cultural history of the Mantaro Valley.

Moving on From Huancayo the Central Highway goes direct to Lima (see page 35), six to seven hours by bus. A poor road with infrequent bus services goes through the beautiful Yauyos region to the Cañete Valley (see page 114). Thirdly, you can turn off the Central Highway at La Oroya (107 km from Huancayo) and carry on to Huánuco (a further 255 km), seven hours direct from Huancayo, via the mining centre of Cerro de Pasco. In Huánuco, connect for the route to Huaraz (see page 121), 11-12 hours by bus, changing in La Unión.

MACHU PICCHU AND THE INCA TRAIL LISTINGS

WHERE TO STAY

\$\$\$\$ Machu Picchu Sanctuary Lodge, at the entrance to the ruins, reservations as for the **Hotel Monasterio** in Cuzco, which is under the same management (Peru Orient Express Hotels), T084-211038, www.sanctuarylodgehotel.com. Comfortable, good service, helpful staff, food well-cooked and presented. Electricity and water 24 hrs a day, prices are all-inclusive, restaurant for residents only in the evening, but the buffet lunch is open to all. Usually fully booked well in advance, try Sunday night as other tourists find Pisac market a greater attraction.

\$\$\$\$ Inkaterra Machu Picchu Pueblo, Km 104, 5 mins' walk along the railway from Aguas Calientes, T084-211122. Reservations: C Andalucía 174, Miraflores, Lima, T01-610 0400, www.inkaterra.com. Beautiful colonial-style bungalows in village compound surrounded by cloud forest, lovely gardens with a lot of steps between the public areas and rooms, pool, restaurant, also campsite with hot showers at good rates, offer tours to Machu Picchu, several guided walks on and off the property, great buffet breakfasts included in price. Also has the **Café Inkaterra** by the railway line and the new **El Mapi Hotel**, Av Pachacútec 109, T084-211011.

\$\$\$\$ Sumaq Machu Picchu, Av Hermanos Ayar Mz 1, Lote 3, Aguas Calientes, T084-211059, www.sumaqhotel peru.com. Award-winning 5-star hotel on the edge of town, between the railway and the road to Machu Picchu. Suites and luxury rooms with heating, restaurant and bar, spa.

\$\$\$ La Cabaña, Av Pachacútec Mz 20, Lote 3, T084-211048, www.lacabanamachu picchu.com. With hot water, café, laundry service, helpful, popular with groups.

\$\$\$-\$\$ Rupa Wasi, Huanacaure 180, T084-211101, www.rupawasi.net. Charming 'eco-lodge' up a small alley off Collasuyo, laid back, comfortable, great views from the balconies, purified water available, organic garden, good breakfasts, half-board available, excellent restaurant, **The Tree House**, and cookery classes. Also now offering Stand-up Paddleboard tours to Lake Piuray, near Cuzco.

RESTAURANTS

\$\$ Indio Feliz, C Lloque Yupanqui 103, T084-211090, www.indiofeliz.com. Great French cuisine, excellent value and service, good pisco sours in the bar, great atmosphere.

\$\$ Inka Wasi, Av Imperio de los Incas 123, T084-213322, www.inkawasirestaurant.com. Very good choice, has an open fire, full Peruvian and international menu available.

The old station and Av Pachútec are lined with eating places, many of them *pizzerías*.

SOUTHEASTERN JUNGLE

The southern selva, in Madre de Dios department, contains the Manu National Park (2.04 million ha), the Tambopata National Reserve (254,358 ha) and the Bahauja-Sonene National Park (1.1 million ha). The forest of this lowland region (260 m) is technically called subtropical moist forest, which means that it receives less rainfall than tropical forest and is dominated by the floodplains of its meandering rivers. The most striking features are the former river channels that have become isolated as oxbow lakes. These are home to black caiman and giant otter. Other rare species living in the forest are jaguar, puma, ocelot and tapir. There are also howler monkeys, macaws, guans, currasows and the giant harpy eagle. As well as containing some of the most important flora and fauna on Earth, the region also harbours gold-diggers, loggers, hunters, drug smugglers and oil-men, whose activities have endangered the unique rainforest. Moreover, the construction of the Interoceánica, a road linking the Atlantic and Pacific oceans via Puerto Maldonado and Brazil, will certainly bring more uncontrolled colonization in the area, as seen so many times in the Brazilian Amazon.

→ ARRIVING IN SOUTHEASTERN JUNGLE

GETTING THERE

Flights to Manu National Park can only be arranged as part of a tour. All arrangements for visiting Manu are to and from Cuzco. There are, however, scheduled 45- to 55-minute flights to Puerto Maldonado for Tambopata. It is also possible to travel overland to the southeastern jungle. The route to Manu is long and slow, part by road, part by river, but it gives opportunities to see the various ranges of habitat in the national park. Puerto Maldonado and Cuzco are now connected by the new Interoceánica highway and buses take 10-11 hours.

The multiple-use zone of Manu Biosphere Reserve is accessible to anyone and several lodges exist in the area (see Listings, page 88). The Reserved Zone is accessible by permit only. Entry is strictly controlled and visitors must visit the area under the auspices of an authorized operator with an authorized guide. Permits are limited and reservations should be made well in advance. The entrance fee to the Reserved Zone is 150 soles per person (about US$55) and is included in package tour prices.

It is possible to get from Manu to Puerto Maldonado (see page 86), but there is no regular transport and tours to Manu rarely extend to Puerto Maldonado and Tambopata as all arrangements for visiting Manu have to be made in Cuzco. To make the trip, though, you would have to find a boat going down the Madre de Dios River, then take a colectivo to Puerto Carlos, where you cross the Inambari River to pick up transport to Puerto Maldonado on the Interoceánica highway.

MOVING ON

It is possible to get from Manu to **Puerto Maldonado** (see page 86), but there is no regular transport as tours to Manu rarely extend to Puerto Maldonado and Tambopata. From Puerto Maldonado (Tambopata) you can return by direct flight to **Lima** (2¾ to three hours), with one night in the capital before your flight home.

TOURIST INFORMATION

In Lima Asociación Peruana para la Conservación de la Naturaleza (APECO) ① *Parque José Acosta 187, p 2, Magdalena del Mar, T01-264 0094, comunicapeco@apeco.org.pe.* Pronaturaleza ① *Doña Juana 137, Urb Los Rosales, Santiago de Surco, T01-271 2662, and in Puerto Maldonado, Jr Cajamarca cuadra 1 s/n, T082-571585, comunicaciones@pronaturaleza.org.*

In Cuzco Perú Verde ① *Ricardo Palma J-1, Santa Mónica, Cuzco, T084-226392, www.peruverde.org.* This is a local NGO that can help with information and has free video shows about Manu National Park and Tambopata National Reserve. Friendly and helpful and with information on research in the jungle area of Madre de Dios. The **Amazon Conservation Association (ACCA)** ① *Av Oswaldo Baca 402, Urb Magisterio, Cuzco, T084-222329 and Jr Cusco 499, Puerto Maldonado, T082-573237, www.amazonconservation.org,* is another NGO whose mission is to protect biodiversity by studying ecosystems and developing conservation tools to protect land while supporting local communities. Further information can be obtained from the **Manu National Park Office** ① *Av Micaela Bastidas 310, Cuzco, T084-240898, pqnmanu@terra.com.pe, open 0800-1400,* where they issue the permit for the Reserved Zone.

BEST TIME TO VISIT

The climate is warm and humid, with a rainy season from Novemer to March and a dry season from April to October. Cold fronts from the South Atlantic, called *friajes*, are characteristic of the dry season, when temperatures drop to 15-16° C during the day, and 13° C at night. Always bring a sweater at this time. The best time to visit is during the dry season when there are fewer mosquitoes and the rivers are low, exposing the beaches. This is also a good time to see nesting birds and to view animals at close range, as they stay close to the rivers and are easily seen. Note that this is also the hottest time. A pair of binoculars is essential and insect repellent is a must.

➔ MANU BIOSPHERE RESERVE

No other reserve can compare with Manu for the diversity of life forms; it holds over 1000 species of birds and covers an altitudinal range from 200 to 4100 m above sealevel. Giant otters, jaguars, ocelots and 13 species of primates abound in this pristine tropical wilderness, and uncontacted indigenous tribes are present in the more remote areas, as are indigenous groups with limited access.

The reserve is one of the largest conservation units on Earth, encompassing the complete drainage of the Manu River. It is divided into the **Manu National Park** (1,692,137 ha), where only government sponsored biologists and anthropologists may visit with permits from the Ministry of Agriculture in Lima; the **Reserved Zone** (257,000 ha) within the Manu National Park, set aside for applied scientific research and ecotourism; and the **Cultural Zone** (92,000 ha), which contains acculturated native groups and colonists, where the locals still follow their traditional way of life. Among the ethnic groups in the Cultural Zone are the Harakmbut, Machiguenga and Yine in the Amarakaeri Reserved Zone, on the east bank of the Alto Madre de Dios. They have set up their own ecotourism activities. Associated with Manu are other areas protected by conservation groups, or local people (for example the Blanquillo reserved zone) and some cloud forest parcels along the road. The **Nahua-Kugapakori Reserved Zone**, set aside for these two nomadic native groups, is the area between the headwaters of the Río Manu and headwaters of the Río Urubamba, to the north of the alto Madre de Dios.

→ PUERTO MALDONADO

Puerto Maldonado is an important starting point for visiting the southeastern jungles of the Tambopata Reserve or departing for Bolivia or Brazil. It overlooks the confluence of the rivers Tambopata and Madre de Dios and, because of the gold mining and timber industries, the immediate surrounding jungle is now cultivated. A bridge, as part of the Interoceánica highway, has been built across the Río Madre de Dios. Even before its

completion, business activity in the town was growing fast. There are tourist offices at the airport and at **Dircetur** ⓘ *Urb Fonavi, take a moto-taxi to the Posta Médica which is next door.*

The beautiful and tranquil **Lago Sandoval** is a one-hour boat ride along the Río Madre de Dios, and then a 5-km walk into the jungle (parts of the first 3 km are a raised wooden walkway; boots are advisable). Entry to the lake costs US$9.50. You must go with a guide; this can be arranged by the boat driver. Boats can be hired at the Madre de Dios port for about US$25 a day, minimum two people (plus petrol) to go to Lago Sandoval (don't pay the full cost in advance).

JUNGLE TOURS FROM PUERTO MALDONADO

Trips can be made to **Lago Valencia**, 60 km away near the Bolivian border, four hours there, eight hours back. It is an oxbow lake with lots of wildlife. Many excellent beaches and islands are located within an hour's boat ride. Mosquitoes are voracious. If camping, take food and water.

It is quite easy to arrange a boat and guide from Puerto Maldonado to the **Tambopata National Reserve** (TNR) ⓘ *SERNANP, Av 28 de Julio 482, Puerto Maldonado, T082-573278, rntambopata@sernanp.gob.pe*, between the rivers Madre de Dios, Tambopata and Heath. The area was first declared a reserve in 1990 and is a very reasonable alternative for those who do not have the time or money to visit Manu. It is a close rival in terms of seeing wildlife and boasts some superb oxbow lakes. There are a number of lodges here that are excellent for lowland rainforest birding. **Explorers' Inn** is perhaps the most famous, but the **Posada Amazonas/Tambopata Research Centre** and **Tambopata EcoLodge** are also good. In an effort to ensure that more tourism income stays in the area, a few local families have established their own small-scale *casas de hospedaje*, which offer more basic facilities and make use of the nearby forest.

SOUTHEASTERN JUNGLE LISTINGS

WHERE TO STAY

Lodges in Manu

In the Manu Reserved Zone the only accommodation is in the comfortable **Manu Lodge** (www.manuperu.com) 3 hrs upriver from Boca Manu towards Cocha Salvador, run by **Manu Nature Tours** and only bookable as part of a full package deal with transport; or in the comfortable but rustic **Casa Machiguenga** in the Cocha Salvador area (owned and operated by Machiguenga Indians, contact **APECO**, address under Tourist information, page 85). Several companies have tented safari camp infrastructures, some with shower and dining facilities, but all visitors sleep in tents. Many tours go to the park overland, and stay en route in one of a number of lodges in the cloudforest sections of the Reserve, such as **Cock of the Rock Lodge** (www.inkanatura.com) or **Manu Cloud Forest Lodge** (www.manu peru.com). Sample prices: 3 days/2 nights in a cloud forest lodge: US$750; a 4 day/ 3 night package at a rainforest lodge from $1,000-1,500 (prices change all the time).

Amazonia Lodge, on the Río Alto Madre de Dios just across the river from Atalaya, T084-816131, www.amazonialodge.com; in Cuzco at Matará 334, p 3, T084-231370. An old tea hacienda run by the Yabar Calderón family, famous for its bird diversity and fine hospitality, a great place to relax, meals included, birding or natural history tours available, contact Santiago in advance and he'll arrange a pick-up.

Manu Learning Centre, Fundo Mascoitania, a 600-ha reserve within the Cultural Zone, T84-262433, www.crees-expeditions.com. 45 mins from Atalaya by boat, a conservation and volunteer programme run by the crees foundation, now welcoming tourists here and at their new, luxury lodge, **Romero Rainforest Lodge**, a day away by boat.

Manu Wildlife Center, 2 hrs down the Río Madre de Dios from Boca Manu, near the Blanquillo macaw lick. Book through **Manu Expeditions** (www.manu expeditions.com), which runs it in conjunction with the conservation group **Peru Verde**, www.manuwildlifecenter.com. 22 double cabins, with private bathroom and hot water. Also canopy towers for birdwatching and a tapir lick. **Manu Expeditions** also owns the **Romero Lodge** at the confluence of the Manu and Madre de Dios rivers.

Pantiacolla Lodge, 30 mins down-river from Shintuya. Owned by the Moscoso family, bungalow accommodation in 900 ha of forest from 350-1200 m above sea level. Book through **Pantiacolla Tours**, T084-238323, www.pantiacolla.com.

Hotels in Puerto Maldonado

$$$ Wasai Lodge & Expeditions, Plaza Grau 1, T082-572290, www.wasai.com. In a beautiful location overlooking the Madre de Dios River, with forest surrounding cabin-style rooms, shower, small pool with waterfall, good restaurant (local fish a speciality). They can organize local tours and also have the **Wasaí Tambopata Lodge** on the Río Tambopata (day rate US$80, various packages available).

$$$-$$ Cabañaquinta, Moquegua 422, T082-571045, www.hotelcabanaquinta.com. A/c or fan, frigobar, laundry, free drinking water, good restaurant, lovely garden, very comfortable, airport transfer. Request a room away from the Interoceanic Highway.

Lodges in Tambopata

Explorers Inn, www.explorersinn.com, or book through **Peruvian Safaris**, Alcanfores 459, Miraflores, Lima, T01-447 8888, www.peruviansafaris.com. Just before the La Torre control post, adjoining the TNR, in the part where most research work has been done, 58 km from Puerto Maldonado. 2½ hrs up the Río Tambopata (1½ hrs return), one of the best places in Peru for seeing jungle birds (580-plus species have been recorded), butterflies (1230-plus species), also giant river otters. A 2-night tour costs US$230 per person, but you probably need more than a 2-day tour to benefit fully from the location. Offers tours through the adjoining community of La Torre. The guides are biologists and naturalists undertaking research in the reserve. They provide interesting wildlife treks, including to the famous Tombopata macaw clay lick (*collpa*).

Posada Amazonas Lodge, on the Tambopata river, 1½ hrs by vehicle and boat upriver from Puerto Maldonado. Book through **Rainforest Expeditions**, Av Aeropuerto, La Joya 6 km, Puerto Maldonado, T1-877-231-9251, www.perunature.com. A collaboration between the tour agency and the local native community of Infierno. Attractive rooms with cold showers, visits to Lake Tres Chimbadas, with good birdwatching including the Tambopata *collpa*. Offers trips to a nearby indigenous primary health care project where a native healer gives guided tours of the medicinal plant garden. Service and guiding is very good. The **Tambopata Research Centre**, is the company's more intimate, but comfortable lodge, about 6 hrs further upriver. Rooms are smaller than Posada Amazonas, shared showers, cold water. The lodge is next to the Colorado macaw clay lick. 2 hrs from Posada Amazonas, Rainforest Expeditions also has the **Refugio Amazonas**, close to Lago Condenados. It is the usual stopover for those visiting the *collpa*. 3 bungalows accommodate 70 people in en suite rooms, large, kerosene lit, open bedrooms with mosquito nets, well-designed and run, atmospheric. There are many packages at the different lodges and lots of add-ons.

Tambopata Eco Lodge, on the Río Tambopata, to make reservations Nueva Baja 432, Cuzco, T084-245695, operations office Jr Gonzales Prada 269, Puerto Maldonado, T082-571397, www.tambopatalodge.com. Rooms with solar-heated water, good guides, excellent food. Trips go to Lake Condenado, some to Lake Sachavacayoc, and to the Collpa de Chuncho, guiding mainly in English and Spanish, naturalists programme provided.

DREAM TRIP 2
Lima→Cuzco→Titicaca→South coast 21 days

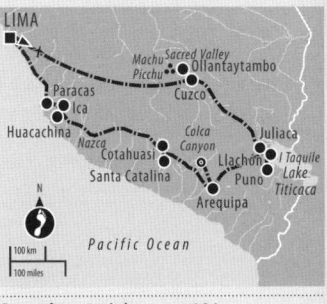

DREAM TRIP 2
Lima→Cuzco→Titicaca→South coast

After spending the first six nights in Lima and in and around Cuzco, the next leg of this trip moves southeast to Lake Titicaca. Take a tourist bus or train over the Altiplano to see the interesting villages and ruins en route to the lake. The main city on the shore is Puno, which is one of the best places to buy textiles, dubbed the 'folklore capital' of Peru. Motorboats zip in and out of the port to the inhabited islands and nearby villages. With mountains in the distance and blue waters under a cloudless sky, this is one of the most unforgettable parts of Peru.

The journey heads west to Arequipa, whose Spanish churches, mansions and 19th-century Plaza de Armas shine with white, volcanic stonework. Its most famous colonial jewel, Santa Catalina Convent, is a gorgeous little city-within-a-city, painted in bright colours. Within relatively easy reach is the Colca Canyon, second only in depth to its neighbour Cotahuasi. There is excellent trekking and riding among the villages and terraces. Hot springs and some of the finest lodges in Peru provide relaxation but, above all, visitors come here for the remarkable close-up view of condors riding the early morning thermals near the town of Cabanaconde.

The next stop is the coastal desert, which was home to a number of ancient civilizations who left their mark in a variety of ways. It would be hard to imagine a stranger set of monuments than the enigmatic Nazca Lines. The whole area is revealing new secrets as more sites are uncovered. Further north is Paracas, named after another culture, famous for its textiles and the burials that have been found in the sands. Today, the desert provides many opportunities for adventure, especially out of neighbouring Ica, where vineyards open their doors for tastings. But it is offshore where we round off the trip, at the marine reserve of the Islas Ballestas, home to thousands of seabirds and sea lions.

LAKE TITICACA AND THE ISLANDS

Straddling Peru's southern border with Bolivia are the sapphire-blue waters of mystical Lake Titcaca, a huge inland sea that is the highest navigable lake in the world. Its shores and islands are home to the Aymara and Quechua, who are among Peru's oldest peoples. Here you can wander through traditional villages where Spanish is a second language and where ancient myths and beliefs still hold true. This is most evident on the islands of Taquile and Amantaní, which are reached by boat from Puno. Almost every trip will call at the tourist-oriented, floating reed islands of Los Uros.

→ PUNO AND AROUND

On the northwest shore of Lake Titicaca, Puno is capital of its department and Peru's folklore centre with a vast array of handicrafts, festivals and costumes and a rich tradition of music and dance. Puno gets bitterly cold at night: from June to August the temperature at night can fall to -25°C, but generally not below -5°C.

ARRIVING IN PUNO

Getting there Puno does not have an airport so all flights go to Juliaca, which is an hour away by a good road. Tourist buses from Cuzco (eg **Inka Express**, www.inkaexpress. com.pe) stop at Andahuaylillas, its elaborately decorated church known as the Sistine Chapel of the Andes; Raqchi, with the impressive remains of the Temple of Viracocha; Sicuani (lunch stop); La Raya, the highest pass on the route; and Pucará, famous for its ceramic bulls. There are also trains from Cuzco; Puno station is quite central and within walking distance of the centre, but if you have got heavy bags, it's a good idea to hire a three-wheel cycle cart (trici-taxi). The bus station (Terminal Terrestre) and the depots for local buses are further away, southeast of the centre, but trici-taxis and conventional taxis serve this area.

Moving on Scheduled flights from Juliaca to **Arequipa** (see page 101) take 50 minutes; to the journey time you will have to add the hour's bus or taxi ride from Puno. Many buses run from Puno to Arequipa. They take six to seven hours via Juliaca and the better companies usually run at night. Note that even the most reputable companies are not immune from hold-ups and accidents at night; seek local advice before travelling on a night bus.

Tourist information i perú ① *Jr Lima y Deústua, near Plaza de Armas, T051-365088, iperupuno@promperu.gob.pe, daily 0830-1930.* Helpful English-speaking staff, good information and maps. Municipal website: www.munipuno.gob.pe. **Dircetur** ① *Ayacucho 684, T051-364976, puno@mincetur.gob.pe,* also has a desk at the Terminal Terrestre. **Indecopi** ① *Jr Deústua 644, T051-363667, jpilco@indecopi. gob.pe,* is the office of the consumer protection bureau. **Tourist police** ① *Jr Deústua 558, T051-354764, daily 0600-2200.* Report any scams, such as unscrupulous price changes, and beware high-pressure sales techniques to make you buy tours.

PLACES IN PUNO

The **Cathedral** ① *Mon-Fri 0800-1200, 1500-1800, Sat-Sun until 1900*, completed in 1657, has an impressive baroque exterior, but an austere interior. Across the street from the Cathedral is the **Balcón del Conde de Lemos** ① *Deústua y Conde de Lemos, art gallery open Mon-Fri 0800-1600*, where Peru's Viceroy stayed when he first arrived in the city. The **Museo Municipal Dreyer** ① *Conde de Lemos 289, Mon-Sat 1030-2200, Sun 1600-2200, US$5 includes 45-min guided tour*, has been combined with the private collection of Sr Carlos Dreyer. A short walk up Independencia leads to the **Arco Deústua**, a monument honouring those killed in the battles of Junín and Ayacucho. Nearby is a mirador giving fine views over the town, the port and the lake beyond. The walk from Jirón Cornejo following the Stations of the Cross up a nearby hill, with fine views of Lake Titicaca, has been recommended, but be careful and don't go alone (the same applies to any of the hills around Puno, eg Huajsapata).

Avenida Titicaca leads to the port from where boats go to the islands. From its intersection with Avenida Costanera towards the pier, one side of the road is lined with the kiosks of the **Artesanos Unificados de Puno**, selling crafts (see below). Closer to the port are food kiosks. On the opposite side of the road is a shallow lake where you can hire **pedal boats** ① *US$0.70 per person for 20 mins*. At the pier are the ticket counters for transport to the islands. The **Malecón Bahía de los Incas**, a lovely promenade along the waterfront, extends to the north and south; it is a pleasant place for a stroll and for birdwatching. The **Yavari** ① *0815-1715, www.yavari.org, free but donations of US$6 welcome to help with maintenance costs*, the oldest ship on Lake Titicaca, is berthed near the entrance to the Sonesta Posadas del Inca hotel: you have to go through the hotel to get to it. Alternatively, a boat from the port costs US$2 return, with wait. The Yavari was

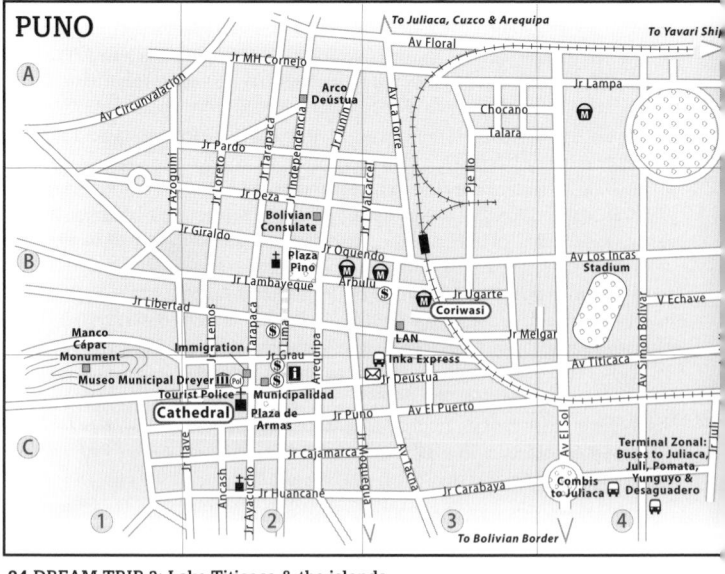

built in England in 1862 and was shipped in kit form to Arica, then by rail to Tacna and by mule to Lake Titicaca. The journey took six years. The ship was launched on Christmas Day 1870. After a century of working life it fell into disuse, but has been restored over the last 25 years. Another old ship is the **MN Coya** ① *moored in Barrio Guaje, beyond the Hotel Sonesta Posada del Inka, T051-368156, has a restaurant on board*, built in Scotland and launched on the lake in 1892. Berthed next to *Coya* is Hull (UK)-built MS *Ollanta*, which sailed the lake from 1926 to the 1970s.

Puno is the best place in Peru to buy alpaca wool articles; bargaining is appropriate. Along the avenue leading to the port is the large **Mercado Artesanal Asociación de Artesanos Unificados** ① *daily 0900-1800*. Closer to the centre are **Mercado Coriwasi** ① *Ugarte 150, daily 0800-2100*, and **Central Integral de Artesanos del Perú (CIAP)** ① *Jr Deústua 576, Mon-Sat 1000-1800*. The **Mercado Central**, in the blocks bound by Arbulú, Arequipa, Oquendo and Tacna, has all kinds of food, including good cheeses, as well as a few crafts.

Equally important culturally are Puno's festivals: at the **Fiesta de la Virgen de la Candelaria** in the first two weeks in February, bands and dancers from all the local towns compete in a *Diablada*, or Devil Dance. There are festivities at night on the streets as well as official functions in the stadium. Check the dates in advance as Candelaria may be moved if pre-Lenten carnival coincides with it. A candlelit procession through darkened streets takes place on **Good Friday**. **Festividad de las Cruces** (3 May) is celebrated with masses, a procession and the **Alasita** festival of miniatures; 29 June is the colourful **Festival of San Pedro**, with a procession at Zepita (see page 96). On **4-5 November** there is a pageant dedicated to the founding of Puno and the emergence of Manco Cápac and Mama Ocllo, the legendary founders of the Inca dynasty, from the waters of Lake Titicaca.

AROUND PUNO

Anybody interested in religious architecture should visit the villages along the western shore of Lake Titicaca. An Inca sundial can be seen near the village of **Chucuíto** (19 km), which has an interesting church, La Asunción, and houses with carved stone doorways.

Juli, 80 km, has some fine examples of religious architecture. **San Pedro** ① *on the plaza, open 0630-1130, 1400-1600, except Tue when only for mass at 0700 and Sun for mass at 0730, 1100 and 1800, free, but donations appreciated*, is the only functioning church. It contains a series of paintings of saints, with the Via Crucis scenes in the same frame, and gilt side altars above which some of the arches have baroque designs. Now a museum, **San Juan Letrán** ① *daily 0800-1600, US$1.50*, has two sets of 17th-century paintings of the lives of St John the Baptist and of St Teresa, contained in sumptuous gilded frames.

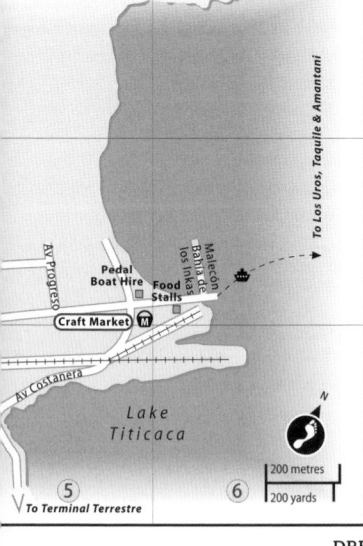

It also has intricate *mestizo* carving in pink stone. **La Asunción** ① *daily 0800-1630, US$1.20,* is also a museum. The nave is empty, but its walls are lined with colonial paintings with no labels. The original painting on the walls of the transept can be seen. Its fine bell tower was damaged by earthquake or lightning. Outside is an archway and atrium which date from the early 17th century. Needlework, other weavings, handicrafts and antiques are offered for sale in town. Colectivo Puno-Juli US$1.50; return from Juli outside market at Ilave 349.

A further 20 km along the lake is **Pomata** (bus from Juli US$0.75, US$2 from Puno), whose red sandstone church of **Santiago Apóstol** ① *daily 0700-1200, 1330-1600, US$1, but if guardian is not there, leave money on table*, has a striking exterior and beautiful interior, with superb carving and paintings. At **Zepita**, near Desaguadero, the 18th-century Dominican church is also worth a visit.

Near Puno are the *chullpas* (pre-Columbian funeral towers) of **Sillustani** ① *32 km from Puno on a good road, US$2, take an organized tour; about 3-4 hrs, leave 1430, US$15-18, tours usually stop at a Colla house on the way, to see local products,* in a beautiful setting on a peninsula in Lake Umayo. John Hemming writes: "Most of the towers date from the period of Inca occupation in the 15th century, but they are burial towers of the Aymara-speaking Colla tribe. The engineering involved in their construction is more complex than anything the Incas built – it is defeating archaeologists' attempts to rebuild the tallest 'lizard' *chullpa*." There is a museum, and handicraft sellers wait at the exit. Photography is best in the afternoon light, though this is when the wind is strongest. The scenery is barren, but impressive. There is a small community at the foot of the promontory.

LLACHON

At the eastern end of the Península de Capachica, which encloses the northern side of the Bahía de Puno, the pretty farming villages of Llachón, Santa María and Ccotos have become a focus of community-based tourism. On Capachica there are currently six organizations, each with a dozen or more families and links to different tour operators in Puno, Cuzco or abroad. The scenery is very pretty, with sandy beaches, pre-Inca terracing, trees and flowers. The view of the sunset from the Auki Carus hill is reckoned to be better even than from Taquile. Visitors share in local activities and 70% of all produce served is from the residents' farms. Throughout the peninsula the dress of the local women is very colourful, with four-cornered hats called *monteros*, matching vests and colourful *polleras*.

The peninsula is good for hiking, mountain biking and sailing; boats can be hired. Tours to the peninsula often include kayaking around the coast or to other islands. Off the east coast of the peninsula is the island of **Ticonata**, whose community tourism association offers accommodation in round houses and various activities (www.ticonatatours.com). It's a short boat ride from Ccotos or Chifrón on the peninsula or from Amantaní island (see opposite). Motor boats from Puno take 3½ hours.

THE UROS
ⓘ *US$2 entry.*

The Uros, the people of the 'floating islands' in Puno Bay, fish, hunt birds and live off the lake plants, most important of which are the reeds they use for their boats, houses and the very foundations of their islands. Visitors to the floating islands encounter more women than men. These women wait every day for the tour boats to sell their handicrafts. The few men one does see might be building or repairing boats or fixing their nets. The rest are out on the lake, hunting and fishing. The Uros cannot live from tourism alone and it is better to buy handicrafts or pay for services than just to tip. They glean extra income from tourists by offering overnight accommodation in reed houses, selling meals and providing Uro guides for two-hour tours. Organized tour parties are usually given a boat-building demonstration and the chance to take a short trip in a reed boat. Some islanders will also greet boatloads of tourists with a song and will pose for photos. The islanders, who are very friendly, appreciate gifts of pens, paper, etc for their two schools. This form of tourism on the Uros Islands is now well established and, whether it has done irreparable harm or will ultimately prove beneficial, it takes place in superb surroundings. Take drinking water as there is none on the islands.

TAQUILE
ⓘ *US$3 to land. Contact Munay Taquile, the island's community-based travel agency, Titicaca 508, Puno, T051-351448, www.taquile.net*

Isla Taquile, 45 km from Puno, on which there are numerous pre-Inca and Inca ruins, and Inca terracing, is only about 1 km wide, but 6-7 km long. Ask for the (unmarked) **museum of traditional costumes**, which is on the plaza. There is a co-operative shop on the plaza that sells exceptional woollen goods, which are not cheap, but of very fine quality. Each week different families sell their products. Shops on the plaza sell postcards, water and dry goods. The principal festivals are from 2-7 June, and the **Fiesta de Santiago** from 25 July to 2 August, with many dances in between. Native guides in Taquile, some speaking English and/or German, charge US$5 for two-hour tours. If you are staying over, you are advised to take some food, particularly fruit, bread and vegetables, water, plenty of small-value notes, candles and a torch, toilet paper and a sleeping bag. Take precautions against sunburn and take warm clothes for the cold nights. It is worth spending a night on Taquile to observe the daily flurry of activity around the boatloads of tourists: demonstrations of traditional dress and weaving techniques, the preparation of trout to feed the hordes. When the boats leave, the island breathes a gentle sigh and people slowly return to their more traditional activities.

AMANTANI
ⓘ *US$3 to land.*

Another island worth visiting is Amantaní, very beautiful and peaceful. There are six villages and ruins on both of the island's peaks, **Pacha Tata** and **Pacha Mama**, from which there are excellent views. There are also temples and on the shore there is a throne carved out of stone, the **Inkatiana**. On both hills, a fiesta is celebrated on 15-20 January, **Pago a la Tierra or San Sebastián**. The festivities are very colourful, musical and hard-drinking. There is also a festival on 9 April, **Aniversario del Consejo** (of the local council), and a **Feria de**

ON THE ROAD
Mother Earth

Pachamama, or Mother Earth, occupies a very privileged place in Aymara culture because she is the generative source of life. The Aymara believe that man was created from the land, and thus he is fraternally tied to all the living beings that share the earth. According to them, the earth is our mother, and it is on the basis of this understanding that all of human society is organized, always maintaining the cosmic norms and laws.

Women's and men's relationship with nature is what the Aymara call ecology, harmony and equilibrium. The Aymara furthermore believe that private land ownership is a social sin because the land is for everyone. It should be shared and not used for the benefit of a few.

Vicenta Mamani Bernabé of the Andean Regional Superior Institute of Theological Studies states: "Land is life because it produces all that we need to live. Water emanates from the land as if from the veins of a human body, there is also the natural wealth of minerals, and pasture grows from it to feed the animals. Therefore, for the Aymaras, the Pachamama is sacred and since we are her children, we are also sacred. No one can replace the earth, she is not meant to be exploited, or to be converted into merchandise. Our duty is to respect and care for the earth. This is what white people today are just beginning to realize, and it is called ecology. Respect for the Pachamama is respect for ourselves as she is life. Today, she is threatened with death and must be liberated for the sake of her children's liberation."

Artesanías, 8-16 August. The residents make beautiful textiles and sell them quite cheaply at the Artesanía Cooperativa. They also make basketwork and stoneware. The people are Quechua speakers, but understand Spanish. Islanders arrange dances for tour groups (independent travellers can join in), visitors dress up in local clothes and join the dances. Small shops sell water and snacks.

ANAPIA AND YUSPIQUE

In the Peruvian part of the Lago Menor (the 'minor lake' at the southeastern end of Titicaca) are the islands of **Anapia**, a friendly, Aymara-speaking community, and **Yuspique**, on which are ruins and vicuñas. The community has organized committees for tourism, motor boats, sailing boats and accommodation with families. To visit Anapia independently, take a colectivo from Yunguyo, near the border with Bolivia, to Tinicachi and alight at Punta Hermosa, just after Unacachi. Boats to Anapia leave Punta Hermosa on Sunday and Thursday at 1300 (they leave Anapia for Yunguyo market on the same days at 0630); bus from Puno Sunday, Tuesday, Thursday, US$6. It's two hours each way by boat. On the island ask for José Flores, who is very knowledgeable about Anapia's history, flora and fauna. He sometimes acts as a guide.

LAKE TITICACA AND THE ISLANDS LISTINGS

WHERE TO STAY

Puno

$$$ Intiqa, Jr Tarapacá 272, T051-366900, www.intiqahotel.com. Built around a sunny courtyard with good restaurant. Stylish, rooms have heaters, professional staff. Offers tours and is associated with **La Casa de Wiracocha**, at No 260, for select Peruvian handicrafts.

$ Inka's Rest, Pasaje San Carlos 158, T051-368720, www.inkasresthostel.com. Several sitting areas, hot water, heating, double or twin rooms with private or shared bath and a dorm, cooking and laundry facilities, a place to meet other travellers, reserve ahead.

The islands

$$$$ Hotel Isla Suasi, T01-951 310070, a Casa Andina Private Collection hotel, capc-islasuasi@casa-andina.com (Casa Andina have properties in Puno also, www.casa-andina.com). The hotel is the only house on this tiny, tranquil, private island. There are beautiful terraced gardens, best Jan-Mar. You can take a canoe around the island to see birds and the island has vicuñas, a small herd of alpacas and vizcachas. The sunsets from the highest point are beautiful. Facilities are spacious, comfortable and solar-powered, rooms with bath, hot water, hot water bottles. Price includes full board, national drinks, entrance to island, all transport (suite boat from Puno 2¼ hrs direct), services and taxes. Massage room and sauna, internet extra.

$$$$ Titilaka Lodge, Comunidad de Huencalla s/n, on a private peninsula near Chucuíto, T01-700 5111 (Lima), www.titilaka.com. Luxury boutique hotel offering all-inclusive packages

in an exclusive environment on the edge of the lake. Plenty of activities available.

$$ MN Yavari, Muelle del Hotel Sonesta Posadas del Inca, T051-369329 (in Lima T01-255 7268), www.yavari.org. B&B is available on board the steamship, 3 twin bunk rooms with shared bath. Price per person.

Community tourism

Overnight stays at Llachón and the islands are organized by the communities. At Llachón and the Capachica Peninsula, families offer accommodation on a rotational basis and, as the community presidents change each year, the standard of facilities changes from year to year and family to family. See also www.ticonata tours.com for Ticonata. For the Uros community, Oscar Coyla, T051-951 824378 is the representative. Accommodation costs US$5 per person, simple meals extra, or US$10 per person full board including tour. On Taquile The **Community Tourism Agency Munay Taquile** (see page 97) can arrange accommodation in a *Casa Rural* (a room in a private home), *Albergue Rural*, or *Hotel Rural* (both bigger than a *casa rural*, with better facilities for tourists). Someone will approach you when you get off the boat if you don't have anything booked in advance. Lodging rates US$15-25 per person full board. On Amantaní, the **Comité Turístico de Amantaní** can be reached on T051-951 430637. The lodging rate is up to US$25 per person full board. If you are willing to walk to more distant communities, you might get a lower price and you are helping to share the income. **$$ Kantuta Lodge**, T051-630238, or 951 636172, www.kantutalodge.com. Run by Segundino Cari and family, full board.

WHAT TO DO

Agencies organize trips to the islands, Llachón, Sillustani, and other places. The standard island tour is 2 days, 1 night, visiting the Uros, staying in either Taquile or Amantaní and then visiting the other island the next day (from US$26.50 per person). Choose an agency that allows you to pay direct for your lodging so you know that the family is benefiting.

All Ways Travel, Casa del Corregidor, Deústua 576, p 2, T051-353979, and at Tacna 281, p 2, T051-355552, www.titicacaperu.com. Very helpful, kind and reliable, speak German, French, English and Italian. They offer many tours, including a cultural tour to the islands of Anapia and Yuspique in Lake Wiñaymarka, beyond the straits of Tiquina.

Edgar Adventures, Jr Lima 328, T051-353444, www.edgaradventures.com. English, German and French spoken, very helpful and knowledgeable. Tours include kayaking tour of Llachón. Community-minded, promoting responsible tourism. Consistently recommended.

AREQUIPA AND COLCA

The colonial city of Arequipa, with its guardian volcano, El Misti, is the ideal place to start exploring southern Peru. It is the gateway to two of the world's deepest canyons, Colca and Cotahuasi, whose villages and terraces hold onto a traditional way of life and whose skies are home to the magnificent condor.

→ AREQUIPA

The city of Arequipa, 1011 km from Lima, stands in a beautiful valley at the foot of El Misti volcano, a snow-capped, perfect cone, 5822 m high, guarded on either side by the mountains Chachani (6057 m) and Pichu-Pichu (5669 m). The city has fine Spanish buildings and many old and interesting churches built of sillar, a pearly white volcanic material almost exclusively used in the construction of Arequipa. The city was re-founded on 15 August 1540 by an emissary of Pizarro, but it had previously been occupied by Aymara Indians and the Incas. It is the main commercial centre for the south and is a busy place. Its people resent the general tendency to believe that everything is run from Lima. It has been declared a World Cultural Heritage site by UNESCO.

ARRIVING IN AREQUIPA

Getting there The **airport** is 7 km west. It takes about half an hour to town. The main **bus terminal** is south of the centre, 15 minutes from the centre by colectivo, 10 minutes by taxi.

Moving on Three bus companies run on a paved road from Arequipa to Chivay, the main town in the **Colca Canyon** (see page 105). None is very good; it may be better to go with tourist transport and arrange to return with another company. The journey takes six hours. Buses and combis go from Chivay's bus terminal to villages in the canyon, including **Cabanaconde** (see page 107), from where you can return to **Arequipa** (eight hours).

From Arequipa to **Nazca** (see page 110) by bus takes nine hours. Several companies operate on this route, the majority continuing to Lima. Most buses go at night. Note that even the most reputable companies are not immune from hold-ups and accidents at night; seek local advice before travelling on a night bus.

Getting around The main places of interest and the hotels are within walking distance of the Plaza de Armas. If you are going to the suburbs, take a bus or taxi. A cheap tour of the city can be made in a *Vallecito* bus, 1½ hours for US$0.50. It is a circular tour that goes down Calles Jerusalén and San Juan de Dios. Alternatively an **open-top bus** ① *US$17 for 4 hrs, Bus Tour, T054-203434, www.bustour.com.pe,* tours the city and nearby attractions from Portal San Agustín, Plaza de Armas at 0900 and 1400 daily.

Best time to visit The climate is delightful, with a mean temperature before sundown of 23°C, and after sundown of 14°C. The sun shines on 360 days of the year. Annual rainfall is less than 150 mm.

Security There have been recent reports of taxi drivers in collusion with criminals to rob both tourists and locals. Ask hotels, restaurants, etc, to book a safe taxi for you. Theft can be a problem in the market area and the park at Selva Alegre. Be very cautious walking anywhere at night. The police are conspicuous, friendly, courteous and efficient, but their resources are limited.

Tourist information i perú: central office is in the Plaza de Armas ① *Portal de la Municipalidad 110, T054-223265, iperuarequipa@promperu.gob.pe, Mon-Sat 0830-1930, Sun 0830-1600,* and in the airport arrivals hall ① *T054-444564, only open when flights are arriving.* Municipal tourist office is in the Municipalidad ① *on the south side of the Plaza de Armas, No 112 next to iperu, T054-211021.* Indecopi ① *Hipólito Unanue 100-A, Urb Victoria, T054-212054, mlcornejo@indecopi.gob.pe.* The Tourist Police ① *Jerusalén 315, T054-201258, open 24 hrs,* are very helpful with complaints or giving directions.

PLACES IN AREQUIPA

The elegant **Plaza de Armas** is faced on three sides by arcaded buildings with many restaurants, and on the fourth by the massive **Cathedral**, founded in 1612 and largely rebuilt in the 19th century. It is remarkable for having its façade along the whole length of the church (entrance on Santa Catalina and San Francisco). Inside is the fine Belgian organ and elaborately carved wooden pulpit. In the June 2001 earthquake that devastated much of southern Peru, one of the cathedral's twin towers famously collapsed. It has been rebuilt. The cathedral has a good **museum** ① *www.museocatedralarequipa.org.pe, Mon-Sat 1000-1700,* with sections on the building and its art works. Behind the Cathedral there is an alley with handicraft shops and places to eat.

Santa Catalina Convent ① *Santa Catalina 301, T054-608282, www.santacatalina.org.pe, 0900-1700 (high season from 0800, last admission 1600), evening visits till 2000 on Tue and Thu, US$12.* This is by far the most remarkable sight in Arequipa, opened in 1970 after four centuries of mystery. The convent has been beautifully refurbished, with period furniture, pictures of the Arequipa and Cuzco schools and fully equipped kitchens. It is a complete miniature walled colonial town of over 2 ha in the middle of the city at Santa Catalina 301, where about 450 nuns lived in total seclusion, except for their women servants. The few remaining nuns have retreated to one section of the convent, allowing visitors to see a maze of cobbled streets and plazas bright with geraniums and other flowers, cloisters and buttressed houses. These have been painted in traditional white, orange, deep red and blue. On Tuesday and Thursday evenings the convent is lit with torches, candles and blazing fireplaces, very beautiful. There is a good café, which sells cakes, sandwiches, baked potatoes and a special blend of tea. There are tours of 1½ hrs, no set price, many of the guides speak English or German (a tip of US$6 is expected).

Museo Santuarios de Altura ① *La Merced 110, T054-215013, www.ucsm.edu.pe/ santury, Mon-Sat 0900-1800, Sun 0900-1500, US$6 includes a 20-min video of the discovery in English followed by a guided tour in English, French, German, Italian or Spanish (tip the guide), discount with student card, tour lasts 1 hr.* It contains the frozen Inca mummies found on Mount Ampato; the mummy known as 'Juanita' is fascinating as it is so well preserved. From January to April, Juanita is often jetting round the world, and is replaced by other child sacrifices unearthed in the mountains.

Arequipa is said to have the best preserved colonial architecture in Peru, apart from Cuzco. As well as the many fine churches, there are several fine seignorial houses with large carved tympanums over the entrances. Built as single-storey structures, they have mostly withstood earthquakes. They have small patios with no galleries, flat roofs and small windows, disguised by superimposed lintels or heavy grilles. Good examples are the 18th-century **Casa Tristán del Pozo**, or **Gibbs-Ricketts house** ⓘ *San Francisco 108, Mon-Sat 0915-1245, 1600-1800*, with its fine portal and puma-head waterspouts (now a bank);

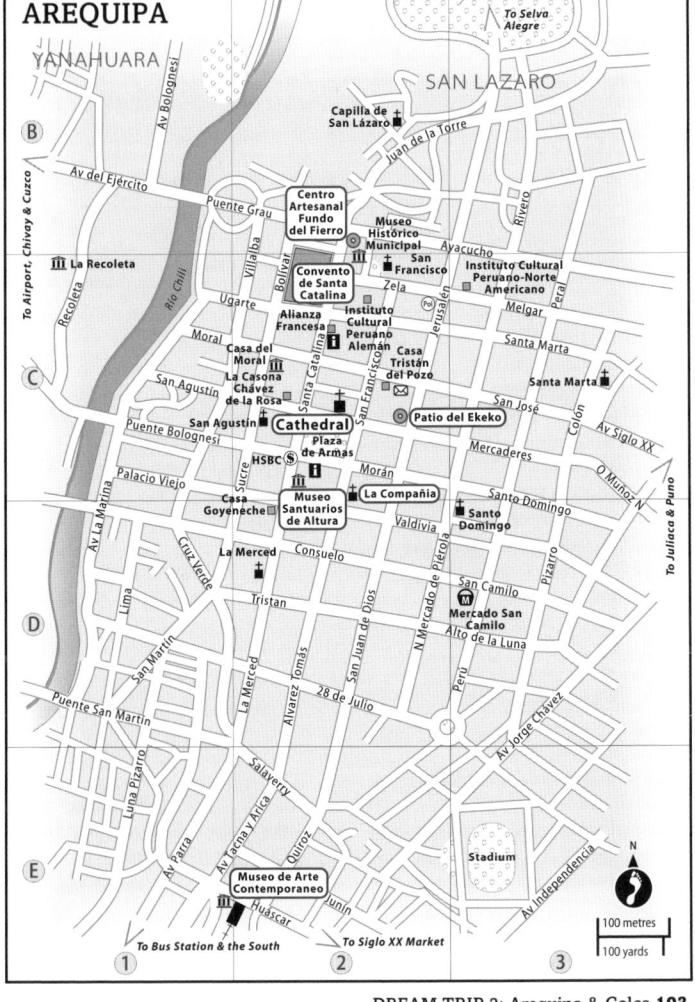

Casa del Moral ⓘ *Moral 318 y Bolívar, Mon-Sat 0900-1700, Sun 0900-1300, US$1.80, US$1 for students,* also known as Williams house, now a bank and has a museum; **Casa Goyeneche** ⓘ *La Merced 201 y Palacio Viejo,* also a bank office, ask the guards to let you view the courtyard and fine period rooms. The oldest district is **San Lázaro**, a collection of tiny climbing streets and houses quite close to the **Hotel Libertador**, where you can find the ancient **Capilla de San Lázaro**.

Among the many fine churches is **La Compañía** ⓘ *General Morán y Alvarez Thomas,* the main façade (1698) and side portal (1654) are striking examples of the florid Andean *mestizo* style. To the left of the sanctuary is the **Capilla Real** (Royal Chapel) ⓘ *Mon-Fri 0900-1230, 1500-1930, Sat 1130-1230, 1500-1800, Sun 0900-1230, 1700-1800, with mass every day at 1200, free but donations box by the main altar.* Its San Ignacio chapel has a beautiful polychrome cupola. Also well worth seeing is the church of **San Francisco** ⓘ *Zela 103, US$1.65,* opposite which is the interesting **Museo Histórico Municipal** ⓘ *Plaza San Francisco 407, Mon-Fri 0900-1700, US$0.70,* with much war memorabilia and some impressive photos of the city in the aftermath of several notable earthquakes. **La Recoleta** ⓘ *Jr Recoleta 117, T054-270966, Mon-Sat 0900-1200, 1500-1700, US$1.50,* a Franciscan monastery built in 1647, stands on the other side of the river, on Recoleta. A seldom-visited gem, it contains a variety of exhibits. As well as several cloisters and a religious art museum, the pre-Columbian art museum contains ceramics and textiles produced by cultures of the Arequipa area. Most impressive however is the museum of Amazon exploration, featuring many artefacts as well as photos of early Franciscan missionaries in the Amazon. The library, containing many antique books, is available for supervised visits at 45 minutes past the hour for 15 minutes when the museum is open.

The central **San Camilo market**, between Perú, San Camilo, Piérola and Alto de la Luna, is worth visiting, as is the Siglo XX market, to the east of the rail station. **Fundo del Fierro**, the large handicraft market behind the old prison on Plaza San Francisco, is also worth a visit. For a different shopping experience, try the **Patio del Ekeko** ⓘ *Mercaderes 141,* a commercial centre with upmarket alpaca textiles, handicrafts and fine jewellery shops, **La Ibérica** chocolate shop (also at Morán 160), café, internet, cinema and, upstairs, the **Museo de Arte Textil** ⓘ *Mon-Sat 1000-2030, Sun 1000-1530.*

The **Museo de Arte Contemporáneo** ⓘ *Tacna y Arica 201, T054-221068, Tue-Fri 1000-1700, Sat-Sun 1000-1400, US$1,* in the old railway station, is dedicated to painting and photography from 1900 onwards. The building is surrounded by gardens and has a Sunday market. The **archaeological museum** of the Universidad de San Agustín ⓘ *Alvarez Thomas y Palacio Viejo, T054-288881, Mon-Fri 0815-1700,* has an interesting collection of ceramics and mummies, tracing the region's history from pre-Columbian times to the Republican era.

EXCURSIONS NEAR AREQUIPA

At **Yanahuara**, 2 km northwest, is a 1750 *mestizo*-style church, with a magnificent churrigueresque façade, all in *sillar* (opens 1500). On the same plaza is a mirador, through whose arches there is a fine view of El Misti with the city at its feet, a popular spot in the late afternoon. The **Museo Pre Inca de Chiribaya** ⓘ *Miguel Grau 402, Mon-Sat 0830-1900, Sun 0900-1500,* has a good collection of vessels and well-preserved textiles from a culture that had a high importance in the area before the arrival of the Incas. To get to Yanahuara, cross the Puente Grau, turn right up Avenida Bolognesi.

Some 3 km past **Tingo**, beside the Río Sabandía on the Huasacanche road, is **La Mansión del Fundador** ① *0900-1700, US$4.50*. Originally owned by the founder of Arequipa, Don Garcí Manuel de Carbajal, it has been restored as a museum with original furnishings and paintings; also has cafetería and bar.

About 8 km southeast of Arequipa is the **Molino de Sabandía** ① *US$3.75, ring bell for admission; round trip by taxi US$6*. This is the first stone mill in the area, built in 1621. It has been fully restored and the guardian diverts water to run the grinding stones when visitors arrive. Adjoining Sabandía is **Yumina** ① *tourist fee of US$6 payable, which may be asked for on the bus to Chivay*, with many Inca terraces, which are still in use.

Climbing El Misti and Chachani At 5822 m, El Misti volcano offers a relatively straightforward opportunity to scale a high peak. There are three routes for climbing the volcano; all take two days. The northeast route starts from the Aguada Blanca reservoir, reached by 4WD, from where a four-hour hike takes you to the Monte Blanco camp at 4800 m. Then it's a five- to six-hour ascent to the top. Two hours takes you back down to the trail. The southwest route involves taking a 4WD vehicle to the trailhead at Pastores (3400 m), followed by a hike of five or six hours to a camp at 4700 m. A five-hour climb takes you to the summit, before a three-hour descent to the trail. A southern route (Grau) also starts at 3400 m, with a camp at 4610 m, followed by a five-hour hike to the summit and a two-hour descent. Be prepared for early starts and take plenty of water, food and protection against the weather. Favoured months are May to September.

Climbing Chachani (6057 m), northwest of El Misti, is also popular. This peak retains it's icy covering longer than El Misti, though this is fast disappearing. Remember that both summits are at a very high altitude and that this, combined with climbing on scree, makes it hard going for the untrained. Always contact an experienced guiding agency or professional guide in Arequipa as you should never climb alone.

→COLCA CANYON

① *You must buy a tourist ticket for US$26.50 (valid 10 days), at a checkpoint on the road to Chivay when entering the canyon.*

The Colca Canyon is deep: twice as deep as the Grand Canyon. The Río Colca descends from 3500 m above sea level at Chivay to 2200 m at Cabanaconde. In the background looms the grey, smoking mass of Sabancaya, one of the most active volcanoes in the Americas, and its more docile neighbour, Ampato (6288 m). Unspoiled Andean villages lie on both sides of the canyon, inhabited by the Cabana and Collagua peoples, and some of the extensive pre-Columbian terraced fields are still in use. High on anyone's list for visiting the canyon is an early-morning trip to the **Cruz del Cóndor**, to see these majestic birds at close quarters. From January to April is the rainy season, but this makes the area green, with lots of flowers. This is not the best time to see condors. May to December is the dry, cold season when there is more chance of seeing the birds. Conditions vary annually, though.

From Arequipa there are two routes to **Chivay**, the first village on the edge of the canyon: the old route, via Cayma, and the new route, through Yura, following the railway, longer but quicker. It can be cold in the morning, reaching 4825 m in the Pata Pampa pass, but the views are worth it. Cyclists should use the Yura road: better condition and less of a climb at the start. The main road from Arequipa to Chivay has been paved. The old dirt route runs north from Arequipa, over the Altiplano. About an hour out of Arequipa is the **Aguada Blanca National Vicuña Reserve**. If you're lucky, you can see herds of these rare animals near the road. This route affords fine views of the volcanoes Misti, Chachani, Ampato and Sabancaya. The road from Chivay to Puno via Pata Pampa, Patahuasi, Imata and Juliaca has been improved with a daily tourist transport service.

Chivay is the chief linking point between the two sides of the canyon; there is a road bridge over the river here (others at Yanque and Lari). The road continues northeast to **Tuti** (small handicrafts shop), and **Sibayo** (*pensión* and grocery store). A long circuit back to Arequipa heads south from Sibayo, passing through **Puente Callalli**, **Chullo** and **Sumbay**. This is a little-travelled road, but the views, with vicuña, llamas, alpacas and Andean duck, are superb. Crossing the river at Chivay going west to follow the canyon on the far side, you pass the villages of **Coporaque**, **Ichupampa** (a footbridge crosses the river between the two villages and foot and road bridges connect the road between Coporaque and Ichupampa with Yanque), **Lari**, **Madrigal** (footbridge to Maca) and **Tapay** (connected to Cabanaconde by a footbridge).

CHIVAY TO CABANACONDE

Chivay (3600 m) is the gateway to the canyon. The **Maria Reiche Planetarium and Observatory** ⓘ *in the grounds of the Casa Andina hotel, 6 blocks west of the Plaza between Huayna Capac and Garcilazo, www.casa-andina.com, US$6, discounts for students*, makes the most of the Colca's clear Southern Hemisphere skies with a powerful telescope and two 55-minute presentations per day at 1830 (Spanish) and 1930 (English). There is a very helpful **tourist office** in the Municipalidad on the west side of the plaza (closed at weekends). The tourist police, also on the plaza, can give advice about locally trained guides. **Traveller's Medical Center** (TMC) ⓘ *T054-531037, Ramón Castilla 232, tmc. colcaperu@hotmail.com*. There is a Globalnet ATM close to the plaza.

The hot springs of **La Calera** ⓘ *US$3.50 to bathe, half price just to go in, regular colectivos (US$0.25), taxi (US$1.50) or a 1-hr walk from town*, are 4 km away and are highly recommended after a hard day's trekking.

From Chivay, the main road goes west along the Colca Canyon. The first village encountered is **Yanque** (8 km, excellent views), with an interesting church containing superbly renovated altarpieces and paintings, a museum on the opposite side of the plaza, and a bridge to the villages on the other side of the canyon. A large thermal swimming pool is 20 minutes' walk from the plaza, beside the renovated colonial bridge on the Yanque–Ichupampa road, US$0.75. The road continues paved to **Achoma** (Hospedaje Cruz del Cóndor on the plaza and a campsite) and **Maca**, which barely survived an earthquake in November 1991. Then comes the tiny village of **Pinchollo**, with Hospedaje Refugio del Geyser ⓘ *C Melgar s/n, behind municipality, T054-959-007441/958-032090, basic with good local information*. From here it is a 30-minute walk on a dirt track to the geyser **Hatun Infiernillo**. The mirador, or **Cruz del Cóndor** ⓘ *where you may be asked to show your tourist ticket*, is at the deepest point of the canyon. The view is wonderful and condors can be seen rising on the morning thermals (0900, arrive by 0800 to get a good spot) and sometimes in the late afternoon (1600-1800). Camping here is officially forbidden, but if you ask the tourist police in Chivay they may help. Milagros' 0630 bus from Chivay stop here very briefly at around 0800 (ask the driver to stop), or try hitching with a tour bus at around 0600. Buses from Cabanaconde stop at about 0700 (**Andalucía**) or 0830 (**Reyna**), which leave Cabanaconde's plaza 30 minutes earlier.

From the mirador it is a 20-minute ride in tourist transport, 40 minutes by local bus on a paved road to **Cabanaconde** (3287 m), a friendly, typical village, but very basic (it does have 24-hour electricity). It is the last village in the Colca Canyon. The views are superb and condors can be seen from the hill just west of the village, a 15-minute walk from the plaza, which also gives views of the agrcultural terraces, arguably the most attractive in the valley, to the south of the village. Cabanaconde is an excellent base for visiting the region, with interesting trekking, climbing, biking and horse riding. Many are keen to encourage respectful tourism in the area and several locally owned tourism businesses have opened in the village.

There's a friendly **tourist information office** (T054-280212) willing to give plenty of advice, if not maps. It's a good place to find trekking guides and muleteers (US$30 a day mule and guide).

Two hours below Cabanaconde is **Sangalle**, an 'oasis' of palm trees and swimming areas and three campsites with basic bungalows and toilets (three to 4½ hours back up, ask for the best route in both directions, horses can be hired to carry your bag up, US$5.85), a beautiful spot, recommended. A popular hike involves walking east on the Chivay road to the Mirador de Tapay (before Cruz del Cóndor), then descending to the river on a steep track (four hours, take care). Cross the bridge to the north bank. At the village of San Juan de Chuccho you can stay and eat at a basic family hostel, of which there are several. Hostal Roy and Casa de Rebelino are both good. US$2 will buy you a good meal. From here pass **Tapay** (also possible to camp here) and the small villages of Malata and Cosnirhua, all the time heading west along the north side of the Río Colca (take a guide or ask local directions). After about three hours walking, cross another bridge to the south bank of the Río Colca, follow signs to Sangalle, spend the night and return to Cabanconde on the third day. This route is offered by many Arequipa and local agencies.

GOING FURTHER
Cotahuasi, deeper than Colca

West of Arequipa, a road branches off the Pan-American Highway to Corire, Aplao (small museum containing Wari cultural objects from the surrounding area) and the Río Majes valley. The **world's largest field of petroglyphs**, covering 5 sq km, at Toro Muerto is near Corire. The designs range from simple llamas to elaborate human figures and animals and are thought to be Wari (AD 700-1100) in origin. The sheer scale of the site, some 6000 sculpted rocks, is awe-inspiring and the view is wonderful. Take plenty of water and sun protection. At least an hour is needed to visit the site. Beyond Aplao the road heads north through **Chuquibamba**, where the paving ends, traversing the western slopes of Nevado Coropuna (6425 m), before winding down into **Cotahuasi**, a peaceful colonial town in a sheltered hanging valley beneath Cerro Huinao. Its streets are narrow, the houses whitewashed.

Several kilometres away a canyon has been cut by the Río Cotahuasi, whose waters are formed by the Río Huayllapaña flowing from the north, above Pampamarca, and the Río Huarcaya from the west, above Tomepampa. The river cuts its way westwards and then southwards through the deepest parts of the canyon, below Quechualla. It flows into the Pacific as the Río Ocuña, having joined with the Río Marán along the way.

At its deepest, at Ninochaca (just below the village of Quechualla), the canyon is 3354 m deep, 163 m deeper than the Colca Canyon and the deepest in the world. From this point the only way down the canyon is by kayak and it is through kayakers' reports since 1994 that the area has come to the notice of tourists. It was declared a Zona de Reserva Turística in 1988 and there is pressure to make parts of it into a national park. The vertiginous gradient of the canyon walls and the aridity of its climate allow little agriculture but there are several charming citrus-growing villages downstream, among them **Chaupa**, **Velinga** and **Quechualla**.

In Inca times a road ran along much of the canyon's course, linking Cuzco and the Pacific coast at what is now called **Puerto Inca** (the archaeological site can be visited; there is a hotel close by, T054-692596, www.puertoinka.com.pe). The road was 240 km long, with a staging post every 7 km so that, with a change of runner at every post, messages could be sent in 24 hours. It was also used for taking fish to the ancient Inca capital. Parts of the road are still intact and there are numerous remains of *andenes*, or terraces, which supported settlement along the route. There are also Huari and other pre-Inca ruins. Note that much of the canyon is not on the tourist route and information is hard to come by. Several tour operators in Arequipa run tours to Toro Muerto and four-day trips to Cotahuasi.

AREQUIPA AND COLCA LISTINGS

WHERE TO STAY

Arequipa

$$$$ Casa Andina Private Collection, Ugarte 403, T054-226907, www.casa-andina.com. Luxury hotel in a restored 18th-century mansion, the former **Casa de la Moneda**. 5 large suites in the colonial building, 36 rooms in a modern extension. Gourmet restaurant, room service, business centre, roof terrace with views. There are also Casa Andina Classic hotels in the city and at Chivay.

$$$-$$ Casa de Mi Abuela, Jerusalén 606, T054-241206, www.lacasademiabuela.com. Safe, hot water, laundry, swimming pool, rooms at the back are quieter and overlook the beautiful garden, English spoken, parking, restaurant and piano bar, tours and transport organized in own agency (Giardino, T054-221345, www.giardino tours.com), which has good information.

$$ La Casa de Avila, San Martín 116, Vallecito, T054-213177, www.casadeavila.com. Rooms with hot water on 2 floors around spacious, sunny garden, computers for guests' use, can arrange airport/ bus station pick-up, recommended Spanish courses held in the garden and other activities.

$$ Posada el Castillo, Pasaje Campos 105, Vallecito, T054-201828, www.posadael castillo.com. Dutch-Peruvian-owned, in an old house decorated with utensils found in the renovation, 20 mins by taxi from city centre. Variety of rooms and suites, some with balcony and view of El Misti, wonderful breakfast in new annexe, pool, lovely gardens, a good choice.

$$-$ Casa de Melgar, Melgar 108, T054-222459, www.lacasademelgar.com. 18th-century building, excellent rooms with bath, hot water (solar), safe, courtyard, good breakfast buffet.

Colca Canyon

$$$$ Colca Lodge, across the river from Yanque, T054-531191, office at Mariscal Benavides 201, Selva Alegre, Arequipa, T054-202587, www.colca-lodge.com. Very relaxing, with beautiful hot springs beside the river, spend at least a day to make the most of the activities on offer. Day passes available.

$$$$ Las Casitas del Colca, Av Fundo La Curiña s/n, Yanque, T959-672688, www. lascasitasdelcolca.com. Luxury cottages made of local materials with underfloor heating and plunge pools. Has a restaurant, vegetable garden and farm, offers cookery courses, the Spa offers a variety of treatments, swimming pool.

$$$-$$ Kuntur Wassi, C Cruz Blanca s/n, on the hill above the plaza, Cabanaconde, T054-696665, www.arequipa colca.com. Excellent, 3-star, fine traditional meals on request. Creative design with rooms spaced between rock gardens and waterfalls. Viewing 'tower' and conference centre above. Owners Walter and María very welcoming and knowledgeable about treks.

RESTAURANTS

Arequipa

$$$ Paladar 1900, San Francisco 227, T054-203862, www.elpaladar1900.com.pe. Stylish, contemporary design, the cuisine is modern Peruvian with Middle Eastern influences and more. In the same group are El Turko kebab places and the Fez Istanbul Café.

$$$ Zig Zag, Zela 210, T054-206020, www. zigzagrestaurant.com. In a colonial house, European (mostly Alpine) and local dishes, meats include ostrich and alpaca, delicious.

Café Valenzuela, Morán 114, www.cafe valenzuela.com.pe. Fantastic Peruvian coffee (also sells beans and ground coffee), a favourite with the locals.

SOUTH COAST

The Pan-American Highway runs north all the way from the Chilean border to Lima, mostly along the coast. One of its major detours is inland towards Arequipa, from where it heads back to the Pacific near the town of Camaná. It's a long haul of almost 400 km through coastal desert and the occasional river valley to the next inland section at Nazca. This part of Peru's desert coast has its own distinctive attractions. The most famous, and perhaps the strangest, are the mysterious Nazca Lines, whose origin and function continue to puzzle scientists the world over. But Nazca is not the sole archaeological resource here: remains of other pre-Columbian civilizations include outposts of the Inca empire itself. Pisco and Ica are the main centres between Nazca and Lima. The former, which is near the famous Paracas marine reserve, is named after the latter's main product, the pisco grape brandy, and a number of places are well-known for their bodegas.

→ NAZCA AND AROUND

Set in a green valley amid a perimeter of mountains, Nazca's altitude puts it just above any fog that may drift in from the sea. The sun blazes the year round by day and the nights are crisp. Nearby are the mysterious, world-famous Nazca Lines. Overlooking the town is Cerro Blanco (2078 m), the highest sand dune in the world, popular for sandboarding and parapenting.

ARRIVING IN NAZCA
Getting there Buses from Arequipa (or anywhere else) arrive at their own offices in Nazca, most at the west end of town.

Moving on Many buses run from Nazca to Lima, 444 km via the Pan-American Highway, in seven hours (see page 35; see also notes on page 102 about travelling at night), stopping in Ica (see page 113) after two hours. From Ica, you can take colectivos or local buses for the short journeys to Paracas (see page 113), 45 minutes, or Pisco (see page 114). These are better in this instance than major companies, which leave passengers at a junction (*cruce*) on the Pan-American Highway because neither Paracas nor Pisco is on the main road. Taxis or minivans run to the town centres from the junction. Buses from Paracas or Pisco to Lima take between four and five hours.

Tourist information Tourist police ① *Av Los Incas cuadra 1, T056-522105.*

NAZCA TOWN
In the town of Nazca there are two important museums. **Museo Antonini** ① *Av de la Cultura 600, eastern end of Jr Lima, T056-523444, cahuachi@terra.com.pe, 0900-1900, ring the bell, US$5.75, including guide. 10-min walk from the plaza, or short taxi ride,* houses the discoveries of Professor Orefici and his team from the huge pre-Inca city at Cahuachi (see page 112), which, Orefici believes, holds the key to the Nazca Lines. Many tombs survived the *huaqueros* (grave robbers) and there are displays of mummies, ceramics, textiles, amazing *antaras* (panpipes) and photos of the excavations. In the garden is a prehispanic aqueduct. Recommended. The **Maria Reiche Planetarium** ① *Hotel Nazca Lines, T056-522293, shows usually at 1900 and 2115 in English, 2000 in Spanish; US$7.50 (students half price).*

Introductory lectures are given every night about the Nazca Lines, based on Reiche's theories, which cover archaeology and astronomy. The show lasts about 45 minutes, after which visitors are able to look at the moon, planets and stars through telescopes. There is a small market at Lima y Grau and the Mercado Central at Arica y Tacna. The **Virgen de la Guadalupe** festival takes place 29 August-10 September.

NAZCA LINES

Cut into the stony desert about 22 km north of Nazca, above the Ingenio Valley on the Pampa de San José, along the Pan-American Highway, are the famous Nazca Lines. Large numbers of lines, not only parallels and geometrical figures, but also designs such as a dog, an enormous monkey, birds (one with a wingspan of over 100 m), a spider and a tree. The lines, best seen from the air, are thought to have been etched on the Pampa Colorada sands by three different groups – the Paracas people 900-200 BC, the Nazcas 200 BC-AD 600 and the Huari settlers from Ayacucho at about AD 630.

The Nazcas had a highly developed civilization, which reached its peak about AD 600. Their polychrome ceramics, wood carvings and adornments of gold are on display in many of Lima's museums. The Paracas was an early phase of the Nazca culture, renowned for the superb technical quality and stylistic variety in its weaving and pottery. The Huari empire, in conjunction with the Tiwanaku culture, dominated much of Peru from AD 600-1000.

Origins of the lines The German expert, Dr Maria Reiche, who studied the lines for over 40 years, mostly from a step ladder, died in 1998, aged 95. She maintained that they represent some sort of vast astronomical pre-Inca calendar. In 1976 Maria Reiche paid for a platform, the mirador, from which three of the huge designs can be seen – the Hands, the Lizard and the Tree. Her book, *Mystery on the Desert*, is on sale for US$10 (proceeds to conservation work) in Nazca. In January 1994 Maria Reiche opened a small **museum** ⓘ *US$1, 5 km from town at the Km 421 marker, take micro from in front of Ormeño terminal, US$0.75, frequent.* Viktoria Nikitzhi, a colleague of Maria Reiche, gives one-hour lectures about the Nazca Lines at **Dr Maria Reiche Center** ⓘ *US$5, Av de los Espinales 300, 1 block from Ormeño bus stop, T056-969 9419, viktorianikitzki@hotmail.com.* She also organizes tours in June and December (phone in advance to confirm times; also ask about volunteer work). See the Planetarium, above. Another good book is *Pathways to the Gods: the mystery of the Nazca Lines*, by Tony Morrison (Michael Russell, 1978).

Other theories abound: claims that the lines are the tracks of running contests (Georg A von Breunig, 1980, and English astronomer Alan Sawyer); that they represent weaving patterns and yarns (Henri Stirlin) and that the plain is a map demonstrating the Tiwanaku Empire (Zsoltan Zelko). Johan Reinhard proposes that the lines conform to fertility practices throughout the Andes, in common with the current use of straight lines in Chile and Bolivia.

Another theory is that the ancient Nazcas flew in hot-air balloons, based on the idea that the lines are best seen from the air (Jim Woodman, 1977 and, in part, the BBC series 'Ancient Voices', 1998). A related idea is that the lines were not designed to be seen physically from above, but from the mind's eye of the flying shaman. Both theories are supported by pottery and textile evidence, which shows balloonists and a flying creature emitting discharge from its nose and mouth. There are also local legends of flying men. The depiction in the desert of creatures such as a monkey or killer whale also indicates the qualities needed by the shaman in his spirit journeys.

After six years' work at La Muña and Los Molinos, Palpa (43 km north of Nazca), and using photogrammetry, Peruvian archaeologist Johny Isla and Markus Reindel of the Swiss-Liechtenstein Foundation deduced that the lines on both the Palpa and Nazca plains are offerings dedicated to the worship of water and fertility, two elements that also dominate on ceramics and on the engraved stones of the Paracas culture. Isla and Reindel believe that the Palpa lines predate those at Nazca and that the lines and drawings themselves are scaled-up versions of the Paracas drawings. This research proposes that the Nazca culture succumbed not to drought, but to heavy rainfall, probably during an El Niño event.

OTHER EXCURSIONS

The Nazca area is dotted with over 100 cemeteries, and the dry, humidity-free climate has perfectly preserved invaluable tapestries, cloth and mummies. At **Chauchilla** ① *30 km south of Nazca, last 12 km a sandy track, US$3*, grave robbing *huaqueros* ransacked the tombs and left bones, skulls, mummies and pottery shards littering the desert. A tour takes about two hours. Gold mining is one of the main local industries and a tour usually includes a visit to a small family processing shop where the techniques used are still very old-fashioned.

The **Paredones** ruins and aqueduct ① *US$3.55 entry also includes 4 other archaeological sites: El Telar Geoglyphs, Acueductos de Cantayoc, Las Agujas Geoglyphs and Acueductos de Ocongalla*, also called Cacsamarca, are Inca on a pre-Inca base. The ruins are not well preserved. The underground aqueducts, built 300 BC-AD 700, are still in working order and worth seeing.

The **Cantayoc Aqueducts**, **Las Agujas** and **El Telar Geoglyphs** can be visited on a 30 minutes to one hour walk through Buena Fe (or organize a taxi from your hotel), to see markings in the valley floor and ancient aqueducts that descend in spirals into the ground. The markings consist of a triangle pointing to a hill and a *telar* (cloth) with a spiral depicting the threads. Climb the mountain to see better examples.

Cahuachi ① *US$3.55, to visit the ruins of Cahuachi costs US$17 per person on a tour, US$12-15 in private taxi, minimum 2 people (see also the Museo Antonini, page 110)*, one hour to the west of the Nazca Lines along a rough dirt track, comprises some 30 pyramids. Only 5% of the site has been excavated so far, some of which has been reconstructed. It could be larger than Chan Chán, making it the largest adobe city in the world. About 4 km beyond Cahuachi is a site called **El Estaquería**, thought to have been a series of astronomical sighting posts, though more recent research suggests the wooden pillars were used to dry dead bodies and therefore it may have been a place of mummification.

Reserva Nacional de San Fernando is a gathering place for birds, continental and oceanic mammals. Originally a project, it was established in 2011 as a National Reserve to protect migratory and local wildlife such as the Humboldt penguin, sea lions, the Andean fox, condor, guanaco, dolphins and whales. San Fernando is located in the highest part of the Peruvian coastal desert, in the same place as Cerro Blanco, the highest dune in the world. Here is where the Nazca Plate lifts the South American Plate, generating moist accumulation in the ground with resulting seasonal winter flora and a continental wildlife corridor between the high coastal mountains and the sea. Full-day and two-day/one-night tours are offered by some agencies in town.

The Ica valley, with its wonderful climate, is home to that equally wonderful grape brandy, pisco. Most beaches have very strong currents and can be dangerous for swimming; if unsure, ask locals. Further north, the Paracas Peninsula, near Pisco, is one of the world's great marine bird reserves and was home to one of Peru's most important ancient civilizations.

ICA AND HUACACHINA

Ica, 140 km northeast of Nazca, is Peru's chief wine centre and is famous for its *tejas*, local sweets filled with *manjarblanco*. It suffered less damage than Pisco in the earthquake of 2007, but one side of the Plaza de Armas collapsed. The **Museo Regional** ① *Av Ayabaca, block 8, T056-234383, Mon-Wed 0800-1900, Thu-Sun 0900-1800, US$4, students US$2.15, tip guides US$4-5, take bus 17 from the Plaza de Armas (US$0.50)*, has mummies, ceramics, textiles and trepanned skulls from the Paracas, Nazca and Inca cultures; a good, well-displayed collection of Inca *quipus* and clothes made of feathers. Behind the building is a scale model of the Nazca Lines with an observation tower; a useful orientation before visiting the lines. The kiosk outside sells copies of motifs from the ceramics and textiles. **Dircetur** is at ① *Av Grau 148, T056-238710, ica@mincetur.gob.pe*. See www.helloica.com. Some tourist information is available at travel agencies.

Wine bodegas that you can visit are: **La Caravedo**, Panamericana Sur 298, T01-9833 4729, with organic production and sophisticated presentation; **El Carmen**, 3 km north of Ica (has an ancient grape press made from a huge tree trunk); **El Catador** ① *Fondo Tres Esquinas 102, T056-962629, elcatadorcristel@yahoo.es, 1000-1800, US$1.50, 10 km outside Ica, in the district of Subtanjalla, combi from the 2nd block of Moquegua, every 20 mins, US$0.75, taxi takes 10 mins, good tours in Spanish*. The shop sells home-made wines, pisco and crafts associated with winemaking. In the evening it is a restaurant-bar with dancing and music, best visited during harvest, late February to early April. Near El Catador is **Bodega Alvarez**, whose owner, Umberto Alvarez, is very hospitable. The town of Ocucaje is a popular excursion from Ica for tours of the **Ocucaje winery** ① *Ctra Panamericana Sur, Km 335.5, T01-251 4570, www.ocucaje.com*, which makes wines and pisco.

About 5 km from Ica, round a palm-fringed lake and amid amazing sand dunes, is the oasis and summer resort of **Huacachina** ① *take a taxi from Ica for US$1.75*, a popular hang-out for people seeking a change from the archaeology and chill of the Andes. Plenty of cheap hostels and bars have opened, playing pop and grunge as opposed to pan-pipe music. Paddleboats can be rented and sandboarding on the dunes has become a major pastime. For the inexperienced, note that sandboarding can be dangerous. Dune buggies also do white-knuckle, rollercoaster tours for US$20 (plus a small municipal fee), most start between 1600 and 1700 for sunsets, some at 1000, 2½ hours.

PARACAS NATIONAL RESERVE

① *US$1.85 per person; agency tours cost US$8.75 in a bus*.

On the coast 70 km from Ica is the bay of **Paracas**, sheltered by the Paracas Peninsula. The name means 'sandstorm' (these can last for three days, especially in August; the wind gets up every afternoon, peaking at around 1500). Paracas can be reached by local bus or colectivo from Ica. In town is the **Museo Histórico de Paracas** ① *Av Los Libertadores Mz JI Lote 10, T955-929514, www.museohistoricoparacas.com*, with exhibits from the pre-Columbian cultures of the region.

The peninsula, a large area of coast to the south and the Ballestas Islands are a National Reserve, and one of the best marine reserves, with the highest concentration of marine birds in the world. It's advisable to visit the peninsula as part of a tour: it is not safe to walk alone and it is easy to get lost. The **Julio C Tello** site museum was being rebuilt in 2013 after the 2007 earthquake. Tours follow a route through the Reserve, including to a mirador overlooking **La Catedral** rock formation, a sea arch that collapsed in 2007. Longer tours venture into the deserts to the south. About 14 km from the museum is the pre-Columbian **Candelabro** traced in the hillside, a geoglyph at least 50 m long, best seen from the sea. The tiny fishing village of **Lagunilla** is 5 km from the museum across the neck of the peninsula.

BALLESTAS ISLANDS

Trips to the **Islas Ballestas** leave from the jetties in Paracas town. The islands are spectacular, eroded into numerous arches and caves (*ballesta* means bow, as in archery), which provide shelter for thousands of seabirds, some of which are very rare, and hundreds of sea lions. The book *Las Aves del Departamento de Lima* by Maria Koepcke is useful (see also www.avesdelima.com/playas.htm). You will see, close up, thousands of inquisitive sea lions, guano birds, pelicans, penguins and, if you're lucky, dolphins swimming in the bay. Most boats are speedboats with life jackets, some are very crowded; wear warm clothing and protect against the sun. The boats pass Puerto San Martín and the Candelabra en route to the islands.

PISCO AND AROUND

The largest port between Callao and Matarani is a short distance to the west of the Pan-American Highway and 237 km south of Lima. In August 2007, an earthquake of 7.9 on the Richter scale struck the coast of Peru south of Lima killing 519 people, with 1366 injured and 58,500 homes destroyed. Hardest hit was the province of Ica; in the city of Pisco almost half of all buildings were destroyed. Also affected was **Chincha Alta**, 35 km north of Pisco, where the negro/criollo culture thrives. The famous festival, **Verano Negro**, is at the end of February while, in November, the **Festival de las Danzas Negras** is held in El Carmen, 10 km south. In October 2011, another earthquake, this time of 6.9 on the Richter scale, occurred off the coast of Ica, leaving one person dead, 1705 homeless and 515 damaged or destroyed houses.

A 317-km paved road goes to Ayacucho in the Sierra (see box, page 81), with a branch to Huancavelica. At Castrovirreyna it reaches 4600 m. The scenery on this journey is superb. **Tambo Colorado**, one of the best-preserved Inca ruins in coastal Peru, is 38 km from the San Clemente junction, up the Pisco Valley. It includes buildings where the Inca and his retinue would have stayed. Many of the walls retain their original colours. On the other side of the road is the public plaza and the garrison and messengers' quarters. The caretaker will act as a guide and he has a small collection of items found on the site.

CAÑETE VALLEY

A paved road runs inland from Cañete, mostly beside the Río Cañete, to **Lunahuaná** (40 km). It is 8 km beyond the Inca ruins of **Incawasi**, which dominated the valley. In the week it's very quiet, but on Sunday the town is full of life, with pisco tastings from the valley's bodegas, food and handicrafts for sale in the plaza and lots of outdoor activities. Several places offer rafting and kayaking: from November-April rafting is at levels 4-5.

May-October is low water, levels 1-2 only. A festival of adventure sports is held every February and the **Fiesta de la Vendimia**, grape harvest, first weekend in March. At the end of September/beginning October is the **Fiesta del Níspero** (medlar festival). There are several hotels (mid-range and cheap), and *restaurantes campestres* in the area. There's a **Tourist office** ① *in the Municipalidad, T056-284 1006, mlunah@mixmail.com, opposite the church, open daily.*

Beyond Lunahuaná the road ascending the Cañete Valley leaves the narrow flood-plain and runs 41 km, paved, through a series of gorges to the San Jerónimo bridge. A side road heads to Huangáscar and the village of **Viñac**, where Mountain Lodges of Peru (see page 79) has its **Viñak-Reichraming Lodge** (**$$$** per person full board, T01-421 6952, www.refugiosdelperu.com), a wonderful place to relax or go horseriding or walking (superb views, excellent food). The main road carries on to the market town of **Yauyos** (basic accommodation, 5 km off the road). After the attractive village of **Huancaya** (several *hospedajes*, T01-810 6086/7, municipal phone, and ask for details) the valley is transformed into one of the most beautiful upper valleys in all Peru, on a par with Colca. Above Huancaya the high Andean terrain lies within the **Reserva Paisajística Nor Yauyos-Cochas** ① *SERNANP contact Juan Carlos Pilco, pilco_traveler@hotmail.com; regional office RPNYC, Av Francisco Solano 107, San Carlos, Huancayo T064-213064*, and the river descends through a series of absolutely clear, turquoise pools and lakes, interrupted by cascades and white-water rapids. The valley has perhaps the best pre-Columbian terracing anywhere in Peru. Further upstream **Llapay** is a good base because it is in the middle of the valley (**$ Hostal Llapay**, basic but very friendly, will open at any hour, restaurant). Beyond Llapay, the Cañete Valley narrows to an exceptionally tight canyon, with a road squeezed between nothing but rock and rushing water for the steep climb to the 4600-m pass. Beyond, the road drops to Huancayo (see box, page 81).

SOUTH COAST LISTINGS

WHERE TO STAY

Nazca
$$$ Majoro, Panamericana Sur Km 452, T056-522490, www.hotelmajoro.com. A charming old hacienda about 5 km from town past the airstrip so quite remote, beautiful gardens, pool, slow and expensive restaurant, quiet and welcoming, good arrangements for flights and tours.
$$$-$$ Oro Viejo, Callao 483, T056-521112, www.hoteloroviejo.net. Has a suite with jacuzzi, and comfortable standard rooms, hot showers. Nice garden, swimming pool, bar, parking and restaurant. Recommended.

Ica
$$$ Villa Jazmín, Los Girasoles Mz C-1, Lote 7, Res La Angostura, T056-258179, www.villajazmin.net. Modern hotel in a residential area near the sand dunes, 8 mins from the city centre, solar-heated water, restaurant, buffet breakfast, pool, tours arranged, airport and bus transfers, helpful staff, tranquil and very good.

Paracas
$$$$ Hotel Paracas Luxury Collection Resort, Av Paracas 173, T056-581333, www.libertador. com.pe. The reincarnation of the famous **Hotel Paracas**, as a resort with spa, pools, excellent rooms in cottages around the grounds, access to beach, choice of restaurants, bar.
$$ Brisas de la Bahía, Av Principal, T056-531132, www.brisasdelabahia.com. Good, family-run *hostal*, convenient position for waterfront and bus stops, ask for a back room, good breakfast.
$$ Mar Azul, Alan García Mz B lote 20, T056-534542, www.hostalmarazul.com. Family-run, overlooking the sea although most rooms face away from ocean, comfortable, hot water, breezy roof terrace with sea view for breakfast (included), helpful owner. Also offers local tours.

WHAT TO DO

Boat trips from Paracas
Boat trips to the Islas Ballestas leave from Paracas last 2 hrs and cost from US$17-27 per person. Many agencies offer these excursions and most pool customers together.
There are agencies all over town offering trips to the Islas Ballestas, the Paracas reserve, Ica, Nazca and Tambo Colorado. A 2-hr boat tour to the islands is US$17-27 per person; a full day tour taking in sights on land as well as a boat trip is about US$60. Usually, agencies will pool clients together in 1 boat. Do not book tours on the street. An agency that does not pool clients is **Huacachina**, based in Ica, with an office in Paracas, T056-256582, www.huacachinatours.com.

Zarcillo Connections, Av Principal de ingreso al Chaco, Paracas, T056-536636, www.zarcilloconnections.com. With long experience for trips to the Paracas National Reserve, Tambo Colorado, trekking and tours to Ica, Chincha and the Nazca Lines and surrounding sites. Also has its own hotel, **Zarcillo Paradise**, in Paracas.

Desert trips
Desert Adventures, Huacachina, T056-228458, www.desertadventure.net. Frequently recommended for sandboarding and camping trips into the desert by 4WD and buggies, French, English and Spanish spoken. Also to beaches, Islas Ballestas and Nazca Lines flights.
Ica Desert Trip, Bolívar 178, T237373, www.icadeserttrip.com. Roberto Penny

Cabrera (speaks Spanish and English) offers 1, 2 and 3-day trips off-road into the desert, archaeology, geology, etc. 4 people maximum, contact by email in advance. Take toilet paper, something warm for the evening, a long-sleeved loose cotton shirt for daytime and long trousers. Recommended, but not for the faint-hearted.

Flights over the Nazca Lines

There are flights over the Nazca Lines from both Nazca and Pisco. Nazca is the traditional base for flights, which last 30-45 mins and cost US$90-130 per person. The safety record from Nazca has been patchy. Larger planes can fly from the new airport at Pisco, from where flights last 1 hr 35 mins and cost US$180-210 per person.

DREAM TRIP 3
Lima➔Cordillera Blanca➔Trujillo➔Cajamarca
21 days

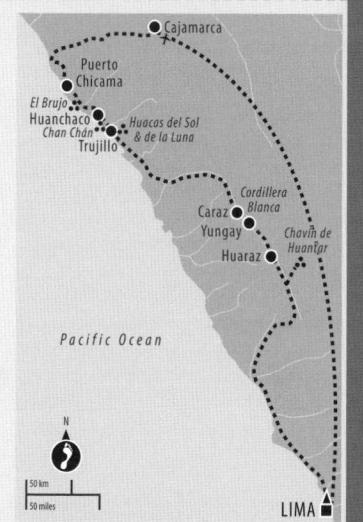

GOING FURTHER

In surfing season (Mar-Oct) you may prefer to move on from Trujillo by bus (1½ hrs) to **Puerto Chicama** (page 137) for 2/3 nights, then go to **Pacasmayo** (1 hr) to catch the bus to **Cajamarca** (4½ hrs).

Huancayo page 82
Bus from Huaraz via La Unión (4½ hrs) and Huánaco (7 hrs) to Huancayo (7 hrs)

DREAM TRIP 3
Lima→Cordillera Blanca→Trujillo→Cajamarca

Leaving Lima for the Cordillera Blanca brings a great change of pace. Snow-capped mountains dominate the town of Huaraz, which is the focal point for the Callejón de Huaylas, a high valley with a string of villages along the course of the Río Santa. Turquoise lakes that form in the terminal moraines are the perfect destination for a hike of a day or more, and long-distance hikes over the passes that separate the white crests have long attracted hikers. On the eastern slopes of the Cordillera Blanca is the Callejón de Conchucos, on the main road to which is the archaeological site of Chavín de Huantar, seat of the hugely influential Chavín culture. Southeast of Huaraz, another group of mountains, the Cordillera Huayhuash, is more than a match for its neighbour in beauty, majesty and challenging treks and climbs.

On the coast to the north of the Cordilleras is a region of vast ruins built by two of Peru's highly skilled pre-Inca civilizations, the Moche and the Chimú. The former's temples, called the Huaca de la Luna and the Huaca Cao Viejo at two different sites, are revealing fabulous, multi-coloured friezes. The Chimú's capital, Chan Chán, is the largest adobe city in the world. Much of it has been lost to the elements, but it remains an impressive monument. All these sites are within easy reach of Trujillo, which has its own fine colonial centre. On the coast nearby is the popular seaside town of Huanchaco, with its surfer-fishermen using age-old techniques and their modern equivalents on high-tech boards.

Head north again to end this trip in Cajamarca, surrounded by hills, dairy farms and hot springs. It was here that the conquistadors had their first significant victory over the Inca emperor, Atahualpa. The city's colonial centre contains a building reputed to be the ransom chamber that Atahualpa promised to fill with gold, to no avail.

HUARAZ AND CORDILLERA BLANCA

This trip begins with four nights in the capital, Lima, as in Dream Trip 1 (see pages 35-51). You can travel by road north from Lima, in which case you could break the journey at Caral (see page 49) instead of visiting the ruins on a day trip from Lima, but this would involve several changes of bus. The quick option is to fly from the barren coast into the mountains.

The spectacular Cordillera Blanca is an area of jewelled lakes and snowy mountain peaks attracting mountaineers and hikers in their thousands. Huaraz is the natural place to head for. It has the best infrastructure and the mountains, lakes and trails are within easy reach. This region, though, also has some sites of great archaeological significance, the most notable of which must be Chavín de Huantar, one of Peru's most important pre-Inca sites. Mining is bringing new prosperity to the area.

→HUARAZ

The main town in the Cordillera Blanca, 420 km from Lima, Huaraz is expanding rapidly as a major tourist centre, but it is also a busy commercial hub, especially on market days. It is a prime destination for hikers and a mecca for international climbers.

ARRIVING IN HUARAZ
Getting there The airport for Huaraz is in Anta district, 21 km north of the town. The daily flight from Lima takes one hour, then it's a 15- to 20-minute drive to town.

North from Lima the Pan-American Highway parallels the coast. Buses take the paved road that branches east off the Pan-American Highway north of Pativilca, 203 km from Lima. The road climbs increasingly steeply to the chilly pass at 4080 m (Km 120). Shortly after, Laguna Conococha comes into view, where the Río Santa rises. After crossing a high plateau the main road descends gradually for 47 km to Catac, from where it is 36 km to Huaraz. There is no central bus terminal in Huaraz; each company has its own terminal.

Moving on Buses and, more commonly, minivans run to all parts of the Cordillera Blanca region. To the north the road winds along the Callejón de Huaylas between the towering Cordillera Negra, snowless and rising to 4600 m, and the snow-covered Cordillera Blanca. Southwards, a branch road heads east to Chavín (see page 125) before veering north up the Callejón de Conchucos. Roads cross the Cordillera Blanca between the two north–south routes. For the Cordilleras Huayhuash and Raura, take the same road south but continue to Conacocha, where a road branches east to Chiquián. This is the road that eventually links up with the Central Highlands route (see Going further, page 81).

There are two routes to Trujillo (see page 131). The main bus companies return to the coast at Casma and then head north on the Panamericana to Trujillo, five to six hours, most at night. (Note that even the most reputable companies are not immune from hold-ups and accidents at night; seek local advice before travelling on a night bus.) The alternative is to go via Caraz (see page 127) and the spectacular Cañón del Pato to the fishing port of Chimbote, where you change buses.

Tourist offices iPerú ⓘ *Pasaje Atusparia, of 1, Plaza de Armas, T043-428812, iperuhuaraz@promperu.gob.pe, Mon-Sat 0800-1830, Sun 0830-1400. Also at Jr San Martín cuadra 6 s/n, open daily 0800-1100, and at Anta airport when flights arrive.* **Tourist Police** ⓘ *on 2nd floor of main iPerú building, T043-421341 ext 315, Mon-Fri 0900-1300, 1600-1900, Sat 0900-1300,* is the place to report crimes and mistreatment by tour operators,

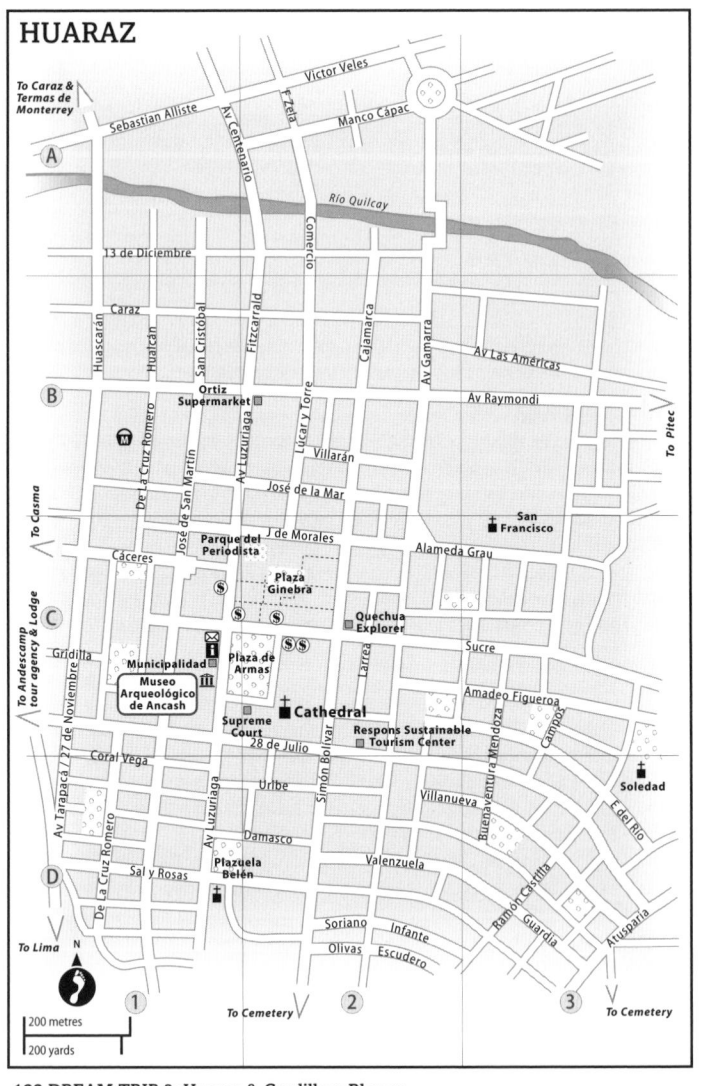

hotels, etc. **Indecopi** ① *Jr José de Sucre 767 y Bolívar, p 2, T043-423899, jcvela@indecopi. gob.pe*. Huaraz has its share of crime, especially since the arrival of mining and during the high tourist season. Women should not go to surrounding districts and sites alone. See also www.andeanexplorer.com.

PLACES IN AND AROUND HUARAZ

Huaraz, capital of Ancash department, was almost completely destroyed in the earthquake of May 1970. The Plaza de Armas has been rebuilt. A new **Cathedral** is still being built. The setting, at the foot of the Cordillera Blanca, is spectacular. The main thoroughfare, Avenida Luzuriaga, is bursting at the seams with travel agencies, climbing equipment hire shops, restaurants, cafés and bars. A good district for those seeking peace and quiet is La Soledad, six blocks uphill from the Plaza de Armas on Avenida Sucre. Here, along Sucre as well as Jirón Amadeo Figueroa, every second house seems to rent rooms, most without signs. **Museo Arqueológico de Ancash** ① *Ministerio de Cultura, Plaza de Armas, Mon-Sat 0900-1700, Sun 0900-1400*, contains stone monoliths and *huacos* (ceremonial vessels) from the Recuay culture, well labelled. The **Sala de Cultura SUNARP** ① *Av Centenario 530, Independencia, T043-421301, Mon-Fri 1700-2000, Sat 0900-1300, free*, often has interesting art and photography exhibitions by local artists.

About 8 km to the northeast is **Willkawain** ① *US$1.50, take a combi from 13 de Diciembre and Comercio, US$0.55 direct to Willkawain*. The ruins (AD 700-1000, Huari Empire) consist of one large three-storey structure with intact stone roof slabs and several small structures. About 500 m past Willkawain is Ichiwillkawain with several similar but smaller structures. Take a torch if it's late. If walking, go past the Hotel Huascarán. After crossing a small bridge take a second right marked by a blue sign, it is about two hours' uphill walk; ask directions as there are many criss-crossing paths used regularly by local people. North of Huaraz, 6 km along the road to Caraz, are the thermal baths at **Monterrey** (at 2780 m) ① *lower pool US$0.85; upper pool, which is nicer (closed Mon for cleaning), US$1.35; also individual and family tubs US$1.35 per person for 20 mins; crowded at weekends and holidays*. There are restaurants and hotels. City buses along Avenida Luzuriaga go as far as Monterrey (US$0.22), until 1900; taxi US$2-3.

→ CORDILLERA BLANCA

Apart from the range of Andes running along the Chile–Argentina border, the highest mountains in South America lie along the Cordillera Blanca and are perfectly visible from many spots. From Huaraz alone, you can see more than 23 peaks of over 5000 m, of which the most notable is Huascarán (6768 m), the highest mountain in Peru. Although the snowline is receding, the Cordillera Blanca still contains the largest concentration of glaciers found in the world's tropical zone, and the turquoise-coloured lakes, which form in the terminal moraines, are the jewels of the Andes. Here also is one of Peru's most important pre-Inca sites, at Chavín de Huantar.

PARQUE NACIONAL HUASCARAN

Established in July 1975, the park includes the entire Cordillera Blanca above 4000 m, with an area of 3400 sq km. It is a UNESCO World Biosphere Reserve and part of the World Heritage Trust. The park's objectives are to protect the flora, fauna, geology, archaeological sites and scenic beauty of the Cordillera. Take all your rubbish away with you when camping. The park office charges visitors US$1.65 for a day visit. For visits of up to seven days (ie for trekking and climbing trips) a permit costing US$23 (65 soles) must be bought. If you stay longer than seven days, you will need another permit. Some offices say the permit is valid for a month, but check before assuming this. Fees for visiting the national park are collected at rangers' posts at Llanganuco and Huascarán (for the Llanganuco to Santa Cruz trek), and at Collón on the way up the Quebrada Ishinca. The **park office** ① *Jr Federico Sal y Rosas 555, by Plazuela Belén, T043-422086, pnhuascaran@sernanp.gob.pe; Mon-Fri 0830-1300, 1430-1700*, is principally administrative.

SERNANP plans to implement new regulations governing the Huascarán National Park. Local guides will be mandatory for everywhere except designated 'Recreation Zones' (areas accessible by car). Tourists will be required to hire a licensed tour operator for all activities and those operators may only employ licensed guides, cooks, arrieros (muleteers) and porters. Anyone wishing to trek, climb or ski in Huascarán should seek advice from SERNANP or a local tour operator to see if these rules are being applied.

TREKKING AND CLIMBING IN THE CORDILLERA BLANCA

The Cordillera Blanca offers popular backpacking and trekking, with a network of trails used by the local people and some less well-defined mountaineers' routes. Most circuits can be hiked in five days. Although the trails are easily followed, they are rugged with high passes, between 4000 and 5000 m, so backpackers should be fit and acclimatized to the altitude, and carry all equipment. Essential items are a tent, warm sleeping bag, stove, and protection against wind and rain (the weather is unreliable and you cannot rule out rain and hail storms even in the dry season). Less stamina is required if you hire mules to carry equipment. The season is from May to September, although conditions vary from year to year. The rainy season in Huaraz is December to March.

Advice to climbers The height of the Cordillera Blanca and the Callejón de Huaylas ranges and their location in the tropics create conditions different from those in the Alps or even the Himalayas. Fierce sun makes the mountain snow porous and glaciers move more rapidly. Deglaciation is rapidly changing the face of the Cordillera. Older maps do not provide a reliable indication of the extent of glaciers and snow fields (according to some studies 15% of the range's glaciers have disappeared since the 1970s), so local experience is important. If the new SERNANP rules preventing independent treks or climbs have not been instigated (see above), move in groups of four or more, reporting to the Casa de Guías (see page 130) or the office of the guide before departing, giving the date at which a search should begin, and leaving your embassy's telephone number, with money for the call. International recommendations are for a 300 m per day maximum altitude gain. Be wary of agencies wanting to sell you trips with very fast ascents (but ask around if this is what you want). The **Departamento de Salvamento de Alta Montaña** (DEPSAM) ① *Jr Bolognesi 410, Caraz, T043-391163/391669*, has a rescue team with 24-hour phone service and vhf/uhf radio dispatch. They have the use of a helicopter and trained search-and-rescue dogs. At present, they will rescue anyone – climbers, trekkers, tourists – without asking for cash up front. Insured climbers will be billed, but rescues for the uninsured are currently free. This policy is likely to change. They will only take the injured person as far as Caraz or Huaraz hospitals, from where additional costly medical evacuation may be required. It therefore remains imperative that all climbers carry adequate insurance (it cannot be purchased locally). Be well prepared before setting out on a climb. Wait or cancel your trip when the weather is bad. Every year climbers are killed through failing to take weather conditions seriously. Climb only when and where you have sufficient experience.

Note Before heading out on any route, always enquire locally about public safety. The Cordillera Blanca is generally safe, but muggings have taken place on the way to Laguna Churup, to the Mirador Rataquenua above Huaraz, the mirador above Monterrey, and on the walk from Willkawain to Monterrey. On all treks in this area, respect the locals' property, leave no rubbish behind, do not give sweets or money to children who beg and remember your cooking utensils and tent would be very expensive for a *campesino*, so be sensitive and responsible.

HUARAZ TO CHAVIN

South of Huaraz is **Olleros** (3450 m). The spectacular and relatively easy three to four-day hike to Chavín, along a pre-Columbian trail, starts from Olleros. Some basic meals and food supplies available. At 38 km via the main road from Huaraz is **Catac** (two basic hotels and a restaurant), where a paved road branches east for Chavín.

A good place to see the impressive *Puya raimondii* plants is the Pumapampa Valley. A 14 km gravel road from Pachacoto goes to the park entrance (4200 m), where there is a park office. You can spend the night here. Another good spot, and less visited, is the **Queshque Gorge**. Follow the Río Queshque from Catac (see above); it's easy to find. The giant *Puya raimondii*, named after Antonio Raimondi, the Italian scholar who discovered it, is a rare species, considered to be one of the oldest plants in the world. Often mistakenly referred to as a cactus, it is actually the largest member of the bromeliad family and is found in only a few isolated areas of the Andes. At its base, the *puya* forms a rosette of long, spiked, waxy leaves, 2 m in diameter. The distinctive phallic spike of the plant can reach a height of 12 m during the flowering process. This takes its entire lifespan – an incredible 100 years – after which time the plant withers and dies. As the final flowering begins, usually during May for mature plants, the spike is covered in flowers. As many as 20,000 blooms can decorate a single plant. During this season, groups of *Puya raimondii* will bloom together, creating a spectacular picture against the dramatic backdrop of the Cordillera Blanca.

From Catac to Chavín is a magnificent journey. The road passes Lago QuerocQocha, has good views of the Yanamarey peaks and, at the top of the route, is cut through a huge rock face, entering the Cahuish tunnel at 4516 m. On the other side it descends the Tambillo Valley, then the Río Mosna gorge before Chavín.

CHAVIN DE HUANTAR

ⓘ *Tue-Sun 0800-1700, US$3.85, students half price, Spanish-speaking guides will take groups for an extra charge.*

Chavín de Huantar, a fortress temple, was built about 800 BC. It is the only large structure remaining of the Chavín culture which, in its heyday, is thought to have held influence in a region between Cajamarca and Chiclayo in the north to Ayacucho and Ica in the south. In December 1985, UNESCO designated Chavín a World Heritage Site. The site is in good condition despite the effects of time and nature. The main attractions are the marvellous carved stone heads and designs in relief of symbolic figures and the many tunnels and culverts which form an extensive labyrinth throughout the interior of the pyramidal structure. The carvings are in excellent condition, and the best are now in the new Museo

Nacional Chavín. The famous Lanzón dagger-shaped stone monolith of 800 BC is found inside one of the temple tunnels. In order to protect the site some areas are closed to visitors. All the galleries open to the public have electric lights. The guard is also a guide and gives excellent explanations of the ruins. The **Museo Nacional Chavín** ① *1 km north of town and 1.6 km from the site, Tue-Sun, 0900-1700, US$3.75* has a comprehensive collection of items, gathered from several deposits and museums, including the Tello obelisk dating from the earliest period of occupation of Chavín (c 100 BC) and representing a complex deity.

In high season, the site is busy with tourists all day through. You will receive an information leaflet in Spanish at the entrance.

THE TOWN OF CHAVIN

Just north of the ruins, Chavín (3140 m), painted colonial yellow and white, has a pleasant plaza with palm and pine trees. Several good, simple hotels and restaurants have benefited recently from the influence of the nearby mines. The local fiesta is celebrated 13-20 July.

CHAVIN TO POMABAMBA

From Chavín one circuit by road back to Huaraz is via Huari, San Luis, Yanama and Yungay (see page 128) but the bus service is infrequent. The road north from Chavín descends into the Mosna river canyon. The scenery is quite different from the other side of the Cordillera Blanca, very dry and hot. After 8 km it reaches **San Marcos**, a small, friendly town with a nice plaza and a few basic restaurants and *hostales*. After 32 km is **Huari**, perched on a hillside at 3150 m, with various basic hotels and restaurants. The Fiesta of **Nuestra Señora del Rosario** is celebrated the first two weeks of October (main day 7th).

There is a spectacular **two- to three-day walk** from Huari to Chacas via Laguna Purhuay. Alberto Cafferata of Caraz writes: "The Purhuay area is beautiful. It has splendid campsites, trout, exotic birds and, at its north end, a 'quenual' forest with orchids. This is a microclimate at 3500 m, where the animals, insects and flowers are more like a tropical jungle, fantastic for ecologists and photographers." A day walk to Laguna Purhuay is possible for those who don't want the longer walk to Chacas, but this does not allow time to walk above the lake. A new road has been built to the lake where there are kayaks and boat rides.

In **Chacas**, 10 km south of San Luis by a new road, is a fine church. The local fiesta (Virgen de la Asunción) is on 15 August, with bullfights, a famous *carrera de cintas* (belt race) and fireworks. There are hostels (**$**), shops, good restaurants and a small market. The road from Chacas is paved over the Punta Olímpica to Carhuaz (see below). It is a terrific mountain crossing and includes a new tunnel. The journey time San Luis-Chacas-Carhuaz-Huaraz is three hours.

It is a three-day hike from Chacas to Marcará via the Quebradas Juytush and Honda (lots of condors to be seen). The Quebrada Honda is known as the Paraíso de las Cascadas because it contains at least seven waterfalls. From Huari the road climbs to the Huachacocha pass at 4350 m and descends to **San Luis** at 3130 m, 60 km from Huari (**$ Hostal Puñuri**, Ramón Castilla 151, T043-830408, with bath and hot water, a few basic restaurants, shops and a market).

Some 20 km north of San Luis, a road branches left to **Yanama**, 45 km from San Luis, at 3400 m. The village retains many traditional features and is beautifully surrounded by snow-capped peaks. A day's hike to the ruins above the town affords superb views.

A longer circuit to Huaraz can be made by continuing from San Luis 62 km to **Piscobamba**. There are a couple of basic hotels, also a few shops and small restaurants. Beyond

Piscobamba by 22 km, is **Pomabamba**, worth a visit for some very hot natural springs (the furthest are the hottest). There are various hotels (**$**) near the plaza and restaurants.

From Pomabamba a dusty road runs up the wooded valley crossing the puna at Palo Seco, 23 km. The road then descends steeply into the desert-like Sihuas Valley, passing through the village of Sicsibamba. The valley is crossed half an hour below the small town of **Sihuas**, a major connection point between the Callejón de Conchucos, Callejón de Huaylas, the upper Marañón and the coast. It has a few **$** hotels and places to eat.

CARAZ

This pleasant town is a good centre for walking and parasailing and the access point for many excellent treks and climbs. Tourist facilities are expanding as a more tranquil alternative to Huaraz, and there are great views of Huandoy and Huascarán as well as the northern Cordilleras in July and August. In other months, the mountains are often shrouded in cloud. Caraz has a milder climate than Huaraz and is more suited to day trips. The ruins of **Tunshukaiko** are 1 km from the Plaza de Armas in the suburb of Cruz Viva, to the north before the turn-off for Parón. There are seven platforms from the Huaraz culture, dating from around 2000-1800 BC. There is a new museum on San Martín, a block up from the plaza. The tourist office, at Plaza de Armas, in the municipality, T043-391029, has limited information. On 20 January is the fiesta **Virgen de Chiquinquirá**. In the last week of July is **Semana Turística**.

TREKS FROM CARAZ

A good day hike with good views of the Cordillera Blanca is to **Pueblo Libre** (about four hours round trip, or you can take a colectivo back to Caraz). A longer day walk of six to seven hours in total with excellent views of Huandoy and Huascarán follows the foothills of the Cordillera Blanca, from Caraz south. It ends at Puente Ancash on the Caraz–Yungay road, from where transport goes back to Caraz.

A large stand of *Puya raimondii* can be seen in the Cordillera Negra west of Caraz. Beyond Pueblo Libre the road, which continues via Pamparomas and Moro, joins the coastal highway between Casma and Chimbote. After 45 km (two hours) are the *Puya raimondii* plants at a place called **Winchos**, with views of 145 km of the Cordillera Blanca and to the Pacific. The plants are usually in flower May or October. Take warm clothing, food and water. You can also camp near the puyas and return the following day. The most popular way to get there is to rent a bike (US$15 per day), go up by public transport, and ride back down in four or five hours. Or form a group (eg via the bulletin board at Pony's Expeditions, Caraz) and hire a car, which will wait for you (US$60 for eight, including guide). From Caraz, a combi for Pamparomas leaves from Ramón Castilla y Jorge Chávez around 0900, two hours, US$3 (get there at about 0800 as they often leave early). From the pass (El Paso) or El Cruce it is a short walk to the plants. Return transport leaves between 1230 and 1300. If you miss the bus, you can walk back to Pueblo Libre in four hours, to Caraz in six to eight hours, but it is easy to get lost and there are not many people to ask directions along the way.

Laguna Parón From Caraz a narrow, rough road goes east 32 km to beautiful Laguna Parón ① *US$3.50*, in a cirque surrounded by several, massive snow-capped peaks, including Huandoy, Pirámide Garcilazo and Caraz. The gorge leading to it is spectacular. It is a long day's trek for acclimatized hikers (25 km) up to the lake at 4150 m, or a four- to five-hour walk from the village of Parón, which can be reached by combi. Camping is possible. There is no trail around the lake and you should not attempt it as it is slippery and dangerous, particularly on the southern shore; tourists have been killed here.

Santa Cruz Valley One of the finest treks in the area is the three- to five-day route over the path from the Santa Cruz Valley, by Mount Huascarán to the Lagunas de Llanganuco (described below). The most popular way to do this famous hike starts at Cashapampa in the Santa Cruz Valley. You climb up to the pass of Punta Unión, 4750 m, then down to Vaquería or the Llanganuco lakes. Many recommend this 'anticlockwise' route as the climb is gentler, giving more time to acclimatize, and the pass is easier to find, although on the other hand, if you start in Vaquería and finish in Cashapampa you ascend for one day rather than three in the other direction. You can hire an *arriero* and mule in Cashapampa, US$10 per day for the *arriero*, US$6 per day for a mule. Campsites are at Llamacorral and Taullipampa before Punta Unión, and Quenoapampa (or Cachina Pampa) after the pass. You can end the hike at Vaquería on the Yanama–Yungay road and take a minibus or, better, an open truck from there (a beautiful run). Or end the walk a day later with a night at the Paccha Pampa campsite, at the Llanganuco lakes, from where cars go back to Yungay.

YUNGAY
The main road goes on 12 km south of Caraz to Yungay, which was completely buried during the 1970 earthquake by a massive mudslide; a hideous tragedy in which 20,000 people lost their lives. The earthquake and its aftermath are remembered by many residents of the Callejón de Huaylas. The original site of Yungay, known as Yungay Viejo, desolate and haunting, has been consecrated as a *camposanto* (cemetery). The new settlement is on a hillside just north of the old town, and is growing gradually. It has a pleasant plaza and a concrete market, good on Wednesday and Sunday. The **Virgen del Rosario** fiesta is on 17 October and 28 October is the anniversary of the founding of the town. The tourist office is on the corner of the Plaza de Armas.

LAGUNAS DE LLANGANUCO
The Lagunas de Llanganuco are two lakes nestling 1000 m below the snowline beneath Huascarán and Huandoy. The first you come to is Laguna Chinancocha (3850 m), the second Laguna Orconcocha (3863 m). The park office is situated below the lakes at 3200 m, 19 km from Yungay. Accommodation is provided for trekkers who want to start the Llanganuco–Santa Cruz trek from here. From the park office to the lakes takes about five hours (a steep climb). For the last 1½ hours, a nature trail, Sendero María Josefa (sign on the road), takes 1½ hours to walk to the western end of Chinancocha where there is a control post, descriptive trail and boat trips on the lake. Walk along the road beside the lake to its far end for peace and quiet among the quenual trees, which provide shelter for 75% of the birdlife found in the park.

CARHUAZ
After Yungay, the main road goes to **Mancos** (8 km south, 30 minutes) at the foot of Huascarán. There is a dormitory at *La Casita de mi Abuela*, some basic shops and restaurants. From Mancos it is 14 km to Carhuaz, a friendly, quiet mountain town with a pleasant plaza. There is very good walking in the neighbourhood (eg to thermal baths; up the Ulta Valley). Market days are Wednesday and Sunday (the latter is much larger). The local fiesta of **Virgen de las Mercedes**, 14-24 September, is rated as among the best in the region.

HUARAZ AND CORDILLERA BLANCA LISTINGS

WHERE TO STAY

$$$$-$$$ Andino Club, Pedro Cochachín 357, Huaraz, some way southeast from the centre (take a taxi after dark), T043-421662, www.hotelandino.com. Good international standard hotel with restaurant, safe parking, Swiss run, upper floors have views of Huascarán. New section has suites with sauna, among other details (more expensive).

$$$$-$$$ Llanganuco Lodge, Lago Keushu, Llanganuco Valley, T943-669580, www.llanganucolodge.com. Small mountain lodge, close to Huascarán park entrance. Luxury and standard rooms, new rooms being built in 2013. Room rate is seasonal and full board with a packed lunch, modern, excellent food in restaurant, helpful staff, fine views and limitless possibilities for trekking (equipment rental and logistics), British-owned.

$$$ Hostal Colomba, Francisco de Zela 210, Huaraz, just off Centenario across the river, T043-421501, www.huarazhotel.com. Lovely old hacienda, family-run, garden with playground and sports, safe parking, gym and well-equipped rooms sleeping 1-6, comfortable beds, restaurant.

$$$ The Lazy Dog Inn, 30 mins' drive from Huaraz (US$10-14 by taxi), close to the boundary of Huascarán National Park, 3.1 km past the town of Marian, close to the Quebrada Cojup, T943-789330, www.thelazydoginn.com. Eco-tourism lodge actively involved in community projects,

water recycling systems and composting toilets. Beautifully designed in warm colours, great location gives access to several mountain valleys. Owners Wayne and Diana can organize horse-riding and hiking trips, excellent home cooked breakfast and dinner included in price.

$$ Andes Lodge Peru, Jr Chavín s/n, Yanama, T043-765579, www.andeslodgeperu.com. Family-run guesthouse, good rooms, hot water, full board available, excellent food and services, activities arranged, fabulous views, consistently recommended.

$$-$ La Alameda, Av Noé Bazán Peralta 262, Caraz, T043-391177, www.hotellaalameda.com. Comfortable rooms, hot water, breakfast, restaurant, bar, laundry, parking, gardens.

$$-$ La Casa de Zarela, J Arguedas 1263, Huaraz, T043-421694, www.lacasadezarela.hostel.com. A short walk from the centre, free transfer from bus terminal with reservation, with bath and hot water, use of kitchen, laundry facilities, bar, TV lounge, popular with climbers and trekkers, owner Zarela who speaks English organizes groups and is very knowledgeable.

$ La Perla de los Andes, Daniel Villar 179, Plaza de Armas, next to the cathedral, Caraz, T043-392007, http://huaraz.com/perladelosandes/. Comfortable rooms, hot water, helpful, average restaurant, has a large new annex 1 block up San Martín.

RESTAURANTS

$$$ Créperie Patrick, Luzuriaga 422, Huaraz, T043-426037. Excellent crepes, fish, quiche, spaghetti and good wine.
$$ Bistro de los Andes, Luzuriaga 702, Plaza de Armas 2nd floor, Huaraz, T043-429556. Great food, owner speaks English, French and German. Plaza branch has a nice view of the plaza. Wide range of dishes including breakfasts.
Café Café 13 Buhos, Parque Ginebra, Huaraz, T0943-890836. Nice atmosphere in this café/bar, with food, drinks, coffee and its own brand beer.

Café Andino, Lúcar y Torre 538, Huaraz, T043-421203. American-run café and bar, roasts its own coffee, book exchange, extensive lending library in many languages, a nice place to relax, great atmosphere, good meeting place, owner guides treks in Cordilleras Blanca and Huayhuash.
California Café, 28 de Julio 562, Huaraz, T043-428354. Open 0730-1900, Sun 0730-1430. Excellent breakfast, great coffee and chocolate cake, book exchange. Californian owner is a good source of information on trekking in the Cordillera Huayhuash.

WHAT TO DO

There are many tour operators in Huaraz. Day trips to Llanganuco cost US$12 per person and to Chavín US$15 per person. Trekking tours cost US$50-70 per person per day, climbing US$100-140 per person per day. Many companies close in low season.
Casa de Guías, Plaza Ginebra 28-g in Huaraz, T043-427545, www.casadeguias. com.pe. Mon-Sat 0900-1300, 1400-2000. This is the climbers' and hikers' meeting place. Has a full list of all members of the **Asociación de Guías de Montaña del Perú (AGMP)** throughout the country. It is useful with information, books, maps, arrangements for guides, *arrieros*, mules, etc. It operates as an agency and sells tours. Notice board, postcards and posters for sale.

Pony's Expeditions, Sucre 1266, near the Plaza de Armas, Caraz, T043-391642, www.ponyexpeditions.com. Mon-Sat 0800-2200, English, French and Quechua spoken. Owners Alberto and Aidé Cafferata are knowledgeable about treks and climbs. They arrange local tours, trekking and transport (US$30 for up to 4 people) for day excursions, maps and books for sale, also equipment for hire, mountain bike rental (US$15 for a full day); also has **Café de Rat**, upstairs, serving breakfast, vegetarian dishes, pizzas, drinks and snacks, darts, travel books, nice atmosphere.

TRUJILLO AND AROUND

The capital of La Libertad Department, 548 km from Lima, disputes the title of second city of Peru with Arequipa. The compact colonial centre, though, has a small-town feel. The greenness surrounding the city is a delight against the backcloth of brown Andean foothills and peaks. Founded by Diego de Almagro in 1534 as an express assignment ordered by Francisco Pizarro, it was named after the latter's native town in Spain. Nearby are some of Peru's most important Moche and Chimú archaeological sites and a stretch of the country's best surfing beaches.

→ ARRIVING IN TRUJILLO

GETTING THERE

The **airport** is west of the city; the entry to town is along Avenida Mansiche. There is no central bus terminal. **Bus stations** are spread out on four sides of the city beyond the inner ring road, Avenida España. There are few hotels around them, but plenty of taxis. Insist on being taken to your hotel of choice. A new Terminal Terrestre is being built.

MOVING ON

Visiting nearby sites such as the **Huacas del Sol and de la Luna** (see page 135), **Chan Chán** (see page 136) and **Huanchaco** (see page 137) is easy with a taxi. A number of recommended guides run tours to these and other places. Chan Chán and Huanchaco are also on the local combi and micro (small bus) routes. Ask locally for the correct service and where to pick it up. **El Brujo** (see page 136) and **Puerto Chicama** (see page 137) are a bit further away. Each can be reached by public transport, but the simplest way of getting to El Brujo is on a tour (tours go to the other archaeological sites, too).

There are no direct flights from Trujillo to **Cajamarca** (see page 141) at the time of writing, and to fly back to Lima and then on to Cajamarca can take longer than the bus journey, which takes seven hours. Numerous companies operate this route, many overnight. (Note that even the most reputable companies are not immune from hold-ups and accidents at night; seek local advice before travelling on a night bus.)

GETTING AROUND

Trujillo is best explored on foot, but take care when walking around. The city is generally safe, but take care beyond the inner ring road, Avenida España, as well as obvious places around bus stops and terminals, and at ATMs and internet cafés.

TOURIST INFORMATION

Tourist offices i perú ① *Diego de Almagro 420, Plaza de Armas, T044-294561, iperutrujillo@ promperu.gob.pe, Mon-Sat 0900-1800, Sun 1000-1400*. Also useful: **Municipalidad de Trujillo**, Sub-Gerencia de Turismo ① *Av España 742, T044-244212, anexo 119, sgturismo@ munitrujillo.gob.pe*. The **Tourist Police** ① *Independencia 572, in the Ministerio de Cultura building, policia_turismo_tru@hotmail.com, open Mon-Sat 0800-2000*, provide useful information and can help with reports of theft, some speak English. **Indecopi** ① *Santo Toribio de Mogrovejo 518, Urb San Andrés II etapa, T044-295733, sobregon@indecopi.gob.pe*, for tourist complaints. **Gobierno Regional de la Libertad** ① *Dirección de Turismo, Av España 1800, T044-296221*, for information on regional tourism. Useful websites include www.xanga.com/TrujilloPeru and www.laindustria.com.

The focal point is the pleasant and spacious **Plaza de Armas**. The prominent sculpture represents agriculture, commerce, education, art, slavery, action and liberation, crowned by a young man holding a torch depicting liberty. Fronting it is the **Cathedral** ① *0700-*

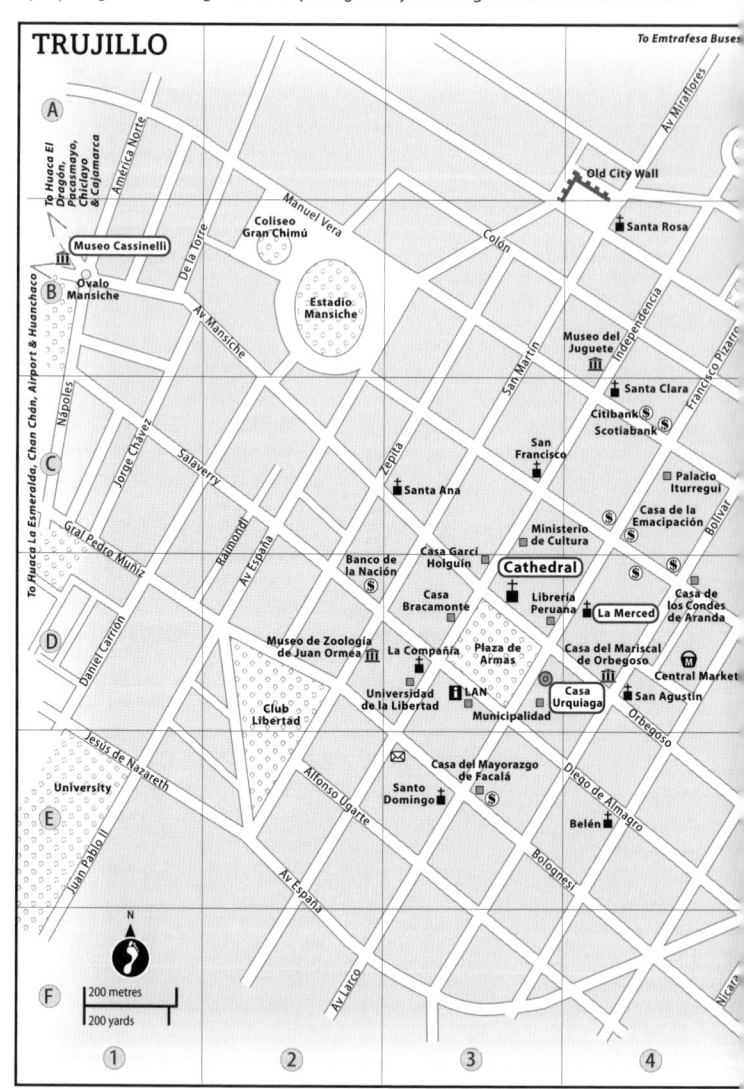

TRUJILLO

To Emtrafesa Buses

Old City Wall

Santa Rosa

Coliseo Gran Chimú

Manuel Vera

Colón

Museo Cassinelli

Ovalo Mansiche

Estadio Mansiche

San Martín

Museo del Juguete

Santa Clara

Citibank
Scotiabank

San Francisco

Palacio Iturregui

Santa Ana

Casa de la Emacipación

Ministerio de Cultura

Banco de la Nación

Casa Garci Holguín

Cathedral

Librería Peruana

La Merced

Casa de los Condes de Aranda

Casa Bracamonte

Museo de Zoología de Juan Orméa

La Compañía

Plaza de Armas

Casa del Mariscal de Orbegoso

Central Market

Universidad de la Libertad

LAN

Casa Urquiaga

San Agustín

Club Libertad

Municipalidad

University

Santo Domingo

Casa del Mayorazgo de Facalá

Belén

N

200 metres
200 yards

To Huaca El Dragón, Pacasmayo, Chiclayo & Cajamarca

To Huaca La Esmeralda, Chan Chán, Airport & Huanchaco

América Norte

De la Torre

Av Mansiche

Nápoles

Jorge Chávez

Salaverry

Zepita

Independencia

Francisco Pizarro

Bolívar

Gral Pedro Muñiz

Raimondi

Av España

Daniel Carrión

Jesús de Nazareth

Juan Pablo II

Alfonso Ugarte

Av España

Diego de Almagro

Orbegoso

Bolognesi

Av Larco

Nicarao

1230, 1700-2000, dating from 1666, with its museum of religious paintings and sculptures next door ① *Mon-Fri 0900-1300, 1600-1900, Sat 0900-1300, US$1.45*. Also on the Plaza are the Hotel Libertador, the colonial-style Sociedad de Beneficencia Pública de Trujillo and the Municipalidad. The **Universidad de La Libertad**, second only to that of San Marcos at Lima, was founded in 1824. Two beautiful colonial mansions on the plaza have been

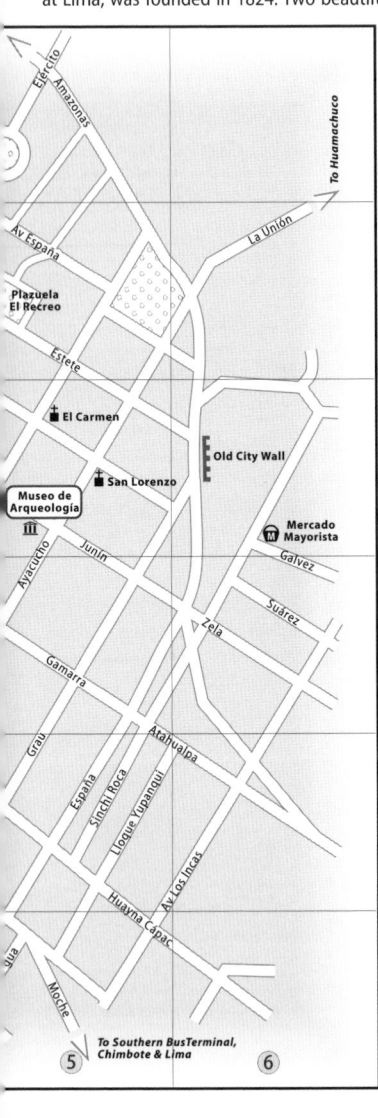

taken over. The Banco Central de Reserva is in the Colonial-style **Casa Urquiaga (or Calonge)** ① *Pizarro 446, Mon-Fri 0930-1500, Sat-Sun 1000-1330, free 30-min guided tour, take passport*, which contains valuable pre-Columbian ceramics. The other is **Casa Bracamonte (or Lizarzaburu)** ① *Independencia 441*, with occasional exhibits. Opposite the Cathedral on Independencia is the **Casa Garci Olguín** (Caja Nuestra Gente), recently restored but boasting the oldest façade in the city and Moorish-style murals. The buildings that surround the plaza, and many others in the vicinity, are painted in bright pastel colours. Near the Plaza de Armas is the spacious 18th-century **Palacio Iturregui**, now occupied by the **Club Central** ① *Jr Pizarro 688, Mon-Sat 0800-1800, free entry to patio, US$1.85 to see the ceramics, 0830-1000*. An exclusive and social centre of Trujillo, it houses a private collection of ceramics.

Other mansions, still in private hands, include **Casa del Mayorazgo de Facalá** ① *Pizarro 314, Mon-Fri 0915-1230* now Scotiabank. **Casa de la Emancipación** ① *Jr Pizarro 610 (Banco Continental), Mon-Sat, 0900-1300, 1600-2000*, is where independence from Spain was planned and it was the first seat of government and congress in Peru. The **Casa del Mariscal de Orbegoso** ① *Orbegoso 553, open 0930-200*, is the Museo de la República owned by the BCP bank.

One of the best of the many churches is the 17th-century **La Merced** ① *Pizarro 550, 0800-1200, 1600-2000, free*, with picturesque moulded figures below the dome. **El Carmen** ① *Colón y Bolívar, open for mass Sun 0700-0730*, church and monastery, has been described as the 'most

ON THE ROAD
Masters of sculpture

One of the most remarkable pre-Inca civilizations was that of the Moche people, who evolved during the first century AD and lasted until around AD 750. Though these early Peruvians had no written language, they left a vivid record of their life and culture in beautifully modelled and painted ceramics.

Compared with the empires of their successors, the Chimú and Inca, the realm of the Moche was very small, covering less than 250 miles of coast from the valleys of Lambayeque to Nepeña, south of present-day Chimbote. Though this was a seemingly inhospitable stretch of coast, the Moche harnessed rivers spilling from the Andean cordillera, channelling them into a network of irrigation canals that watered the arid coastal valleys. The resultant lush fields produced plentiful crops, which, along with the sea's bountiful harvest of fish and seafood, gave the Moche a rich and varied diet. With the leisure allowed by such abundant food, Moche craftsmen invented new techniques to produce their artistic masterpieces. It is these ancient pottery vessels that have made the greatest contribution to our understanding of this great civilization.

These masters of sculpture used clay to bring to life animals, plants and anthropomorphic deities and demons. They recreated hunting and fishing scenes, combat rituals, elaborate ceremonies and sexual intercourse (sometimes with contraception). They depicted the power of their rulers as well as the plight of their sick and invalid.

Ritual combat is a common theme in their work; prisoners of war are apparently brought before congregations where their throats are cut and their blood offered to those present. Decapitation and dismemberment are also shown.

Moche potters were amazingly skilled at reproducing facial features, specializing in the subtle nuances of individual personality. In addition to these 3D sculptures, the Moche potter was skilled at decorating vessels with low-relief designs. Among the most popular scenes are skeletal death figures holding hands while dancing in long processions to the accompaniment of musicians. The potters also developed a technique of painting fine-line scenes on ceramic vessels. Over a period of several centuries the painters became increasingly skilful at depicting complex and lively scenes with multiple figures. Because of their complexity and detail, these scenes are of vital importance in reconstructing Moche life.

The early introduction of moulds and stamps brought efficiency to the production of Moche ceramics. By pressing moist clay into the halves of a mould, it was possible to produce an object much more rapidly than by hand. Similarly, the use of stamps facilitated the decoration of ceramic vessels with elaborate low-relief designs. Mould-making technology thus resulted in many duplications of individual pieces. Since there were almost no unique ceramic objects, elaborate ceramics became more widely available and less effective as a sign of the power, wealth and social status of the élite.

Although among the most sophisticated potters in Spanish America, the Moche did not use ceramics for ordinary tableware. Neither do their ceramics show many everyday activities, such as farming, cooking and pottery making. This is because Moche art expresses the religious and supernatural aspects of their culture and little of everyday life is illustrated for its own sake.

valuable jewel of colonial art in Trujillo' but it is rarely open. Likewise **La Compañía** ⓘ *near Plaza de Armas*, now an auditorium for cultural events.

Museo de Arqueología ⓘ *Junín 682 y Ayacucho, Casa Risco, T044-249322, Mon-Fri 0830-1430, US$1.85*, houses a large and interesting collection of thematic exhibits. The **Museo del Juguete** ⓘ *Independencia 705 y Junín, Mon-Sat 1000-1800, Sun 1000-1300, US$1.85, children US$0.70, café open 0900-2300*, is a toy museum containing examples from prehistoric times to 1950, collected by painter Gerardo Chávez. Downstairs is the Espacio Cultural Angelmira with a café bar; in a restored *casona*, worth a visit. Gerardo Chávez has opened the **Museo de Arte Moderno** ⓘ *Av Industrial, 3.5 km from centre, T044-215668, 0930-1730, Sun 0930-1400, US$3.50, students half price*, which has some fine exhibits, a peaceful garden and friendly staff. The basement of the **Cassinelli garage** ⓘ *Av N de Piérola 607, T044-231801, behind a petrol station, 1000-1300, 1430-1800, US$2.45*, contains a private collection of Mochica and Chimú pottery which is recommended. **Museo de Zoología de Juan Ormea** ⓘ *Jr San Martín 368, Mon-Fri 0700-1850, US$0.70*, has interesting displays of Peruvian animals.

The two most important festivals are the **National Marinera Dance Contest** at the end of January and the **Festival Internacional de La Primavera** (Spring Fair) in the last week of September, with cultural events, parades, beauty pageants and Trujillo's famous **Caballos de Paso** (Paso horses).

→ HUACAS DEL SOL AND DE LA LUNA

ⓘ *0900-1600 (last entry, but site open till sunset), US$3.55 (students US$1.80, children US$0.35), booklet in English or Spanish US$2.85. All tickets are sold at the Museo Huacas de Moche – see page 136. You have to go with a guide on a 1-hr tour in English, French or Spanish. Groups can be up to 25 people and quite rushed. See Proyecto Huaca de la Luna, Jr San Martín 380, Trujillo, T044-221269, www.huacas.com. The visitor centre (T044-834901) has a café showing videos and a souvenir shop and good toilets. In an outside patio craftsmen reproduce ceramics in designs from northern Peru.*

A few kilometres south of Trujillo are the huge and fascinating Moche pyramids, the Huaca del Sol and the Huaca de la Luna. Until the Spaniards destroyed a third of it in a vain search for treasure, Huaca del Sol was the largest man-made structure in the western hemisphere, at 45 m high. It consisted of seven levels, with 11 or 12 phases of construction over the first six centuries AD. Today, about two thirds of the pyramid have been lost and it is closed to the public. Huaca de la Luna, 500 m away, received scant attention until extensive polychrome moulded decorations were uncovered after 1990. The colours on these remarkable geometric patterns and deities have faded little and it is now possible to view impressive friezes of the upper four levels on the northern exterior wall of the huaca. The highest mural is a 'serpent', which runs the length of the wall; beneath it there are repeated motifs of 'felines' holding decapitated heads of warriors, then repeated motifs of 'fishermen' holding fish against a bright blue background and, next, huge 'spider/crab' motifs. The bottom two levels show dancers or officials grimly holding hands and, below them, victorious warriors following naked prisoners past scenes of combat and two complex scenes, similar to those at Huaca Cao Viejo at El Brujo (see page 136). Combined with intricate, brightly painted two-dimensional motifs in the sacrificial area atop the huaca, and with new discoveries in almost every excavation, Huaca de la Luna is now a truly significant site well worth visiting.

The **Templo Nuevo**, or Plataforma III, represents the period 600 to 900 AD and has friezes in the upper level showing the so-called Rebellion of the Artefacts, in which weapons take on human characteristics and attack their owners. Also new is the **Museo Huacas de Moche** ⓘ *5 mins' walk from Huaca de la Luna, daily 0900-1600, US$1, students US$0.75, children US$0.35, www.huacasdemoche.pe*, the site museum. Three halls display objects found in the huacas, including beautiful ceramics, arranged thematically around the Moche themselves, the cermonial complex, daily life, the deities of power and of the mountains and priests who worshipped them. Food is available on Sunday at the nearby town of Moche.

→ EL BRUJO

ⓘ *Open daily 0900-1600, US$3.55 (US$2 with ISIC card, children US$0.35). Shops and toilets at the entrance. See www.fundacionwiese.com.*

A complex collectively known as **El Brujo**, 60 km north of Trujillo, is considered one of the most important archaeological sites on the north coast. Covering 2 sq km, it was a ceremonial centre for up to 10 cultures, including the Moche. Huaca Cortada (or El Brujo) has a wall decorated with high relief stylized figures. Huaca Prieta is, in effect, a giant rubbish tip dating back 5000 years, which once housed the very first settlers. Huaca Cao Viejo has extensive friezes, polychrome reliefs up to 90 m long, 4 m high and on five different levels. The mummy of a tattooed, pregnant woman, La Señora de Cao, dating from AD 450, has also been found. Her mausoleum, with grave goods, can be visited in an excellent, purpose-built museum. In front of Cao Viejo are the remains of one of the oldest Spanish churches in the region. It was common practice for the Spaniards to build their churches near these ancient sites in order to counteract their religious importance. Excavations will continue for many years. Trujillo travel agencies run tours, which cost about US$18 per person. If using public transport you have to take one of the regular buses from Trujillo to Chocope (US$1) and then a colectivo (every 30 minutes) to Magdalena de Cao (US$0.50), then a mototaxi to the site (US$2.55); or it's a 5-km walk. A new road to the site was completed in 2013.

→ CHAN CHAN

ⓘ *5 km from Trujillo. 0900-1600, arrive well before that. Site may be covered up if rain is expected. Tickets cost US$3.80 (US$2 with ISIC card, children US$0.35), include entrance fees for Chan Chán, Huaca El Dragón and Huaca La Esmeralda (for 2 days). Official guides, US$10, wait by the souvenir shops, toilets here too. It is a 25-min walk from the main road to the ticket office, so it's best to take a taxi. On no account walk the 4 km from Chan Chán to Buenos Aires beach (or on the beach) as it is very unsafe.*

These vast, unusually decorated crumbling ruins of the imperial city of the Chimú domains are the largest adobe city in the world. The ruins consist of 10 great compounds built by Chimú kings. The 11- to 12-m-high perimeter walls surrounded sacred enclosures with usually only one narrow entrance. Inside, rows of storerooms contained the agricultural wealth of the kingdom, which stretched 1000 km along the coast from near Guayaquil to the Carabayllo Valley, north of Lima.

Most of the compounds contain a huge walk-in well that tapped the ground water, raised to a high level by irrigation further up the valley. Each compound also included a platform mound that was the burial place of the king, with his women and his treasure, presumably maintained as a memorial. The Incas almost certainly copied this system and transported it to Cuzco where the last Incas continued building huge enclosures. The Chimú surrendered to the Incas around 1471 after 11 years of siege and the cutting off of the irrigation canals.

The dilapidated city walls enclose an area of 28 sq km containing the remains of palaces, temples, workshops, streets, houses, gardens and a canal. What is left of the adobe walls bears either well-restored, or modern fibreglass fabrications of moulded decorations showing small figures of fish, birds, fishing nets and various geometric motifs. Painted designs have been found on pottery unearthed from the debris of a city ravaged by floods, earthquakes, and *huaqueros* (grave looters). The **Ciudadela de Nik-An** (formerly called Tschudi) is the part that visitors see.

The **site museum** ① *US$1, 0830-1630*, on the main road, 100 m before the turn-off, has objects found in the area, displays and signs in Spanish and English.

The partly restored temple, **Huaca El Dragón** ① *0930-1630 (in theory), on the west side of the Pan-American Highway in the district of La Esperanza; combis from Huayna Cápac y Los Incas, or Av España y Manuel Vera marked 'Arco Iris/La Esperanza', taxi costs US$2*, dating from Huari to Chimú times (AD 1000-1470), is also known as **Huaca Arco Iris** (rainbow), after the shape of friezes that decorate it. The poorly preserved **Huaca La Esmeralda** is at Mansiche, between Trujillo and Chan Chán, behind the church and near the Mall Aventura shopping centre. Buses to Chan Chán and Huanchaco pass the church at Mansiche.

→ HUANCHACO

An alternative to Trujillo is **Huanchaco**, a fishing and surfing village, full of hotels, guesthouses, a good selection of seafood and fish restaurants all along the seafront, and several surf schools. It is famous for its narrow pointed fishing rafts, known as *caballitos* (little horses) *de totora*, made of totora reeds and depicted on Mochica, Chimú and other cultures' pottery. Unlike those used on Lake Titicaca, they are flat, not hollow, and ride the breakers rather like surfboards (fishermen offer trips on their *caballitos* for US$1.75, be prepared to get wet; groups should contact Luis Gordillo, El Mambo, T01-461092). You can see fishermen returning on their reed rafts at about 0800 and 1400, when they stack the boats upright to dry in the fierce sun. Overlooking Huanchaco is a huge church (1535-1540) from the belfry of which are extensive views. In the first week of May is the **Festival del Mar**, a celebration of the disembarkation of Taycanamo, the leader of the Chimú period. A procession is made in totora boats. On 29 June, the statue of San Pedro, patron saint of fishermen, is taken out to sea on a huge totora-reed boat. There are also surf competitions. Carnival and New Year are also popular celebrations.

→ PUERTO CHICAMA

Puerto Chicama (Malabrigo), is claimed by surfers as the best surf beach in Peru, with the longest left-hand point-break in the world. The best waves are March-October (high point May-June) and the sand is clean. It is 70 km north of Trujillo, turn off Panamericana at

Paiján. There is a 1-km-long fishing pier and beautiful sunsets. There are a few *hospedajes* and simple places to eat in town (shop early by the market for fresh seafood) and a string of exclusive surfers' hotels and humbler places line the clifftop south of town, Distrito El Hombre. There are direct buses to Puerto Chicama from Avenida Santa Cruz, one block from Avenida América Sur, and Avenida Norte de Piérola 1062 in Trujillo.

TRUJILLO AND AROUND LISTINGS

WHERE TO STAY

Trujillo

$$$$ Libertador, Independencia 485, Plaza de Armas, T044-232741, www.libertador.com.pe. Modern hotel in historic building, a lovely place to stay. Comfortable rooms, excellent service, swimming pool in a flower-filled patio, sauna, cafetería and restaurant, breakfast extra, excellent buffet lunch on Sun.

$$$ Gran Bolívar, Bolívar 957, T044-222090, www.granbolivarhotel.net. In converted 18th-century house, large rooms, restaurant and room service, café, bar, laundry, gym, travel agency, parking.

$$ Colonial, Independencia 618, T044-258261, www.hostalcolonial.com.pe. Attractive but small rooms, hot showers, basic breakfast, good restaurant, especially for set lunch. Recommended.

Huanchaco

$$$ Bracamonte, Los Olivos 160, T044-461162, www.hotelbracamonte.com.pe. Comfortable, modern, contemporary decor, good pool, secure, good restaurant offers lunch *menú* and some vegetarian dishes, English spoken, laundry service, games room. Highly recommended.

$$$-$$ Las Palmeras, Av Larco 1150, sector Los Tumbos, T044-461199, www.laspalmerasdehuanchaco.com. One of the best, rooms with terrace, hot water, dining room, pool and gardens. Rooms on top floor with sea view cost more than ground floor rooms with pool view.

$ Ñaylamp, Av Víctor Larco 123, northern end of seafront in El Boquerón, T044-461022, www.hostalnaylamp.com. Rooms set around a courtyard with patios and garden, others have sea view, dorms, hammocks, good beds, hot water, camping, tents available to hire, laundry, safe, Italian food, good breakfasts.

RESTAURANTS

Trujillo

$$$-$$ El Mochica, Bolívar 462 T044-224401, www.elmochica.com.pe. Long-established, good typical food with live music on special occasions. Also has a branch in Huanchaco.

$$ Chelsea, Estete 675, T949-589784, Chelsea-PUB-Restaurant on Facebook. Restaurant/bar, open 1130-0400, on Sun 1130-1700 for Buffet Criollo, special shows on Fri (live music) and Sat (Marinera dance show). Recommended.

$ Rincón de Vallejo, Orbegoso 303, T044-226232. Open daily 0700-2300. This is a good place to go for typical dishes, it has a daily lunch special and can get very crowded at peak times. It has a 2nd branch at Av España 736.

Café Amaretto, Gamarra 368, T044-221451. Smart, good selection of real coffees, "brilliant" cakes, sweets, snacks and drinks.

Casona Deza, Independencia 630, T948-434866. Open from 0800 (0900 on Sun). Comfortable café/bar selling home-made pasta and pizza and good coffee in an old mansion.

WHAT TO DO

Prices of tours vary and competition is fierce so shop around for the best deal. Few agencies run tours on Sun and often only at fixed times on other days. Their groups are usually large. To **Chan Chán**, **El Dragón** and **Huanchaco**, 4-4½ hrs for US$10 per person. To **Huacas del Sol** and **de la Luna**, 3 hrs for US$10-14 per person. To **El Brujo**, US$35-40 per person, 5-8 hrs. **City tours** cost US$5 per person, 2-2½ hrs. Prices do not include entrance fees.

Guides

Many hotels work on a commission basis with taxi drivers and travel agencies. If you decide on a guide, make your own direct approach and always agree what is included in the price, don't go with cowboy outfits herding up tourists around the plazas and bus terminals. The Tourist Police (see page 131) has a list of guides. **Clara Bravo**, Cahuide 495, T044-243347, www.xanga.com/trujilloperu is an experienced tourist guide who speaks Spanish, English, German and understands Italian; archaeological tour US$20 for 6 hrs, city tour US$7 per person, US$53 per car to El Brujo, with extension to Sipán, Brüning Museum and Túcume possible (tours in Lambayeque involve public transport, not included in cost). Clara works with English chartered accountant **Michael White** (same address, microbewhite@yahoo. com, also speaks German, French and Italian), who provides transport. He is very knowledgeable about tourist sites. Also here is **Casa de Clara**, www.xanga.com/ CasadeClara, a backpackers' *hostal*, good food, use of kitchen with permission and charge for gas, meeting place and lots going on. Other guides: **Luis Ocas Saldaña**, Jr José Martí 2019, T949-339593, guianorteperu@hotmail.com. Very knowledgeable, helpful, covers all of northern Peru. **Gustavo Prada Marga**, at Chan Chán, an experienced guide. **Alfredo Ríos Mercedes**, riosmercedes@ hotmail.com, T949-657978. Speaks English. **Jannet Rojas Sánchez**, Alto Mochica Mz Q 19, Trujillo, T949-344844, jannarojas@ hotmail.com. Speaks English, enthusiastic, works also for Guía Tours. **José Soto Ríos**, Atahualpa 514, dpto 3, T949-251489, speaks English and French.

CAJAMARCA AND AROUND

Leaving the Pacific coast behind, you climb in a relatively short time up to the Sierra. It was here, at Cajamarca, that the defeat of the Incas by the Spaniards began, bringing about cataclysmic change to this part of the world. Cajamarca is a beautiful colonial town and the most important in the northern highlands. It sits at the edge of a green valley that is ideal for dairy farming. Around the Plaza de Armas are many fine old houses, which are being converted into tasteful hotels, restaurants and galleries. It's a great place to buy handicrafts. Outside town are several good haciendas that offer bed, board and rural pursuits, while at the Baños del Inca, just up the road, you can unwind as the steam from the thermal waters meets the cool mountain air.

→ TRUJILLO TO CAJAMARCA

Northeast of Trujillo, Cajamarca can be reached by the old road (now paved) via Huamachuco and Cajabamba, or via Ciudad de Dios. The former road takes two hours from Huamachuco to Cajabamba and three hours from Cajabamba via San Marcos to Cajamarca (as opposed to nine hours via Ciudad de Dios, see page 142). It is also more interesting, passing over the bare *puna* (grassland) before dropping to the Huamachuco Valley.

HUAMACHUCO

This colonial town formerly on the royal Inca Road, 181 km from Trujillo, has the largest main plaza in Peru, with fine topiary, and a controversial modern **cathedral**. There is a colourful **Sunday market**, with dancing in the plaza, and the Founding of Huamachuco festival, second week in August, with spectacular fireworks and the amazing, aggressive male dancers called *turcos*. **Museo Municipal Wamachuko** ① *Sucre 195, Mon-Sat 0900-1300, 1500-1900, Sun 0900-1200, free*, displays artefacts found at nearby Cerro Amaru (a hill-top system of wells and water worship) and **Marca Huamachuco** ① *open daily 0900-1700, US$1, allow 2 hrs, 4 hrs to explore fully*. Access is via a poor vehicle road or a mule track (preferable for walking), off the road to Sanagorán, there is an archway at the turn-off, 5 km from Huamachuco, mototaxi to turnoff US$2; combis to Sanagorán in the morning. These hilltop pre-Inca fortifications rank in the top 10 archaeological sites in Peru. They are 3 km long, dating back to at least 300 BC though many structures were added later. Its most impressive features are: El Castillo, a remarkable circular structure with walls up to 8 m high located at the highest point of the site, and El Convento complex, five circular structures of varying sizes towards the northern end of the hill. The largest one has been partially reconstructed. The extensive Huari ruins of **Wiracochapampa** are 3 km north of town, 45 minutes' walk. Although much of the site is overgrown the **Waman Raymi** festival is held here on the second Sunday in August (a northern version of Cuzco's Inti Raymi).

    Cajabamba is a small market town and a useful stop-over point between Huamachuco and Cajamarca. A new thermal bath complex, **La Grama**, is 30 minutes by combi (US$1) from Cajabamba, with a pool, very hot individual baths and an adjoining small *hostal*.

PACASMAYO

Pacasmayo, 102 km north of Trujillo, is the port for the next oasis north. It has a nice beach front with an old Customs House and a very long pier. Resort **El Faro** is 1 km away, with surfing at the point and kite- and windsurfing closer to town. There are maritime festivals at New Year and Semana Santa. Away from the front it is a busy commercial centre.

Some 20 km further north on the Panamericana is the main road connection from the coast to Cajamarca at a junction called **Ciudad de Dios**. The paved 175 km road branches off the Pan-American Highway soon after it crosses the Río Jequetepeque. The river valley has terraced rice fields and mimosas may often be seen in bloom, brightening the otherwise dusty landscape.

→CAJAMARCA

At Cajamarca Pizarro ambushed and captured Atahualpa, the Inca emperor. This was the first showdown between the Spanish and the Incas and, despite their huge numerical inferiority, the Spanish emerged victorious, executing Atahualpa in the process. The nearby **Yanacocha gold mine** ⓘ *www.yanacocha.com.pe*, has brought new wealth to the town (and major ecological concerns and social problems) and Cajamarca is the hub of tourism development for the whole of the northwest via the Circuito Turístico Nororiental (Chiclayo-Cajamarca-Chachapoyas). **Tourist offices**: **Dirección Regional de Turismo** and **Ministerio de Cultura** ⓘ *in the Conjunto Monumental de Belén, Belén 631, T076-362601, cajamarca@mcultura.gob.pe, Mon-Fri 0900-1300, 1500-1730*. **Sub-Gerencia de Turismo** of the **Cajamarca Municipality** ⓘ *Av Alameda de los Incas, Complejo Qhapac Ñan, T076-363626, www.municaj.gob.pe*, opposite UNC university on the road to Baños del Inca. There's an office of the **University tourist school** ⓘ *Del Batán 289, T076-361546, open Mon-Fri 0830-1300, 1500-2200*, offering free advice and leaflets and the **Indecopi office** ⓘ *Apurímac 601, T076-363315, mcastillo@indecopi.gob.pe*.

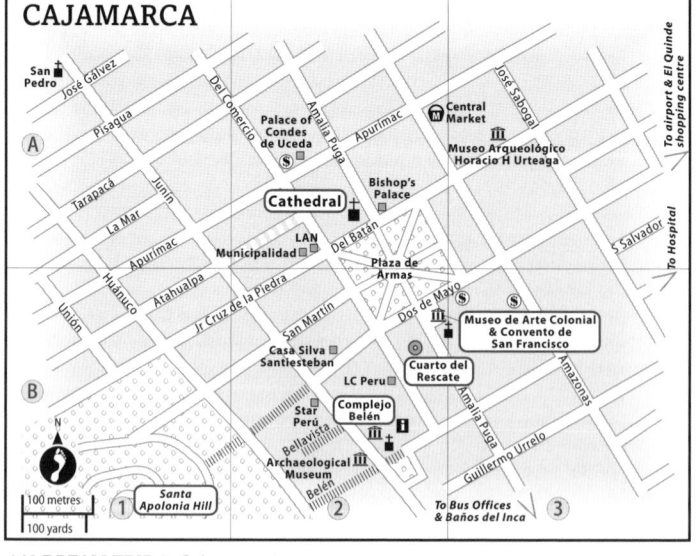

Complejo Belén ① *Tue-Sat 0900-1300, 1500-1800, Sun 0900-1300, US$1.55, valid for more than 1 day, a ticket is also valid for the Cuarto de Rescate, a guide for all the sites costs US$2.85 (US$5.75-8.50 for guides in other languages).* The complex comprises the tourist office and Institute of Culture, a beautifully ornate church, considered the city's finest. See the inside of the dome, where eight giant cherubs support an intricate flowering centrepiece. In the same courtyard is the **Museo Médico Belén**, which has a collection of medical instruments. Across the street is a maternity hospital from the colonial era, now the **Archaeological and Ethnological Museum**, Junín y Belén. It has a range of ceramics from all regions and civilizations of Peru. The **Cuarto de Rescate** ① *entrance at Amalia Puga 750*, is not the actual ransom chamber but in fact the room where Atahualpa was held prisoner. A red line on the wall is said to indicate where Atahualpa reached up and drew a mark, agreeing to have his subjects fill the room to the line with treasure. The chamber is roped off but can be viewed from the outside. Pollution and weather have had a detrimental effect on the stone.

You can also visit the plaza where Atahualpa was ambushed and the stone altar set high on **Santa Apolonia hill** ① *US$0.60, take bus marked Santa Apolonia/Fonavi, or micro A,* where he is said to have reviewed his subjects. There is a road to the top, or you can walk up from Calle 2 de Mayo, using the steep stairway. The view is worth the effort, especially at sunrise (and go in a group).

The **Plaza de Armas**, where Atahualpa was executed, has a 350-year-old fountain, topiary and gardens. The **Cathedral** ① *0800-1000, 1600-1800*, opened in 1776, is still missing its belfry, but the façade has beautiful baroque carving in stone. On the opposite side of the plaza is the 17th-century **San Francisco Church** ① *Mon-Fri 0900-1200, 1600-1800,* older than the Cathedral and with more interior stone carving and elaborate altars. The attached **Museo de Arte Colonial** ① *Mon-Sat 1430-1800, US$1, entrance is behind the church on Amalia Puga y Belén,* is filled with colonial paintings and icons. The guided tour of the museum includes entry to the church's spooky catacombs.

The city has many old colonial houses with garden patios, and 104 elaborately carved doorways: see the **Bishop's Palace**, across the street from the Cathedral; the **palace of the Condes de Uceda**, at Jr Apurímac 719 (now occupied by BCP bank); and the **Casa Silva Santiesteban** (Junín y 2 de Mayo).

Museo Arqueológico Horacio H Urteaga ① *Del Batán 289, Mon-Fri 0700-1445, free, donations accepted,* of the Universidad Nacional de Cajamarca, has objects of the pre-Inca Cajamarca and other cultures. The university maintains an experimental arboretum and agricultural station, the **Museo Silvo-agropecuario** ① *Km 2.5 on the road to Baños del Inca,* with a lovely mural at the entrance.

AROUND CAJAMARCA

About 6 km away are the sulphurous thermal springs of **Los Baños del Inca** ① *0500-2000, T076-348385, US$0.70, combis marked Baños del Inca cost US$0.20, 15 mins, taxis US$2.30.* The water temperature is at least 72° C. Atahualpa tried the effect of these waters on a festering war wound and his bath is still there. The complex is renewed regularly, with gardens and various levels of accommodation. The main baths are divided into five categories, with prices ranging from US$1.75-2.10, all with private tubs and no pool. Sauna US$3.50, massage US$7 (take your own towel; soaps are sold outside). Only spend 20 minutes maximum in the water; obey instructions; many of the facilities allow bathers in shifts, divided by time and/or sex.

Other excursions include **Llacanora**, a typical Andean village in beautiful scenery (13 km southeast; nice walk downhill from Baños del Inca, two hours) and **Ventanillas de Otusco** ⓘ *8 km, 0800-1800, US$1.10, combi US$0.20,* part of an old pre-Inca cemetery, which has a gallery of secondary burial niches. There are good day walks in this area; local sketch maps are available.

A road goes to **Ventanillas de Combayo** ⓘ *occasional combis on weekdays; more transport on Sun when a market is held nearby, 1 hr, some 20 km past the burial niches of Otusco*. These tombs are more numerous and spectacular, being located in an isolated, mountainous area, and distributed over the face of a steep 200-m-high hillside.

Cumbe Mayo, a *pampa* on a mountain range, is 20 km southwest of Cajamarca. It is famous for its extraordinary, well-engineered pre-Inca channels, running for 9 km across the mountain tops. It is said to be the oldest man-made construction in South America. The sheer scale of the scene is impressive and the huge rock formations of Los Frailones ('big monks') and others with fanciful names are strange indeed. On the way to Cumbe Mayo is the Layzón ceremonial centre. There is no bus service; guided tours run from 0900-1300 (recommended in order to see all the pre-Inca sites); taxi US$15. To walk up takes 3-4 hours (take a guide, or a tour, best weather May-September). The trail starts from the hill of Santa Apolonia (Silla del Inca), and goes to Cumbe Mayo straight through the village and up the hill; at the top of the mountain, leave the trail and take the road to the right to the canal. The walk is not difficult and you do not need hiking boots. Take a good torch. The locals use the trail to bring their goods to market.

The **Porcón** rural cooperative, with its evangelical faith expressed on billboards, is a popular excursion, 30 km northwest of Cajamarca. It is tightly organized, with carpentry, bakery, cheese and yoghurt-making, zoo and vicuñas. A good guide helps to explain everything. If not taking a tour, contact **Cooperativa Agraria Atahualpa Jerusalén** ⓘ *Chanchamayo 1355, Fonavi 1, T076-825631*.

Some 93 km west of Cajamarca is the mining town of Chilete, 21 km north of which on the road to San Pablo is **Kuntur Wasi**. The site was devoted to a feline cult and consists of a pyramid and stone monoliths. Extensive excavations are under way and significant new discoveries are being made (excellent site museum). There are two basic *hostales* in Chilete; very limited facilities.

CAJAMARCA AND AROUND LISTINGS

WHERE TO STAY

$$$$ Costa del Sol, Cruz de Piedra 707, T076-362472, www.costadelsolperu.com. On the Plaza de Armas, part of a Peruvian chain, with airport transfer, welcome drink; restaurant, café and bars, pool, spa, casino, business centre.

$$$$-$$$ Laguna Seca, Av Manco Cápac 1098, T076-584300, www.lagunaseca. com.pe. In pleasant surroundings with thermal streams, private hot thermal baths in rooms, swimming pool with thermal water, restaurant, bar, health spa with a variety of treatments, disco, horses for hire.

$$$ El Ingenio, Av Vía de Evitamiento 1611-1709, T076-368733, www.elingenio. com. Colonial-style buildings 1½ blocks from new El Quinde shopping mall. With solar-powered hot water, spacious, comfortable rooms, restaurant, bar and gardens, very relaxed.

$$$ Hostal Fundo Campero San Antonio, 2 km off the Baños road (turn off at Km 5), T076-348237, www.fundosan antonio.com. An old *hacienda*, wonderfully restored, with open fireplaces and gardens, 15 mins' walk along the river to Baños del Inca, riding on *caballos de paso*, own dairy produce, fruit and vegetables, catch your own trout for supper; try the *licor de sauco*.

$$ El Portal del Marqués, Jr del Comercio 644, T076-368464, www.portaldelmarques. com. Attractive converted colonial house, laundry, safe, parking, with new café/ restaurant *El Real Gourmet*, good lunch *menú*. Also has a casino with slot machines.

$$ El Cumbe Inn, Pasaje Atahualpa 345, T076-366858, www.elcumbeinn.com. Includes breakfast and tax, comfortable, variety of rooms, hot water, evening meals on request, small gym, will arrange taxis, very helpful.

RESTAURANTS

$$$ Querubino, Amalia Puga 589, T076-340900, www.elqueribino.com. Mediterranean-style decoration, a bit of everything on the menu, including pastas, daily specials, breakfasts, cocktails, coffees, expensive wines otherwise reasonable, popular.

$$ Salas, Amalia Puga 637, on the main plaza, T076-362867. A Cajamarca tradition, open 0700-2200. Fast service, excellent local food (try their *cuy frito*), best *tamales* in town.

$$-$ El Zarco, Jr del Batán 170, T076-363421, www.elzarco.org. Open Sun-Fri 0700-2300. Very popular, also has short

chifa menu, good vegetarian dishes, excellent fish, popular for breakfast.

Cascanuez, Amalia Puga 554, T076-366089. Great cakes, extensive menu including *humitas*, breakfasts, ice creams and coffees, highly regarded.

Heladería Holanda, Amalia Puga 657 on the Plaza de Armas, T076-340113. Dutch-owned, easily the best ice-creams in Cajamarca, 50 flavours (but not all on at the same time), try *poro poro*, *lúcuma* or *sauco*, also serves coffee. 4 branches, including at Baños del Inca, open 0900-1900. Ask if it is possible to visit their factory. They assist deaf people and single mothers.

WHAT TO DO

Agencies around the Plaza de Armas offer trips to local sites and further (eg Kuntur Wasi, Kuélap), trekking on Inca trails, riding *caballos de paso* and handicraft tours. Cumbe Mayo, US$15-20, 4-5 hrs at 0930. Porcón, US$10-15 per person, 4-5 hrs at 0930. Otusco, US$15, 3-3½ hrs at 1530. City tour, US$10, 3 hrs at 0930 or 1530.

Kuntur Wasi is a full day. There are also 2 day/3 night tours to Kuélap and Cutervo National Park.

Cumbemayo Tours, Amalia Puga 653 on the plaza, T076-362938, www.cumbemayotours.com. Guides in English and French, recommended for all the standard tours.

DREAM TRIP 4
Lima→Chiclayo→Chachapoyas→Amazon jungle
21 days

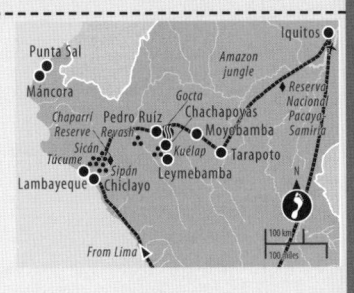

GOING FURTHER

For a longer river journey, take a minibus from Tarapoto to Yurimaguas (page 164, 2½ hrs), stay overnight and go by boat to Lagunas (12 hrs) to enter Pacaya-Samiria. Then take a boat on to Iquitos (2 days) and spend a night there before returning to Lima.

Máncora page 153
Bus from Chiclayo, change in Piura (6 hrs)

DREAM TRIP 4
Lima→Chiclayo→Chachapoyas→Amazon jungle

The largely agricultural department of Lambayeque, set between the Andes and the Pacific, is yet another region where massive adobe-brick temples are revealing a complex, golden past. Sites such as Túcume, Sipán and Sicán are worth visiting for themselves, but the museums built to house their riches at Lambayeque and Ferreñafe are a must. Chiclayo is the modern city from which to start exploring this area.

From here, the route climbs into the Andes to Chachapoyas and its surroundings. Before the Spaniards arrived the area was ruled by the Chachapoyas, who built massive fortified cities – the prime example being Kuélap – and interred their dead in almost inaccessible caves or allowed them to stare out over the cloud-covered valleys and mountains from inscrutable sarcophagi. Another reason to visit this area is to see the waterfalls, such as Gocta, which pour off the green mountains in great steps.

Turning east, the journey goes over the 'eyebrow of the jungle' down to the westernmost reaches of the Amazon basin. It is a beautiful ride to the towns of Moyobamba, famed for its orchids, and Tarapoto, the largest commercial centre in the region and the starting point for journeys into the vast river system beyond. A short flight (or a long river journey from Yurimaguas) takes you to the point furthest from the capital, Iquitos. Standing on the river Amazon and surrounded by jungle, it is an isolated city whose past flourished in the rubber boom and whose present seems to thrive on noise – from motorcycles, music and televisions. It is the best place from which to visit the Peruvian Amazon properly, with lodges offering a variety of packages and luxury craft offering cruises, particularly to the Pacaya-Samiria national park.

After the rainforest a couple of days in Lima will bring you back to the modern world, in preparation for the flight home.

CHICHLAYO AND AROUND

Lambayeque department, sandwiched between the Pacific and the Andes, is a major agricultural zone, especially for rice and sugar cane. The area boasts a distinctive cuisine and musical tradition, and an unparalleled ethnographic and archaeological heritage. Chiclayo's witchcraft market is famous, and excavations at nearby adobe pyramid cities are uncovering fabulous treasures.

→ CHICLAYO

Since its inception in the 16th century, Chiclayo has grown to become a major commercial hub. The city has a distinctive atmosphere and a musical tradition featuring Afro-Indian rhythms, but is best known for the spectacular cache of archaeological treasures that lie on its doorstep.

ARRIVING IN CHICLAYO
Getting there There are daily flights from Lima to Chiclayo (1½ hours). The airport is 1 km from the centre of town and is served by taxis. There is no bus station in Chiclayo. Most companies have their own offices (some share offices), the majority of which are on Avenida Bolognesi, some five blocks south of the centre. Several buses run daily to and from Cajamarca (six hours).

Moving on Direct buses from Chiclayo to **Chachapoyas** (see page 156) take 10-11 hours and are operated overnight by three main companies, Civa, Móvil and Turismo Kuélap. To go by day you have to go to the road junction at **Pedro Ruiz** and change to a shared car or minivan for the one-hour journey on to Chachapoyas.

Tourist information i perú ① *Sáenz Peña 838, T074-205703, iperuchiclayo@promperu. gob.pe, 0900-1900, Sun 0900-1300*; also at the airport (daily). For complaints and tourist protection, **Indecopi** ① *Los Tumbos 245, Santa Victoria, T074-206223, aleyva@indecopi.gob. pe, Mon-Fri 0800-1300, 1630-1930*. The **tourist police** ① *Av Sáenz Peña 830, T074-236700, ext 311, 24 hrs a day*, are very helpful and may store luggage and take you to the sites themselves. There are tourist kiosks on the Plaza and on Balta.

PLACES IN CHICLAYO
In the city centre, on the Plaza de Armas, is the 19th-century neoclassical **Cathedral**, designed by the English architect Andrew Townsend. The private **Club de la Unión** is on the Plaza at the corner of Calle San José. Continue five blocks north on Balta to the **Mercado Modelo**, one of northern Peru's liveliest and largest daily markets. Don't miss the handicrafts stalls (see Monsefú, page 150) and the well-organized section (off C Arica on the south side) of ritual paraphernalia used by traditional curers and diviners (*curanderos*): herbal medicines, folk charms, curing potions, and exotic objects including dried llama foetuses to cure all manner of real and imagined illnesses. At Paseo de Artesanías, 18 de Abril near Balta, stalls sell handicrafts in a quiet, custom-built open-air arcade.

The traditional town of **Monsefú**, 12 km southwest of Chiclayo, is known for its music and handicrafts; good market, four blocks from the plaza. Handicraft stalls open when potential customers arrive. In the second half of July the **Feria de Exposiciones Típico Culturales de Monsefú (FEXTICUM)** celebrates traditional foods, drink, handicrafts, music and dance, and includes an agricultural show. Along the coast beyond Monsefú are three ports serving the Chiclayo area. **Pimentel**, 8 km from Chiclayo, is a beach resort which gets very crowded on Sunday. You can walk along the decaying pier for US$0.25. There are several seafood restaurants. The surfing between Pimentel and the Bayovar Peninsula is excellent, reached from Chiclayo (14.5 km) by road branching off from the Pan-American Highway. Sea-going reed boats (*caballitos de totora*) are used by fishermen and may be seen returning in the late afternoon. Nearby **Santa Rosa** has little to recommend it and it is not safe to walk there from Pimentel. The most southerly is **Puerto Eten**, a quaint port with some nice wooden buildings on the plaza, 24 km by road from Chiclayo. Its old railway station has been declared a national heritage site. In the adjacent roadstead, Villa de Eten, panama hats are the local industry, but it is not as picturesque. The ruined Spanish town of **Zaña**, 51 km south of Chiclayo, was destroyed by floods in 1726, and sacked by English pirates on more than one occasion. There are ruins of five colonial churches and the convents of San Agustín, La Merced and San Francisco.

About 12 km northwest from Chiclayo is Lambayeque, its narrow streets lined by colonial and republican houses, many retaining their distinctive wooden balconies and wrought-iron grille-work over the windows, but many in very bad shape. On Calle 2 de Mayo see especially **Casa de la Logia o Montjoy**, whose 64-m-long balcony is said to be the longest in the colonial Americas. It is being restored. At 8 de Octubre 345 is **Casona Descalzi**, which is well preserved as a good restaurant ① *T284341, 1100-1700 daily*. It has 120 carved iguana heads on the ceiling. Opposite, at No 328, **Casona Cúneo**, and **Casona Iturregui Aguilarte**, No 410, are, by contrast, seriously neglected. Also of interest is the 16th-century **Complejo Religioso Monumental de San Francisco de Asís** and the baroque church of the same name, which stands on **Plaza de Armas 27 de Diciembre**.

The reason most people visit is to see the town's two museums. The older of the two is the **Brüning Archaeological Museum** ① *Av Huamachuco, block 8, T074-282110, 0900-1700, US$3.50, a guided tour costs an extra US$2.75*, in a modern building, specializing in Mochica, Lambayeque/Sicán and Chimú cultures. Three blocks east is the more recent **Museo de las Tumbas Reales de Sipán** ① *Av Juan Pablo Vizcardo y Guzmán 895, T074-283977, www.museotumbasrealessipan.pe, 0900-1700, closed Mon, US$3.55, moto taxi from plaza US$0.35*, shaped like a pyramid. The magnificent treasure from the tomb of 'The Old Lord of Sipán' (see below), and a replica of El Señor de Sipán's tomb are displayed here. A ramp from the main entrance takes visitors to the third floor, from where you descend, mirroring the sequence of the archaeologists' discoveries. There are handicrafts outside and a **tourist office** ① *Tue-Sun 1030-1400, 1500-1730*.

On the plaza in **Mórrope**, on the Pan-American Highway 20 km north of Lambayeque, is one of the earliest churches in northern Peru, **San Pedro de Mórrope** (1545), an adobe and *algarrobo* (carob wood) structure beautifully renovated and painted. It contains the tomb of the cacique Santiago Cazusol. Next to it is the more modern parish church.

→ TUCUME

ⓘ *Open 0900-1700, entry US$3.45, students US$1, children US$0.30, guide US$7, T074-835026, www.museodesitiotucume.com.*

About 24 km north of Lambayeque, not far from the Panamericana and Túcume Nuevo, lie the ruins of this vast city built over 1000 years ago. A short climb to the two miradors on **Cerro La Raya** (or **El Purgatorio**) offers the visitor an unparalleled panoramic vista of 26 major pyramids, platform mounds, walled citadels and residential compounds flanking a ceremonial centre and ancient cemeteries. One of the pyramids, **Huaca Larga**, where excavations are still being undertaken, is the longest adobe structure in the world, measuring 700 m long, 280 m wide and over 30 m high. There is no evidence of occupation of Túcume previous to the Sicán, or Lambayeque people who developed the site AD 1000-1375 until the Chimú conquered the region, establishing a short reign until the arrival of the Incas around 1470. The Incas built on top of the existing structure of **Huaca Larga** using stone from Cerro La Raya. Among the other pyramids that make up this huge complex are: **Huaca El Mirador** (90 m by 65 m, 30 m high), **Huaca Las Estacas**, **Huaca Pintada** and **Huaca de las Balsas**, which is thought to have housed people of elevated status such as priests.

Not much of the site is open to view, only the miradors mentioned above and the walk through the site there, as lots of study is going on. There is a pleasant dry forest walk to Huaca I, with shade, bird- and lizard-watching. **A site museum** contains architectural reconstructions, photographs and drawings.

The town of Túcume Viejo is a 20-minute walk beyond the site. Look for the side road heading towards a new park, opposite which is the ruin of a huge colonial church made of adobe and some brick. The surrounding countryside is pleasant for walks through mango trees and fields of maize. Túcume celebrates the **Fiesta de la Purísima Concepción**, the town's patron saint, eight days prior to Carnival in February, and also in September. This is the most important festival, with music, dancing, fireworks, cockfights, sports events and, of course, much eating and drinking. During the Dance of the Devils (which is common in northern Peru), the participants wear horned masks, forked tails and long capes and are said to represent the diabolical drunken Spanish priests from colonial times. It also features a song and dance dedicated to the native girl who was seen combing the Virgin's hair.

→ FERREÑAFE AND SICAN

The colonial town of **Ferreñafe**, 20 km northeast of Chiclayo, is worth a visit, especially for the **Museo Nacional Sicán** ⓘ *T074-286469, see Museo-Nacional-Sican on Facebook, Tue-Sun 0900-1700, US$2.75, students US$1.10.* This excellent new museum on the outskirts of town houses objects of the Sicán (Lambayeque) culture from near Batán Grande. **Tourist office**: helpful Mincetur office on the Plaza de Armas ⓘ *T074-282843, citesipan@mincetur.gob.pe.*

The entrance to **El Santuario Histórico Bosque de Pómac** ⓘ *free, visitors' centre, dalemandelama@gmail.com, 0900-1700, a guide (Spanish only) can be hired with transport, US$3.45, horses for hire US$6,* which includes the ruins of **Sicán**, lies 20 km beyond

Ferreñafe along the road to Batán Grande (from the Panamericana another entrance is near Túcume). Visiting is not easy because of the arid conditions and distances involved: it is 10 km to the nearest *huaca* (pyramid). At the visitors' centre food and drinks are available and camping is permitted. The guide covers a two-hour tour of the area, which includes at least two huacas, some of the most ancient carob trees and a mirador, which affords a beautiful view across the emerald green tops of the forest with the enormous pyramids dramatically breaking through. Sicán has revealed several sumptuous tombs dating to AD 900-1100. The ruins comprise some 12 large adobe pyramids, arranged around a huge plaza, measuring 500 by 250 m, with 40 archaeological sites in total. The city, of the Sicán, was probably moved to Túcume (see above), 6 km west, following 30 years of severe drought and then a devastating El Niño-related flood in AD 1050-1100. These events appear to have provoked a rebellion in which many of the remaining temples on top of the pyramids were burnt and destroyed. The forest itself has good birdwatching possibilities.

→ SIPAN

ⓘ *Daily 0900-1700, entrance for tombs and museum is US$2.85; guide at site US$7 (may not speak English). To visit the site takes about 3-4 hrs.*

At this imposing complex a short distance east of Chiclayo (turn-off well signed in the centre of Pomalca), excavations since 1987 in one of three crumbling pyramids have brought to light a cache of funerary objects considered to rank among the finest examples of pre-Columbian art. Peruvian archaeologist Walter Alva, leader of the dig, continues to probe the immense mound that has revealed no less than 12 royal tombs filled with 1800-year-old offerings worked in precious metals, stone, pottery and textiles of the Moche culture (circa AD 1-750). In the most extravagant Moche tomb discovered, El Señor de Sipán, a priest, was found clad in gold (ear ornaments, breast plate, etc), with turquoise and other valuables. A site museum features photos and maps of excavations, technical displays and replicas of some finds. A new site museum is under construction.

In another tomb were found the remnants of what is thought to have been a priest, sacrificed llama and a dog, together with copper decorations. In 1989 another richly appointed, unlooted tomb contained even older metal and ceramic artefacts associated with what was probably a high-ranking shaman or spiritual leader, called 'The Old Lord of Sipán'. Three tombs are on display, containing replicas of the original finds. A new museum, **Museo de Sitio Huaca Rajada** ⓘ *daily 0900-1700, US$2.85,* concentrates on the finds at the site, especially Tomb 14 (the 'Sacerdote-Guerrero', or Priest-Warrior), the decorative techniques of the Moche and the roles that archaeologists and local communities play in protecting these precious discoveries. You can wander around the previously excavated areas of the **Huaca Rajada** to get an idea of the construction of the burial mound and adjacent pyramids. For a good view, climb the large pyramid across from the excavated Huaca Rajada.

A 4000-year-old temple, **Ventarrón**, was uncovered about 20 km from Sipán in 2007 by Walter Alva. It predates Sipán by some 2000 years and shows three phases of development. Its murals, which appear to depict a deer trapped in a net, are claimed to be the oldest in the Americas and there is evidence of cultural exchange with as far away as the Amazon. A project to build a site museum and improved access will take until the end of 2013, until then entry, with guide, is US$2.

GOING FURTHER
Máncora and Punta Sal

A long detour north can be made to Máncora, Peru's best-known beach resort (four days including travelling). Although it is six hours beyond Chiclayo, via the city of Piura (scheduled flights from Lima), its warm waters, surfing and bars make it a popular spot for limeños at weekends and holidays and for travellers passing through.

Máncora is a small, attractive resort stretching along 3 km of the Pan-American Highway. Bathing is safe on a long, sandy beach and excellent beaches such as Las Pocitas and Vichayito are being developed to the south. Surfing on this coast is best November-March and boards and suits can be hired from several places on Avenida Piura. **Tourist office** ① *iPerú, Av Piura 250, Thu-Sun 1000-1700*. The main strip of the Panamericana is known as Avenida Piura from the bridge for the first couple of blocks, then Avenida Grau to the end of town. The better hotels are at the southern end of town, with a small concentration of mid-range hotels just over the bridge. Hotels to the left look onto the beach directly in front of the best surf and often have beach entrances as well as road entrances. As the most popular with tourists, they are all quite noisy at night from nearby discos, which go until around 0200 week nights and 0600 at weekends. Prices can increase by up to 100% in high season (December-March). Many hotels have special rates for Christmas, New Year, Easter and Independence Day holidays when the resort is full to bursting. Look after your valuables and protect against mosquitoes at certain times of the year. See www.vivamancora.com for a full list of accommodation and other details.

At 22 km north of Máncora, Km 1187, is the turn-off for **Punta Sal Grande**, marked by a large white arch (El Arco). Punta Sal boasts a 3-km long white sandy beach and a more upmarket clientele than Máncora, with accommodation (and prices) to match. There is no town centre, nor services such as restaurants independent of hotels; it is very quiet in the low season. Taxi from Máncora, 20 minutes, US$14, mototaxi 40 minutes, US$10, otherwise take any combi going between Mancorá and the border town of Tumbes and tell the driver you want to get out at Punta Sal, then look out for the arch marking the entrance. It takes about 30 minutes to walk down to the beach.

East from Pomalca is Chongoyape, just before which is the turning to the **Chaparrí** private ecological reserve, 34,000 ha, set up and run by the Comunidad Muchik Santa Catalina de Chongoyape, 75 km from Chiclayo. Visitors can go for the day or stay at the **EcoLodge Chaparrí** ① *T074-978 896377, www.chaparri.org, US$10.55 for a day visit; see also Listings, page 154*. All staff and guides are locals; for every 10 people you have to have a local guide (this provides work and helps to prevent rubbish). There are no dogs or goats in the area so the forest is recuperating; it contains many bird and mammal species of the dry forest, including white-winged guan and spectacled bear. There is a Spectacled Bear Rescue Centre where bears rescued from captivity live in semi-wild enclosures. The Tinajones reservoir is good for birdwatching.

CHICLAYO AND AROUND LISTINGS

WHERE TO STAY

$$$$ EcoLodge Chaparrí, T984-676249 or in Chiclayo T074-452299, www.chaparri lodge.com. A delightful oasis in the dry forest, 6 beautiful standard en suite rooms, 5 superior rooms, a suite and 4 rooms with shared bath, built of stone and mud, nice and cool, solar power. More rooms are being built. Price is for 3 meals and a local guide for 1 day, 1st-class food. Sechuran foxes visit the gardens; hummingbirds bathe at the pool about 0600 every day. Recommended.

$$$ Casa Andina Select Chiclayo, Villareal 115, Chiclayo, T074-234911, cas-chiclayo@ casa-andina.com. Large, modern hotel for corporate and leisure guests, formerly the Gran Hotel, now part of the Peruvian chain, pool, safe car park, changes dollars, jacuzzi, entertainments, restaurant.

$$$ Hostería San Roque, 2 de Mayo 437, Lambayeque, T074-282860, www.hosteria sanroque.com. In a fine, extensive 19th-century house, beautifully refurbished, helpful staff, bar, swimming pool, lunch

on request. Single, double, triple, quad rooms and dorm for groups of 6, **$**.

$$$ Intiotel, Luis Gonzales 622, Chiclayo, T074-235931, www.intiotel.com. More expensive rooms with jacuzzi, family rooms available, welcome cocktail, airport transfer included, parking, safe and fridge in room, restaurant, helpful staff.

$$ Los Horcones, Caserío San Antonio, Túcume, T951-831705, www.loshorcones detucume.com. Rustic luxury in the shadow of the pyramids, with adobe and algarrobo rooms set in lovely garden with lots of birdlife. Good food, pizza oven, breakfast included, price is per person. Also offers packages of several days, including local craft workshops and excursions. Note that if rice is being grown nearby in Jan-May there may be many mosquitoes.

$ Muchik Hostel, Vicente de la Vega 1127, T074-272119, www.muchik-hostel.com. Singles, doubles and dorm rooms, with fan, use of kitchen, pleasant common area, safe.

RESTAURANTS

$$$ Fiesta, Av Salaverry 1820 in 3 de Octubre suburb, Chiclayo, T074-201970, www.restaurantfiesta gourmet.com. Gourmet local dishes, excellent food and service, beautifully presented, daily and seasonal specials, fabulous juices, popular business lunch place.

$$$ El Huaralino, La Libertad 155, Santa Victoria, Chiclayo, T074-270330. Recommended for its wide variety of international and creole dishes, good service.

$$ Hebrón, Balta 605, T074-222709, www. hebron.com.pe. For more upmarket than average chicken, but also local food and *parrilla*, good salads. Also does an excellent breakfast and a good buffet at weekends.

WHAT TO DO

Lambayeque's museums, Sipán and Túcume can easily be visited by public transport, although you have to check where the buses leave from. They all have different departure points: to **Monsefú**, US$0.75 from Balta y Pedro Ruiz, or Terminal Epsel, Av Quiñónez. To **Lambayeque**, US$0.75, 25 mins, from Pedro Ruíz at the junction with Av Ugarte. Combis to **Sipán** leave from Plaza Elías Aguirre, US$0.75, 1 hr. To **Túcume**, from Av Leguía, 15 m from Angamos, US$1, 45 mins; mototaxi from highway/new town to ruins US$0.50. Colectivos from Chiclayo to the centre of **Ferreñafe** leave every few mins from 8 de Octubre y Sáenz Peña, 15 mins, U$1, take a mototaxi to the museum, 5 mins, US$0.75.

Local operators run full-day tours to Sipán; Túcume and Lambayeque; Sicán including Ferreñafe and Pómac, all about US$22 per person; there are also tours to Zaña and coastal towns (US$18 per person).

Horse riding
Rancho Santana, in Pacora, T979-712145, www.cabalgatasperu.com. Relaxing tours on horseback, half-day (US$16), 1-day (US$23) or 3-day tours, including to Santuario Bosque de Pómac, Sicán ruins and Túcume, Swiss run (Andrea Martin), good horses. Also **$** a bungalow and camping (tents for hire) at the ranch with safe parking for campervans. Frequently recommended.

CHACHAPOYAS REGION

Chiclayo is a convenient starting point for the trip east to the department of Amazonas, which contains the archaeological riches of the Chachapoyans, also known as Sachupoyans. Here lie the great pre-Inca cities of Vilaya (not yet developed for tourism) and the immense fortress of Kuélap, among many others. It is also an area of great natural beauty with waterfalls, notably Gocta, cliffs and caves. At Olmos, about 90 km north of Chiclayo, a road runs east over the 2150-m Porculla Pass to Chamaya and Bagua Grande in the hot, dusty depression of the Marañón river valley. From Bagua the road continues to Pedro Ruiz on the Utcubamba River. While the main road heads up into cloud-covered mountains before the descent to the Amazon lowlands, a side road heads south, following the dramatic gorge of the Utcubamba to the turn-off to Chachapoyas.

→ CHACHAPOYAS AND AROUND

The capital of the Department of Amazonas, founded in 1538, retains its colonial character. The city's importance as a crossroads between the coast and jungle began to decline in the late 1940s, however archaeological and ecological tourism have grown gradually since the 1990s and have brought increasing economic benefits to the region.

ARRIVING IN CHACHAPOYAS
Getting there Buses from Chiclayo and local transport from Pedro Ruiz and other neighbouring towns and villages all arrive at their own terminals, which are mostly north of the Plaza de Armas.

Moving on To get to the Amazon region from Chachapoyas, you have first to go by road to **Tarapoto** (see page 164). Return to **Pedro Ruiz** (see page 159) where you have two options: try to get a seat on a through bus, which may be difficult and at an awkward hour; much simpler, take a shared car or minivan via any of the following places, **Nuevo Cajamarca**, **Rioja** or **Moyobamba** (see page 163). You may have to change a couple of times, but the cars and minivans leave frequently and are quick. The whole journey should take seven or eight hours if you set out early and connections work well. If they don't, the best place to spend the night is Moyobamba. Once in Tarapoto there are daily flights to **Iquitos** (see page 166), which take one hour. See page 164 for Pacaya-Samiria National Park; one way to get to Iquitos is by road and river from Tarapoto through this beautiful region.

Getting around Chachapoyas itself is a small town, easy to walk around. To visit places in the vicinity you can take tours with agencies in the town, or you can you can go by public transport (as mentioned above). Transport often does not go all the way to the archaeological and other sites, so there will almost certainly be some walking to get to your final destination.

The cathedral, with a lovely modern interior, stands on the spacious Plaza de Armas. **Ministerio de Cultura Museum** ① *Ayacucho 904, T01-477045, amazonas@mcultura.gob.pe, Mon-Fri 0800-1300, 1500-1700, free*, contains a small collection of artefacts and mummies, with explanations in Spanish. The **Museo Santa Ana** ① *Jr Santa Ana 1054, T790988, Sun-Fri 0900-1300, 1500-1800, US$2*, has colonial religious art and pre-Hispanic ceramics and textiles. Jirón Amazonas, pedestrianized from the Plaza de Armas uphill to Plaza Burgos, makes a pleasant stroll. Tourist offices: iPerú ① *Jr Ortiz Arrieta 582, Plaza de Armas, T01-477292, iperuchachapoyas@promperu.gob.pe, Mon-Sat 0900-1800, Sun 0900-1300*. A useful site is www.camayocperu.com of the German ethnologist, Doctor Peter Lerche.

Huancas ① *autos leave from Jr Ortiz Arrieta 370, 0600-1800, 20 min, US$1.15 or 2-hr walk*, is a small village to the north of Chacha where rustic pottery is produced. Walk uphill from town to the **Mirador** ① *1 km from the plaza, US$0.40, viewing tower, crafts on sale*, for magnificent views into the deep canyon of the Río Sonche, with tumbling waterfalls. At **Huanca Urco**, 5 km from Huancas, past the large prison complex, are ruins, remains of an Inca road and another mirador with fine views including Gocta Waterfall in the distance.

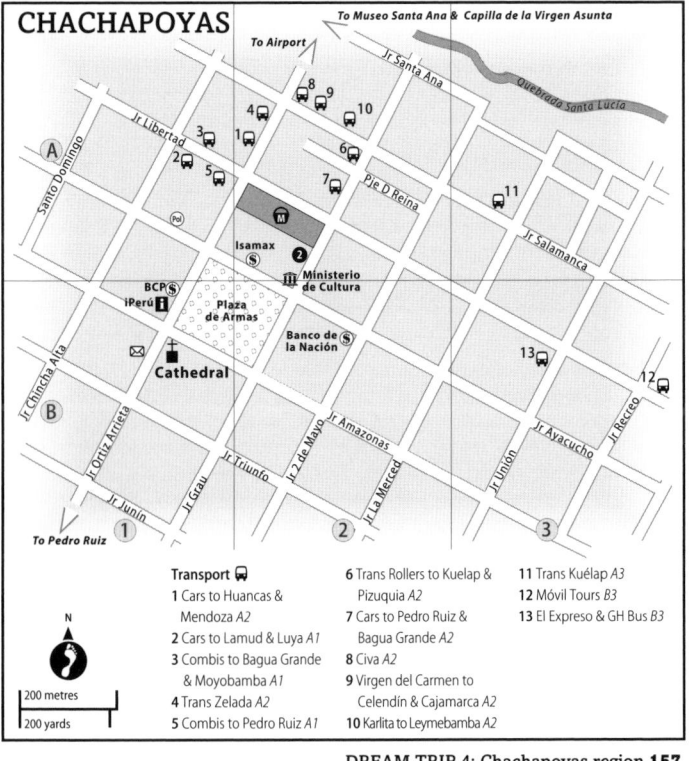

CHACHAPOYAS

To Museo Santa Ana & Capilla de la Virgen Asunta

To Airport

Jr Santa Ana

Quebrada Santa Lucia

Jr Libertad

Santo Domingo

Pje D'Reina

Jr Salamanca

Isamax

Ministerio de Cultura

BCP

iPerú

Plaza de Armas

Banco de la Nación

Cathedral

Jr Chincha Alta

Jr Ortiz Arrieta

Jr Triunfo

Jr Grau

Jr Amazonas

Jr 2 de Mayo

Jr La Merced

Jr Ayacucho

Jr Unión

Jr Recreo

Jr Junín

To Pedro Ruiz

Transport 🚌
1 Cars to Huancas & Mendoza *A2*
2 Cars to Lamud & Luya *A1*
3 Combis to Bagua Grande & Moyobamba *A1*
4 Trans Zelada *A2*
5 Combis to Pedro Ruiz *A1*

6 Trans Rollers to Kuelap & Pizuquia *A2*
7 Cars to Pedro Ruiz & Bagua Grande *A2*
8 Civa *A2*
9 Virgen del Carmen to Celendín & Cajamarca *A2*
10 Karlita to Leymebamba *A2*

11 Trans Kuélap *A3*
12 Móvil Tours *B3*
13 El Expreso & GH Bus *B3*

200 metres

200 yards

N

Levanto, due south of Chachapoyas, was built by the Spaniards in 1538, directly on top of the previous Chachapoyan structures, as their first capital of the area. Nowadays Levanto is an unspoilt colonial village overlooking the massive canyon of the Utcubamba River. Kuélap can, on a clear day, be seen on the other side of the rift. A 30-minute walk from Levanto towards Chachapoyas are the overgrown ruins of **Yalape**, which seems to have been a massive residential complex, extending over many hectares. Local people can guide you to the ruins.

→ TINGO

Situated at the junction of the Tingo and Utcubamba rivers, 37 km south of Chachapoyas and 25 km north of Leymebamba (see below), Tingo is the access for Kuélap. A road climbs steeply from Tingo to Choctámal, where it divides. The left branch climbs east to Lónguita, María, Quizango and Kuélap.

→ KUELAP

ⓘ *0800-1700, US$4.30, guides available for US$7 per group (Rigoberto Vargas Silva has been recommended). A small Centro de Interpretaciones has a good model of the site.*
Kuélap is a spectacular pre-Inca walled city that was re-discovered in 1843. It was built over a period of 600 years, from AD 500 to 1100, and contained three times more stone than the Great Pyramid at Giza in Egypt. The site lies along the summit of a mountain crest, more than 1 km in length. The massive stone walls, 585 m long by 110 m wide at their widest, are as formidable as those of any pre-Columbian city. Some reconstruction has taken place, mostly of small houses and walls, but the majority of the main walls on all levels are original, as is the inverted, cone-shaped 'dungeon'. The structures have been left in their cloud forest setting, the trees covered in bromeliads and moss, the flowers visited by hummingbirds.

→ LEYMEBAMBA AND AROUND

There are plenty of ruins – many of them covered in vegetation – and good walking possibilities around this pleasant town at the source of the Utcubamba River. See www.leymebamba.org. The main attraction in the area is its spectacular museum, see below.

La Congona, a Chachapoyan site, is well worth the effort, with stupendous views. It consists of three hills: on the vegetation-covered conical hill in the middle, the ruins are clustered in a small area, impossible to see until you are right there. The other hills have been levelled. La Congona is the best preserved of three sites in this area, with 30 round stone houses (some with evidence of three storeys) and a watch tower. The two other sites, El Molinete and Pumahuanyuna, are nearby. All three sites can be visited in a day but a guide is advisable. It is a brisk three hours' walk from Leymebamba, first along the rough road to Fila San Cristóbal, then a large trail. The road starts at the bottom of Jirón 16 de Julio.

At **Laguna de los Cóndores**, in 1996, a spectacular site consisting of six burial *chullpas*, containing 219 mummies and vast quantities of ceramics, textiles, woodwork, *quipus* and everyday utensils from the late Inca period, was discovered near a beautiful lake in a lush cloudforest setting. The trip to Laguna de los Cóndores takes 10-12 hours on foot and horseback from Leymebamba. An all-inclusive tour for the three-day muddy trek can be arranged at Leymebamba hotels or with Chachapoyas operators, US$70 per person. The artefacts were moved to the excellent **Museo Leymebamba** ① *outside San Miguel, on the road to Celendín, T041-816803, www.museoleymebamba.org, Tue-Sun about 0930-1630, entry US$5.75. Taxi from Leymebamba US$2.75, mototaxi US$2*. From Leymebamba, walk to the village of 2 de Mayo, ask for the trail to San Miguel, then take the footpath uphill, the road is much longer. It is beautifully laid out and very informative. Across the road is **Kentitambo** (T971-118273, **$$$$-$$$** in two comfortable cabins, restaurant, lovely grounds with hummingbirds), **Kentikafe**, offering snacks, and **Mishqui**, offering meals on request.

The road back to Chachapoyas follows the Utcubamba River north. In the mountains rising from the river are a number of archaeological sites. Before **Yerbabuena** (important Sunday market, basic *hospedaje*), a road heads east to **Montevideo** (basic *hospedaje*) and beyond to the small village of San Pedro de Utac.

The burial *chullpas* of **Revash**, of the Revash culture (AD 1250), are reached from either **San Bartolo** (30-45 minutes' walk) or a trail starting past **Puente Santo Tomás** (1½ to two hours' walk). Both access points are along roads going west from Yerbabuena.The town of **Jalca Grande** (or La Jalca), at 2800 m, is reached along a road going east at **Ubilón**, north of Yerbabuena. Jalca Grande has the remains of a Chachapoyan roundhouse, a stone church tower, a small **museum** ① *entry US$1.80*, with ceramics and textiles, and one very basic *hospedaje*.

→ EAST OF CHACHAPOYAS

In the district of Soloco, south of the Chachapoyas-Mendoza road, is **Parjugsha**, Peru's largest cave complex, about 300 m deep and with some 20 km of galeries (10 km have been explored and connected). **Peru Nativo** operator can arrange visits, spelunking experience is required.

The road east from Chachapoyas continues on to **Mendoza** (2½ hours), centre of the coffee producing region of Rodríguez de Mendoza. It is the starting point of an ethnologically interesting area in the Guayabamba Valley, where there is an unusually high incidence of fair-skinned people. Close by are the caves at Omia, Tocuya thermal baths, Mirador Wimba and Santa Natalia waterfall. For information ask for Michel Ricardo Feijoó Aguilor in the municipal office, mifeijoo@gmail.com; he can help tourists arrange a guide, accommodation etc. A recommended guide is Alfonso Saldana Pelaez, fotoguiaalsape@gmail.com.

→ NORTHWEST OF CHACHAPOYAS

On a turn-off on the Chachapoyas-Pedro Ruiz road, at Km 37, is the village of **Luya**. Here the road divides, one branch goes north to **Lamud**, a convenient base for several interesting sites, such as San Antonio and Pueblo de los Muertos, and the **Quiocta** cave ① *entry US$2, tours from Chachapoyas, or arranged at the Lamud Oficina de Turismo; it's 30 mins by car from Lamud, then a 10-min walk*. The cave is 560 m long, 23 m deep, has four chambers with stalagtites and stalagmites and a stream running through it. There are petroglyphs at the mouth, a man-made wall, human skulls set in depressions and other, partly buried human remains.

The second road goes south and west to Cruzpata, the access for **Karajía** ① *entry US$2, take binoculars*, where remarkable, 2.5-m-high sarcophagi set into an impressive cliff face overlook the valley. The viewpoint is 2½ hours' walk from Luya or 30 minutes from Cruzpata (*autos* from Luya to Cruzpata, 0600-1700, US$3, one hour). **Chipuric** is another site 1½ hours' walk from Luya. In a lush canyon, 1½ hours' walk from the road to Luya is **Wanglic**, a funeral site with large circular structures built under a ledge. Nearby is a beautiful waterfall, a worthwhile excursion. Ask for directions in Luya. Best to take a local guide (US$3.50-5 a day). The road to Luya and Lamud is unpaved.

→GOCTA

① *The easiest way to get to Gocta is with a tour from Chachapoyas; in high season there are also tours from Pedro Ruiz. A taxi from Chachapoyas costs US$30, or US$38 with 5-6 hrs' wait. A taxi from Pedro Ruiz to San Pablo or Cocachimba costs US$2 per person, but there are seldom other passengers to share, or US$10 for the vehicle. Cars wait at 5 Esquinas, along the road to Chachapoyas, 4 blocks from the highway. Arrange return transport ahead or at the tourist offices in San Pablo or Cocachimba.*

South of Pedro Ruíz is the spectacular **Gocta Waterfall** (771 m, the upper waterfall is 231 m, the lower waterfall is 540 m), one of the highest in the world. From Chachapoyas road take the Pedro Ruiz for 40 km to Cocahuayco where there are two roads up to Gocta, along either bank of the Cocahuayco River. The first turn-off leads up to the village of **Cocachimba** (1796 m, 5.3 km, 20 minutes), from which it is a 1½- to 2½-hour, 5.5-km walk to the base of the lower waterfall, of which there is an impressive view. The second turn-off, 100 m further on the main road, leads up to the village of **San Pablo de Valera** (1934 m, 6 km from main road, 20 minutes by car) from which it is a 1-1½-hour walk to a mirador, and then 30-60 minutes to the base of the upper waterfall, 6.3 km in all. Both routes go through about 2 km of lovely forest; the San Pablo trail is somewhat flatter. A trail connecting both banks starts on the San Pablo side at the mirador. It is a much smaller trail than the others, quite steep and not signposted past the mirador. There is a suspension footbridge over the main river. It joins the Cocachimba trail about three-quarters of the way to the base of the lower falls. If you start the hike at San Pablo and finish at Cocachimba you can arrange transport to return to San Pablo at the end of the day. Or you can take transport to San Pablo to begin the hike if lodged in Cocachimba. The ride is about 30 minutes. To see both sides in one day you need to start very early, but this is a great way to get the full experience. Each community offers similar services: entry fee is US$4, guides (compulsory) cost US$11, horses can be hired for US$11 (they can only go part of the way), rubber boots and rain ponchos are available for hire, US$1.20 (it is always wet by the falls). The best time to visit is May to September, the dry season. In the wet season the falls are more spectacular, but it is cold, rainy and the trails may be slippery. Both towns have a community tourist information office: San Pablo, T041-631163, daily 0800-1730, www.goctawaterfall.com, and Cocachimba, T041-630569, daily 0800-1730. More waterfalls in this area are now becoming accessible, including **Yumbilla**, 895 m (124 m higher than Gocta), although in eight tiers.

CHACHAPOYAS REGION LISTINGS

WHERE TO STAY

$$$ Gocta Andes Lodge, Cocachimba, T041-630552 (Tarapoto 042-522225), www.goctalodge.com. Beautifully located lodge overlooking the waterfall, ample rooms with balconies, lovely terrace with pool, restaurant. Packages available with other hotels in the group, such as the **Río Shilcayo** resort near Tarapoto, www.rioshilcayo.com.

$$$-$$ Casa Vieja, Chincha Alta 569, Chachapoyas, T041-477353, www.casavieja peru.com. Converted old house with lovely courtyard, very nicely decorated, all rooms different, comfy beds, family atmosphere, good service, living room and *comedor* with open fire, includes breakfast, Wi-Fi and library. Repeatedly recommended.

$$ Puma Urco, Amazonas 833, Chachapoyas, T041-477871, www. hotelpumaurco.com. Comfortable rooms, includes breakfast, TV, frigobar, Wi-Fi, **Café Café** next door, hotel and café receive good reports, run tours with **Turismo Explorer**.

$$ Vilaya, Ayacucho 734, Chachapoyas, T041-477664, www.hotelvilayachachapoyas. com. Ample carpeted rooms in a smart new hotel (2012), has a cafeteria, bar, Wi-Fi, and parking and offers tours in the region.

$$-$ Revash, Grau 517, Plaza de Armas, Chachapoyas, T041-477391, www.chachapoyaskuelap.com.pe. Traditional house with patio, stylish decor, steaming hot showers, breakfast available, helpful owners, good local information, popular. They sell local crafts and operate **Andes Tours**, daily trips to Kuélap and Gocta, other tours to ruins, caves, trekking and less-visited destinations, combining travel by car, on horseback and walking.

$ Chachapoyas Backpackers, Amazonas 1416, Chachapoyas, T041-477407, www.chachapoyasback packers.com. Simple 2- and 3-bed dorms with shared bath, electric shower, away from the centre, no sign, family run, a good budget option, same owners as Turismo Explorer tour operator.

$$ La Casona, Jr Amazonas 223, Leymebamba, T041-630301, www.casona deleymebamba.com. Nicely refurbished old house with balcony, attractive common area, restaurant upstairs with good view over rooftops, simple rooms with solar hot water, arrange tours and horses.

$ Laguna de los Cóndores, Jr Amazonas 320, ½ a block from the plaza, Leymebamba, T041-797908, www.los condoreshostal.com. Nice courtyard, breakfast available, electric shower, also runs the shelter at Laguna de los Cóndores and offers tours of 1-8 days.

RESTAURANTS

$$ El Tejado, Santo Domingo 424, Chachapoyas, Mon-Thu 1200-1600, 1900-2100, Fri-Sun midday only, but hours vary. Excellent upscale *comida criolla*. Large portions, attentive service, nice atmosphere and setting. Also serves good value *menú ejecutivo* on weekdays.

WHAT TO DO

The cost of full-day trips depends on season (higher Jul-Sep), distance to a site, number of passengers and whether meals are included. Several operators have daily departures to Kuélap, US$15-19, Gocta, US$13.50-15, Quiocta and Karajía, US$19-27, and Museo de Leymebamba and Revash, US$31-39. Hotels can arrange tours (see above).

Nuevos Caminos, at **Café Fusiones**, Chincha Alta 445, Chachapoyas, T041-479170, www.nuevoscaminostravel.com. Alternative community tourism throughout northern Peru, volunteer opportunities.

Perú Nativo, Ortiz Arrieta 508, Plaza Mayor, Chachapoyas, T041-477129, www.peru-nativo.com. Northern Peru specialists, from the coast to Cajamarca to Chachapoyas, private and group tours, trekking, camping, caving, archaeology and fishing. French, German, Spanish and English spoken. Run by French archaeologist Olivier Fabre.

Turismo Explorer, Jr Grau 509, Chachapoyas, T041-478162, www.turismo explorer peru.com. Daily tours to Kuélap, Gocta and other destinations, trekking tours including Laguna de los Cóndores and other archaeological sites, transport service.

Vilaya Tours, T941-708798, www.vilayatours.com. All-inclusive treks to off-the-beaten-path destinations throughout northern Peru. Run by Robert Dover, a very experienced and knowledgeable British guide, book ahead.

CHACHAPOYAS TO THE AMAZON

From Chachapoyas the road heads north through the beautiful Utcubamba canyon for one hour to a crossroads, Pedro Ruíz (two hotels and other lodgings; basic restaurants), where you continue east to Tarapoto and Yurimaguas, making the spectacular descent on a paved road from high Andes to jungle.

The final destination on this route is Iquitos, an urban oasis in the jungle on the banks of the Amazon River. You can only get there by plane or riverboat and its noise and activity may seem totally out of keeping with its natural surroundings, but it is an excellent jumping-off point for exploring the rainforest.

→ EAST TO THE AMAZON

From Pedro Ruiz the main road runs paved all the way to Yurimaguas, the first major river port for boats to Iquitos. All sections are still prone to landslides in the wet season. This is a very beautiful journey, first passing **Laguna Pomacochas**, 2150 m above sea level, near the town of Florida. The blue-green water is surrounded by totora reeds, and boats make trips from the pier. Beyond here you reach a point where the high Andes tumble into the Amazon Basin before your eyes. The descent from the heights to the Río Afluente at 1400 m is known as the **Abra Patricia** and is one of the best birdwatching sites in Northern Peru. As you travel the road you will usually see groups of people with their binoculars tramping beside the highway, stopping at likely sites for rare species. Ideally several days should be taken to see as many birds as possible. **ECOAN** ① *Carretera Fernando Belaunde Terry, Km 364.5, T041-816814, www.ecoanperu.org*, has an **Abra Patricia Reserve and Estación Biológica Lechucita Bigotona** (EBLB – Long-whiskered Owlet Biological Station), which provides lodging in bungalows and meals. This private reserve is aimed at conserving the critically endangered long-whiskered owlet (*Xenoglaux loweryi*) and other rare species. ECOAN has information on many aspects of this area. As the road continues to descend towards Tarapoto, it passes Nueva Cajamarca (reported unsafe for an overnight stay), Rioja, a pleasant town 22 km from Nueva Cajamarca (several hotels), and Moyobamba.

→ MOYOBAMBA

Moyobamba (900 m), capital of San Martín department, is a pleasant town, in the attractive Río Mayo Valley. The area is renowned for its orchids and there is a **Festival de la Orquídea** over three days around 1 November. Among several places to see orchids is **Orquideario Waqanki** ① *www.waqanki.com, 0700-1800, US$0.55*, where the plants have been placed in trees. Just beyond, 5 km southeast of Moyobamba, are **Baños Termales San Mateo** ① *0600-2200, US$0.55*, which are worth a visit. **Puerto Tahuishco** is the town's harbour, a pleasant walk north of the centre, where boat trips can be taken. **Morro de Calzada** ① *Rioja combi to the Calzada turn-off, US$0.55, mototaxi to the start of the trail US$2.50*, is an isolated outcrop clothed in white sand forest, good for birdwatching. A path through the forest leads to the top and a lookout (1½ hours). In the foothills to the west is the **Reserva Ecológica del Río Avisado-Tingana**, see www.tingana.org and www.lloros.org for community tourism projects here.

Tourist offices: Oficina Municipal de Información ① *Jr Pedro Canga 262, at Plaza, T042-562191 ext 541, Mon-Fri 0800-1300, 1430-1715, no English spoken*. Dircetur ① *Jr San Martín 301, T562043, www.turismosanmartin.com, Mon-Fri 0800-1300, 1430-1730*, has leaflets and map, English spoken. Also see www.moyobamba.net.

→ TARAPOTO

Tarapoto (350 m), the largest commercial centre in the region, is a very friendly place. Information from: Oficina Municipal de Información ① *Jr Ramírez Hurtado, at plaza, T526188, itarapoto@hotmail.com, Mon-Sat 0800-1300, 1500-2000, Sun 0900-1300* and Dircetur ① *Jr Angel Delgado Morey, cuadra 1, T042-522567, tarapoto@mincetur.gob. pe*. **Lamas** 22 km from Tarapoto, off the road to Moyobamba, has a native community, descendants of the Chancas people, who live in the Wayku neighbourhood below the centre. There is a small **Museo Los Chankas** ① *Jr San Martín 1157, daily 0830-1300, 1430-1800, US$1.15*, with ethnological and historical exhibits. In the upper part of town is a mirador, opposite is **$ Hospedaje Girasoles**, T042-543439, stegmaiert@yahoo.de, breakfast available, nice views, pizzeria and friendly knowledgeable owners. Cars from Tarapoto: Avenida Alfonso Ugarte, cuadra 11, US$1.45, 30 minutes.

Tarapoto stands at the foot of the forested hills of the **Area de Conservación Regional Cordillera Escalera** (149,870 ha), good for birdwatching and walking. By the conservation area and within easy reach of town are the 9-ha **El Amo del Bosque Sector** ① *Urawasha 5 km walk (9 km by car), T042-524675 (after 1900)*, knowledgeable owner Sr José Macedo, offers guided tours; and 20-ha **Wayrasacha** ① *6 km walk (10 km by car), T042-522261, www.wayrasacha.com.pe*, run by Peruvian-Swiss couple, César Ramírez and Stephanie Gallusser, who offer day trips, overnight stays in a basic shelter and volunteer opportunities, English and French spoken. Within the conservation area, about 15 km from Tarapoto on the spectacular road to Yurimaguas are the 50-m falls of **Ahuashiyacu** ① *US$1.15, tours available or transport from La Banda de Shilcayo*. This is a popular place with locals. There are many other waterfalls in the area. Past Ahuashiyacu, the road climbs to a tunnel (stop at the police control for birdwatching, mototaxi US$6), after which you descend through beautiful forest perched on rocky cliffs to Pongo de Caynarachi (several basic *comedores*), where the flats start.

→ PACAYA-SAMIRIA

Some 2½ hours by minibus (120 km) from Tarapoto is **Yurimaguas**, a very relaxed jungle town on lower Río Huallaga. It is an ideal starting point for river travel in the Peruvian Amazon. A colourful Mercado Central is open from 0500-1200, full of fruit and animals, many, sadly, for the pot. **Concejo Regional** tourist office at ① *Mariscal Castilla 118, of 2, Mon-Fri 0745-1545, www.yurimaguas.net*. Beyond Yurimaguas, all river traffic to Iquitos stops at **Lagunas**, 12 hours, one of the entry points to the **Pacaya-Samiria Reserve** ① *Reserve office in Iquitos, SERNANP, Jorge Chávez 930/942, T065-223555, www. pacayasamiria.org, Mon-Fri 0700-1300, 1500-1700*, has general information and an updated list of the community tourist associations and tour operators authorized to enter the reserve. Entry costs US$2 for a day visit, US$23 for three days, US$46 for seven days, payable at the ranger stations. Pacaya-Samiria Reserve, at 2,080,000 ha, is the country's second largest protected area. It is bounded by the rivers Marañón and Ucuyali, narrowing to their confluence near the town of Nauta. The reserve's waterways and wetlands provide habitat for several cats including puma and jaguar, manatee, tapir, river dolphins, giant otters, black cayman, boas, 269 species of fish and 449 bird species. Many of the animals found here are in danger of extinction.

The reserve can only be visited with an authorized guide arranged through a tour operator or a local community tourism association. Native guides generally speak only Spanish and native tongues. A list of authorized community associations is found in the reserve's web page and iPerú in Iquitos has a list of authorized operators. Most of the reserve is off-limits to tourists, but eight areas have been set up for visitors: these have shelters or camping areas, conditions are generally simple and may require sleeping in hammocks. Trips are mostly on the river and often include fishing. Four circuits are most commonly offered. All are rich in wildlife. 1) The basin of the Yanayacu and Pucate rivers is the most frequently visited; Laguna El Dorado is an important attraction in this area. It is accessed from **Nauta** on the Marañón, two hours by paved road from Iquitos and three hours by *peque peque* (outboard motor boat), or 1½ hours by *deslizador* (speedboat) from there to the reserve. Arrange a tour with an operator. 2) The middle and lower Samiria, accessed from Leoncio Prado (with a couple of *hospedajes*), 24 hours by *lancha* (slow boat) from Iquitos along the Marañón. Several lakes are found in this area. 3) The lower Pacaya, mostly flooded forest, accessed from Bretaña, on the Canal de Puinahua, a shortcut on the Ucayali, 24 hours by *lancha* from Iquitos. This area is less frequently visited than others. 4) The Tibilo-Pastococha area in the western side of the park, also in the Samiria basin, accessed from Lagunas on the Río Huallaga, 10-12 hours by *lancha* or three hours by *deslizador* from Yurimaguas and 48 hours by *lancha* from Iquitos. Another way of visiting the reserve is on a cruise, sailing along the main rivers on the periphery of the park. These tours are offered by some authorized Iquitos operators. Community tours cost US$46-70 per person per day, agency tours arranged in Iquitos start at US$80 per day. With all tours make sure you know exactly what is included in the price: park fees, lodging, food, transport, guide's fees. Also what the trip involves: most of the day in a canoe, walking, hunting, fishing, type of accommodation, etc.

There is a luxury lodge in the buffer zone, about half an hour by boat from Nauta, Hatuchay Hotels' Pacaya-Samiria Amazon Lodge ($$$$, www.hatuchayhotelsperu.com, in Iquitos T065-225769). A beautifully designed, luxurious lodge on a hill overlooking the Marañón, just inside the boundaries of the Reserve but close to road and town. All buildings in indigenous style, with balconies and en-suite bathrooms, restaurant, bar. Community visits and specialist birdwatching trips are included in the price, but boat trips (also included) can be long. Camping trips can be arranged deeper inside the reserve.

Pacaya-Samiria is a worthwhile trip from Iquitos, but should you choose to visit en route from Yurimaguas to Iquitos, starting out from Tarapoto, it is unlikely you will have time to visit a jungle lodge from Iquitos as well.

Iquitos stands on the west bank of the Amazon and is a chief town of Peru's jungle region. Some 800 km downstream from Pucallpa and 3646 km from the mouth of the Amazon, the city is completely isolated except by air and river. Its first wealth came from the rubber boom (late 19th century to second decade of 20th century). The main economic activities are logging, commerce and petroleum and it is the main starting point for tourists wishing to explore Peru's northern jungle. It is hot, dirty and noisy from the tens of thousands of mototaxis and motorcycles that fill the streets.

ARRIVING IN IQUITOS
Getting there There are flights to Iquitos from Tarapoto (not every day), taking just over an hour. By boat, it's a three-day/two-night trip from Yurimaguas.

Moving on Flights from Iquitos to **Lima** (see page 35) take three hours 10 minutes.

Tourist offices i perú ① *Jr Napo 161, of 4, T065-236144, iperuiquitos@promperu.gob.pe, Mon-Sat 0900-1800, Sun 0900-1300*, also at the airport, at flight times. Both offices are helpful. If arriving by air, go first to this desk. They will give you a list of hotels, a map, tell you about the touts outside the airport etc. Both www.iquitos news.com and www.iquitostimes.com have articles, maps and information. See also www.jungle-love. org. **Indecopi** ① *Putumayo 464, T065-243490, jreategui@indecopi.gob.pe, Mon-Fri 0830-1630*, the consumer protection service.

PLACES IN IQUITOS
The incongruous **Iron House/Casa de Fierro** stands on the Plaza de Armas, designed by Eiffel for the Paris exhibition of 1889. It is said that the house was transported from Paris by a local rubber baron and it is constructed entirely of iron trusses and sheets, bolted together and painted silver. It now houses a pharmacy. Of special interest are the older buildings, faced with *azulejos* (glazed tiles). They date from the rubber boom of 1890 to 1912, when the rubber barons imported the tiles from Portugal and Italy and ironwork from England to embellish their homes. The **Casa de Barro** on the Plaza (house of the controversial rubber baron Carlos Fitzcarrald), is now a bank. **Museo Amazónico** ① *Malecón Tarapacá 386, T065-234221, Mon-Sat 0800-1300, 1430-1730, Sun 0800-1230, free, some guides speak English, tip expected*, in the Prefectura, has displays of native art and sculptures by Lima artist Felipe Lettersten. The waterfront by Malecón Maldonado, known as 'Boulevard', is a pleasant place for a stroll and gets busy on Friday and Saturday evenings.

    Belén, the picturesque, lively waterfront district, is worth visiting, but is not safe at night. Most of its huts were built on rafts to cope with the river's 10 m change of level during floods (January to July); now they're built on stilts. On Pasaje Paquito are bars serving local sugar cane rum. The main plaza has a bandstand made by Eiffel. In the high season canoes can be hired on the waterfront for a tour of Belén, US$3 per hour. The market at the end of the Malecón is well worth visiting, though you should get there before 0900 to see it in full swing.

AROUND IQUITOS
There are pleasant beaches at **Tipishca** on the Río Nanay, reached in 20 minutes by boat from Puerto de Santa Clara near the airport, it gets quite busy at weekends, and,

ON THE ROAD
Rubber Barons

The conquest and colonization of the vast Amazon basin was consolidated by the end of the 19th century with the invention of the process of vulcanizing rubber. Many and varied uses were found for this new product and demand was such that the jungle began to be populated by numerous European and North American immigrants who came to invest their money in rubber.

The rubber tree grew wild in the Amazon but the indigenous peoples were the only ones who knew the forests and could find this coveted tree. The exporting companies set up business in the rapidly expanding cities along the Amazon, such as Iquitos. They sent their 'slave-hunters' out into the surrounding jungle to find the native labour needed to collect the valuable rubber resin. These natives were completely enslaved, their living conditions were intolerable and they perished in their thousands, which led to the extinction of many indigenous groups.

The Rubber Barons lived in the new Amazonian cities and travelled around in luxurious boats that plied the great river. Every imaginable luxury was imported for their use: latest Parisian fashions for the women; finest foreign liqueurs for the men; even the best musical shows were brought over from the Old World. But this period of economic boom came to a sudden end in 1912 when rubber grown in the French and British colonies in Asia and Africa began to compete on the world market.

quieter, **Santa Rita**, reached from Puerto de Pampa Chica, on a turn off the road to the airport. Beaches appear when the river is low, July-September. **Pilpintuhuasi Butterfly Farm** ① *near the village of Padre Cocha, T065-232665, www.amazon animalorphanage.org, US$7.75, students US$4, includes guided tour, Tue-Sun 0900-1600, guided tours at 0930, 1100, 1330 and 1500,* as well as butterflies, has a small well-kept zoo, Austrian/Peruvian-run. Colectivo from Bellavista to Padre Cocha takes 20 minutes, walk from there. If the river is high, boats can reach Pilpintuhuasi directly (no need to walk), a speedboat charges US$25 return including waiting time (pay at the end).

Along the road to Nauta, which is 100 km from Iquitos, are several attractions and balnearios. At Km 4.5 is **Centro de Rescate Amazónico** ① *http://gonzalomatosuria. blogspot.com/p/fundacion-iquitos-centro-de-rescate_20.html, open 0900-1500 daily, free, must show ID,* where orphaned manatees are nursed until they can be released: a good place to see this endangered species. The beautiful **Lake Quistococha** in lush jungle is at Km 6.5, with a fish hatchery at the lakeside. There's a two-hour walk through the surrounding jungle on a clearly marked trail, bars and restaurants on the lakeside and a small beach. Boats are for hire on the lake and swimming is safe but take insect repellent against sandflies.

Allpahuayo-Mishana Reserve ① *SERNANP, Jorge Chávez 930/942, T065-223555, rnallpahuayomishana@sernanp.gob.pe, Mon-Fri 0700-1300, 1500-1700, reserve fees: US$8.50, students US$6.25.* On the Río Nanay, some 25 km south of Iquitos by the Nauta road or two hours by boat from Bellavista, this reserve protects the largest concentration of white sand forest (*varillales*) in Peru. Part of the Napo ecoregion, biodiversity here is among the highest in the Amazon basin. It has several endangered species including two primates, several endemic species; the area is rich in birds (475 species have been recorded). Within the reserve are **Zoocriadero BIOAM**, Km 25, a good birdwatching circuit in land belonging to the Instituto Nacional de Innovación Agraria (INIA); **Jardín de Plantas Medicinales y Frutales** ① *at Km 26.8, 0800-1600, guiding 0800-1000*; and at Km 28, **El Irapay** interpretation centre ① *Mon-Sat 0830-1430*, with a trail to Mishana village by the river.

MOVING ON
To Lima

From Iquitos, fly back to Lima (see page 35) for a couple of days to see some of the sights of the city. The contrasts between Peru's Northern Highlands, its Northeastern Amazonian frontier and the capital overlooking the Pacific Ocean are huge, making this one of the most rewarding trips you can do in the country.

CHACHAPOYAS TO THE AMAZON LISTINGS

WHERE TO STAY

Tarapoto

$$$ Puerto Palmeras, Carr Belaúnde Terry Km 614, T042-524100, www.puertopalmeras. com. Large, modern complex, popular with families, lots of activities and entertainment. Nice rooms, helpful staff, good restaurant, pleasant grounds with pool, mountain bikes, horses and small zoo, airport transfers. Private reserve outside town.

$$ La Patarashca, Jr San Pablo de la Cruz 362, T042-528810, www.lapatarashca.com. Very nice hotel with large rooms, cheaper without a/c, rustic, restaurant, electric shower, large garden with hammocks, tours arranged.

$$-$ El Mirador, Jr San Pablo de la Cruz 517, 5 blocks uphill from the plaza, T042-522177, www.elmiradortarapoto. blogspot.com. With bath, electric shower, fan, Wi-Fi, laundry facilities, breakfast available, hammocks on rooftop terrace with nice views, tours arranged. Family-run and very welcoming.

Iquitos

$$$$ El Dorado Plaza, Napo 258 on main plaza, T065-222555, www.grupo-dorado.com. Good accommodation and restaurant, bar, business-type hotel, pool, prices include service, small breakfast, welcome drink and transfer to/from airport. Also owns the less grand **$$$ El Dorado Isabel**, Napo 362, T065-232574.

$$$ Casa Morey, Raymondi y Loreto, Plaza Ramón Castilla, T065-231913, www.casamorey.com. Boutique hotel in a beautifully restored historic rubber-boom period mansion. Great attention to detail, includes airport transfers, ample comfortable rooms, pool, good library.

$$$ La Casa Fitzcarraldo, Av La Marina 2153, T065-601138, www.casafitzcarraldo. com. Prices vary according to room. Includes breakfast and airport transfer, with Wi-Fi, satellite TV, minibar, 1st-class restaurant, treehouse, pool in lovely gardens. The house was the home of Walter Saxer, the executive producer of Werner Herzog's famous film (it is now owned by his daughter), lots of movie and celebrity memorabilia.

$ Green Track Hostel, Ricardo Palma 540, T997-829118, www.greentrack-travel.com. Nice hostel, dorms with a/c or fan, 1 private room with bath, free pick up with advanced booking, English spoken, helpful owners, tours arranged to Tapiche Ohara's Reserve.

RESTAURANTS

Iquitos

$$$ Al Frío y al Fuego, on the water, go to Embarcadero Turístico and their boat will pick you up, T065-224862, www. alfrioyalfuego.com. Mon 1830-2300, Tue-Sat 1130-1600 and 1830-2300, Sun 1130-1600. Good upscale floating restaurant with regional dishes, seafood specialities.

$$$ La Gran Maloca, Sargento Lores 170, opposite Banco Continental, T065-233126. A/c, high class regional food, closes 2000 on Sun, other days 2300.

$$ Yellow Rose of Texas, Putumayo 180. Varied food including local dishes, Texan atmosphere. Open 24 hrs so you can wait here if arriving late at night, good breakfasts, lots of information, also has a bar, Sky TV and Texan saddle seats.

Amazon Bistro, Malecón Tarapacá 268, T065-600785. Upscale French bistro/bar on the waterfront, drinks, snacks, breakfasts and meal of the day. Trendy and popular.

WHAT TO DO

Jungle lodges and cruises
Jungle tours from Iquitos Agencies arrange 1-day or longer trips to places of interest with guides speaking some English. Package tours booked in your home country, over the internet or in Lima are much more expensive than those booked locally. Take your time before making a decision and don't be bullied by the hustlers at the airport (they get paid a hefty commission). You must make sure your tour operator or guide has legal authorization (check with i Perú). Find out all the details of the trip and food arrangements before paying (a minimum of US$50 per day). Speed boats for river trips can be hired by the hour or day at the Embarcadero Turístico, at the intersection of Av de la Marina and Samánez Ocampo in Punchana. Prices vary greatly, usually US$15-20 per hr, US$80 for speedboat, and are negotiable. In fact, all prices are negotiable. Some places, however, do not take commissions, for example **Muyuna**, **Heliconia Lodge** and **Explorama**.

Aqua Expeditions, Iquitos 1167, T601053, www.aquaexpeditions.com. Luxury river cruises of 3, 4, or 7 nights on the M/V *Aria* (from US$2835 per person) and the M/V *Aqua* (from US$2685 per person), both designed by architect Jordi Puig to look like floating town houses rather than boats, with massive picture windows in each a/c suite. Amazing food with local delicacies on the gourmet tasting menu, good shore excursions with knowledgeable local guides. Aqua is an authorized operator in Pacaya-Samiria.

Dawn on the Amazon, Malecón Maldonado 185 y Nauta, T065-223730, www.dawnontheamazon.com. Offer a variety of day tours around Iquitos on the luxurious 20-passenger *Dawn on the Amazon III* (US$199 per person per day). Also offer custom-made cruises for several days. Their wooden vessels are decorated with carvings of jungle themes. They are an authorized operator in Pacaya-Samiria. Also have a bar/restaurant in town at Nauta 101/ Malecón Maldonado 185, T065-234921, www.dawnontheamazoncafe.com.

Delfín, Av Abelardo Quiñones Km 5, San Juan Bautista, T065-262721, www. delfinamazoncruises.com. Luxury cruises in the *Delfín I* and *Delfín II* (the cheaper of the two), 3- and 4-night expeditions to Pacaya-Samiria, with daily activities including kayaking, bird and wildlife watching, fresh organic food, from US$2400 per person.

Explorama Tours, by the riverside docks on Av La Marina 340, T065-252530, www. explorama.com, are highly recommended, with almost 50 years in existence, certainly the biggest and most established. Their sites: **Ceiba Tops**, 40 km (1½ hrs) from Iquitos, is a comfortable resort, 75 a/c rooms with electricity, hot showers, pool with hydromassage and beautiful gardens. The food is good and, as in all Explorama's properties, is served communally. There are attractive walks and other excursions, a recommended jungle experience for those who want their creature comforts, US$340 per person for 1 night/2 days.

Explorama Lodge at Yanamono, 80 km (2½ hrs) from Iquitos, has palm-thatched accommodation with separate bathroom and shower facilities connected by covered walkways, cold water, no electricity, good food and service. US$455 for 3 days/2 nights. **Explornapo Lodge** at Llachapa on the Sucusari creek (a tributary of the Napo), is in the same style as Explorama Lodge, but is further away from Iquitos, 160 km (4 hrs), and is set in 105,000 ha of primary rainforest, so is better for seeing wildlife, US$1,120 for 5 days/4 nights (all 2014 basic prices). Nearby is the impressive canopy walkway 35 m above the forest floor and 500 m long, 'a magnificent experience and not to be missed'. It is associated with the **Amazon Center for Tropical Studies** (ACTS), a scientific station, only 10 mins from the canopy walkway. Close to Explornapo is the ReNuPeRu medicinal plant garden, run by a *curandero* (healer).

Heliconia Lodge, Ricardo Palma 259, T065-231959 (Lima 01-421 9195), www.amazon riverexpeditions.com. On the Río Amazonas, 80 km from Iquitos. Surrounded by rainforest, islands and lagoons full of wildlife, this is a beautiful place for resting, birdwatching, looking for pink dolphins, jungle hikes. Organized packages from 1 to 4 nights, all-inclusive (4 days/3 nights US$475 per person). Good guides, food and flexible excursions according to guests' request. The lodge has a traditional, rustic yet comfortable design, swimming pool, hot water and electricity at certain times of day and 1700 to 2200.

Muyuna Amazon Lodge, Putumayo 163, ground floor, T065-242858, www.muyuna. com. 140 km from Iquitos, on the Yanayacu River, before San Juan village. Packages from 2 to 5 nights available (a 3-night tour costs US$490 per person). Everything is included in the price. Good guides, accommodation, food and service; very well organized and professional, flexible, radio contact, will collect passengers from airport if requested in advance. Amenities are constantly updated with new ecological considerations. It is easy to see animals here and you can even find rareties such as the piuri (Wattled curaçao, *Crax globulosa*). They offer birdwatching trips. Because of the isolated location they guarantee that visitors will see animals. Also visits to the Butterfly Farm and manatee rescue centre and city tours. Highly recommended.

PERU'S PRE-HISPANIC CIVILIZATIONS

EARLIEST SETTLEMENT

It is generally accepted that the earliest settlers in South America were related to people who had crossed the Bering Straits from Asia and drifted through the Americas from about 50,000 BC. Alternative theories of early migrations from across the Pacific and Atlantic have been rife since Thor Heyerdahl's raft expeditions in 1947 and 1969-1970. The earliest evidence of human presence has been found at various sites: in the Central Andes (with a radiocarbon date between 12000 and 9000 BC), northern Venezuela (11000 BC), southeast Brazil, south-central Chile and Argentine Patagonia (from at least 10000 BC). After the Pleistocene Ice Age, 8000-7000 BC, rising sea levels and climatic changes introduced new conditions as many mammal species became extinct and coastlands were drowned. A wide range of crops was brought into cultivation and camelids and guinea pigs were domesticated. It seems that people lived nomadically in small groups, mainly hunting and gathering but also cultivating some plants seasonally, until villages with effective agriculture began to appear, it was orignally thought, between 2500-1500 BC. The earliest ceramic-making in the western hemisphere was thought to have come from what is now Colombia and Ecuador, around 4000 BC, but fragments of painted pottery were found near Santarém, Brazil, in 1991 with dates of 6000-5000 BC.

→ PRE-INDEPENDENCE HISTORY

On the coast of central Peru settled life developed rapidly. The abundant wealth of marine life produced by the Humboldt Current, especially north of today's Lima, boosted population growth and a shift from nomadic to settled farming in this area. The introduction of sophisticated irrigation systems encouraged higher productivity and population growth, leading to organized group labour which could be devoted to building and making textiles from cotton. Evidence from Caral, Aspero and other sites in the Huaura, Supe, Pativilca and Fortaleza river valleys prove that this process happened much earlier than previously imagined. Caral dates from 2627 BC (other sites have older dates) and is a monumental construction. It flourished for some 500 years and appears to have been a city with primarily a religious, rather than a warlike purpose. The archaeological finds point to Caral and neighbouring sites predating the development of pottery in this region, but artefacts show cultural links with other communities, even as far as the Amazon. In the central Andes near Huánuco, also in what is now Peru, more advanced architecture was being built at Kotosh. There is evidence of a pre-ceramic culture here, too, but some of the earliest pottery from the site's later phases was found, showing signs of influence from southern Ecuador and the tropical lowlands. Radiocarbon dates of some Kotosh remains are from 1850 BC and Japanese archaeological excavations there in the 1960s revealed a temple with ornamental niches and friezes.

Chavín and Sechín For the next 1000 years or so up to c900 BC, communities grew and spread inland from the north coast and south along the north highlands. Farmers still lived in simple adobe or rough stone houses but built increasingly large and complex ceremonial centres. As farming became more productive and pottery more advanced, commerce grew and states began to develop throughout central and north-central Peru, with the associated signs of social structure and hierarchies.

Around 900 BC a new era was marked by the rise of two important centres; Chavín de Huántar in the central Andes and Sechín Alto, inland from Casma on the north coast, both now in Peru. The chief importance of Chavín de Huántar was not so much in its highly advanced architecture as in the influence of its cult, coupled with the artistic style of its ceramics and other artefacts. The founders of Chavín may have originated in the tropical lowlands, as some of its carved monoliths show representations of monkeys and felines.

The Chavín cult This was paralleled by the great advances made in this period in textile production and in some of the earliest examples of metallurgy. The origins of metallurgy have been attributed to some gold, silver and copper ornaments found in graves in Chongoyape, near Chiclayo, which show Chavín-style features. But earlier evidence has been discovered at Kuntur Wasi (some 120 km east of the coast at Pacasmayo) where 4000-year-old gold has been found, and in the Andahuaylas region, dating from 1800-900 BC. The religious symbolism of gold and other precious metals and stones is thought to have been an inspiration behind some of the beautiful artefacts found in the central Andean area.

The cultural brilliance of Chavín de Huántar was complemented by its contemporary, Sechín, with which it may have combined forces, Sechín being the military power that spread the cultural word of Chavín. The Chavín hegemony broke up around 500 BC, soon after which the Nazca culture began to bloom in southern Peru. This period, up to about AD 500, was a time of great social and cultural development. Sizable towns of 5-10,000 inhabitants grew on the south coast, populated by artisans, merchants and government and religious officials.

Paracas-Nazca Nazca origins are traced back to about the second century BC, to the Paracas Cavernas and Necropolis, on the coast in the national park near Pisco in Peru. The extreme dryness of the desert here has preserved remarkably the textiles and ceramics in the mummies' tombs excavated. The technical quality and stylistic variety in weaving and pottery rank them among the world's best, and many of the finest examples can be seen in the museums of Lima. The famous Nazca Lines are a feature of the region. Straight lines, abstract designs and outlines of animals are scratched in the dark desert surface forming a lighter contrast that can be seen clearly from the air. There are many theories of how and why the lines were made but no definitive explanation has yet been able to establish their place in South American history. There are similarities between the style of some of the line patterns and that of the pottery and textiles of the same period. Alpaca hair found in Nazca textiles, however, indicates that there must have been strong trade links with highland people.

Moche culture Nazca's contemporaries on the north coast were the militaristic Moche who, from about AD 100-800, built up an empire whose traces stretch from Piura in the north to Huarmey, in the south. The Moche built their capital outside present day Trujillo. The huge pyramid temples of the Huaca del Sol and Huaca de la Luna mark the remains of this city. Moche roads and system of way stations are thought to have been an early inspiration for the Inca network. The Moche increased the coastal population with intensive irrigation projects. Skilful engineering works were carried out, such as the La Cumbre canal, still in use today, and the Ascope aqueduct, both on the Chicama River. The Moche's greatest achievement, however, was its artistic genius. Exquisite ornaments in gold, silver and precious stones were made by its craftsmen. Moche pottery progressed through five stylistic periods, most notable for the stunningly lifelike portrait vases. A wide variety of everyday scenes were created in naturalistic ceramics, telling us more about Moche life than is known about other earlier cultures. Spectacular Moche tombs, discovered at Sipán since 1987, have included semi-precious stones brought from Chile and Argentina, and seashells from Ecuador. The Moche were great navigators.

The cause of the collapse of the Moche Empire around AD 600-700 is unknown, but it may have been started by a 30-year drought at the end of the sixth century, followed by one of the periodic El Niño flash floods (identified by meteorologists from ice thickness in the Andes) and finished by the encroaching forces of the Huari Empire. The decline of the Moche signalled a general tipping of the balance of power in Peru from the north coast to the south sierra.

Huari-Tiwanaku The ascendant Huari-Tiwanaku movement, from AD 600-1000, combined the religious cult of the Tiwanaku site in the Titicaca basin, with the military dynamism of the Huari, based in the central highlands. The two cultures developed independently but they are generally thought to have merged compatibly. Up until their own demise around AD 1440, the Huari-Tiwanaku had spread their empire and influence across much of south Peru, north Bolivia and Argentina. They made considerable gains in art and technology, building roads, terraces and irrigation canals across the country. The Huari-Tiwanaku ran their empire with efficient labour and administrative systems that were later adopted by the Incas. Labour tribute for state projects practised by the Moche were further developed. But the empire could not contain regional kingdoms who began to fight for land and power. As control broke down, rivalry and coalitions emerged, the system collapsed and the scene was set for the rise of the Incas.

Chachapoyas and Chimú cultures After the decline of the Huari Empire, the unity that had been imposed on the Andes was broken. A new stage of autonomous regional or local political organi- zations began. Among the cultures corresponding to this period were the Chachapoyas in northern highlands and the Chimú. The Chachapoyas people were not so much an empire as a loose-knit 'confederation of ethnic groups with no recognized capital' (Morgan Davis 'Chachapoyas: The Cloud People', Ontario, 1988). But the culture did develop into an advanced society with great skill in road and monument building. Their fortress at Kuélap was known as the most impregnable in the Peruvian Andes. The Chimú culture had two centres. To the north was Lambayeque, near Chiclayo, while to the south, in the Moche valley near present-day Trujillo, was the great adobe walled city of Chan Chán. Covering 20 sq km, this was the largest pre-Hispanic Peruvian city. Chimú has been classified as a despotic state that based its power on wars of conquest. Rigid social stratification existed and power rested in the hands of the great lord Siquic and the lord

Alaec. These lords were followed in social scale by a group of urban couriers who enjoyed a certain degree of economic power. At the bottom were the peasants and slaves. In 1450, the Chimú kingdom was conquered by the Inca Túpac Yupanqui, the son and heir of the Inca ruler Pachacútec.

Cultures of the northern Andes What is today Ecuador was a densely populated region with a variety of peoples. One of the most important of these was the **Valdivia culture** (3500-1500 BC) on the coast, from which remains of buildings and earthenware figures have been found. A rich mosaic of cultures developed in the period 500 BC to AD 500, after which integration of groups occurred. In the mid-15th century, the relentless expansion of the Inca empire reached Ecuador. The **Cañaris** resisted until 1470 and the Quitu/Caras were defeated in 1492. Further north, most of the peoples who occupied Colombia were primitive hunters or nomad agriculturists, but one part of the country, the high basins of the Eastern Cordillera, was densely occupied by **Chibcha Indians** who had become sedentary farmers. Their staple foods were maize and the potato, and they had no domestic animal save the dog; the use they could make of the land was therefore limited. Other cultures present in Colombia in the pre-Columbian era were the **Tayrona, Quimbaya, Sinú** and **Calima**. Exhibits of theirs and the Chibcha (Muisca) Indians' goldwork can be seen at the Gold Museum in Bogotá and other cities.

Southern Andes Although there was some influence in southern Bolivia, northern Chile and northern Argentina from cultures such as Tiwanaku, most of the southern Andes was an area of autonomous peoples, probably living in fortified settlements by the time the Incas arrived in the mid-15th century. The conquerors from Peru moved south to the Río Maule in Chile where they encountered the fierce **Mapuches** (Araucanians) who halted their advance.

Archaeological evidence from the Amazon basin and Brazil is more scanty than from the Andes or Pacific because the materials used for house building, clothing and decoration were perishable and did not survive the warm, humid conditions of the jungle. Ceramics have been found on Marajó island at the mouth of the Amazon while on the coast much evidence comes from huge shell mounds, called sambaquis. Theories about structured societies and their large populations are being revised as aerial photography and forest clearance in the Upper Amazon and Xingu regions of Brazil reveal huge interconnected earthworks, canals, roads and other indicators of city-building. Moreover, falling river levels have uncovered rock carvings estimated between 3000 and 7000 years old near Manaus. The Incas made few inroads into the Amazon so it was the arrival of the Portuguese in 1500 which initiated the greatest change on the Atlantic side of the continent.

The origins of the Inca Dynasty are shrouded in mythology and shaky evidence. The best known story reported by the Spanish chroniclers talks about Manco Cápac and his sister rising out of Lake Titicaca, created by the sun as divine founders of a chosen race. This was in approximately AD 1200. Over the next 300 years the small tribe grew to supremacy as leaders of the largest empire ever known in the Americas, divided into the four quarters of Tawantinsuyo, all radiating out from Cuzco: Chinchaysuyo, north and northwest; Cuntisuyo, south and west; Collasuyo, south and east; Antisuyo, east.

At its peak, just before the Spanish Conquest, the Inca Empire stretched from the Río Maule in central Chile, north to the present Ecuador-Colombia border, contained most of Ecuador, Peru, west Bolivia, north Chile and northwest Argentina. The area was roughly equivalent to France, Belgium, Holland, Luxembourg, Italy and Switzerland combined, 980,000 sq km. For a brief description of **Inca Society**, see under Cuzco. The first Inca ruler, Manco Cápac, moved to the fertile Cuzco region, and established Cuzco as his capital. Successive generations of rulers were fully occupied with local conquests of rivals, such as the Colla and Lupaca to the south, and the Chanca to the northwest. At the end of Inca Viracocha's reign the hated Chanca were finally defeated, largely thanks to the heroism of one of his sons, Pachacútec (Pachacuti Inca Yupanqui), who was subsequently crowned as the new ruler.

From the start of Pachacútec's own reign in 1438, imperial expansion grew in earnest. With the help of his son and heir, Topa Inca, territory was conquered from the Titicaca basin south into Chile, and all the north and central coast down to the Lurin Valley. In 1460-71, the Incas also laid siege to the Chimú. Typical of the Inca method of government, some of the Chimú skills were assimilated into their own political and administrative system, and some Chimú nobles were even given positions in Cuzco.

Perhaps the pivotal event in Inca history came in 1527 with the death of the ruler, Huayna Cápac. Civil war broke out in the confusion over his rightful successor. One of his legitimate sons, Huáscar, ruled the southern part of the empire from Cuzco. Atahualpa, Huáscar's half-brother, governed Quito, the capital of Chinchaysuyo. In 1532, soon after Atahualpa had won the civil war, Francisco Pizarro arrived in Tumbes with 167 conquistadores, a third of them on horseback. Atahualpa's army was marching south, probably for the first time, when he clashed with Pizarro at Cajamarca. **Francisco Pizarro**'s only chance against the formidable imperial army he encountered at Cajamarca was a bold stroke. He drew Atahualpa into an ambush, slaughtered his guards and many of his troops, promised him liberty if a certain room were filled with treasure, and finally killed him on the pretext that an Inca army was on its way to free him. Pushing on to Cuzco, he was at first hailed as the executioner of a traitor: Atahualpa had ordered the death of Huáscar in 1533, while himself captive of Pizarro, and his victorious generals were bringing the defeated Huáscar to see his half-brother. Panic followed when the conquistadores set about sacking the city, and they fought off with difficulty an attempt by Manco Inca to recapture Cuzco in 1536.

Pizarro's arrival in Peru had been preceded by Columbus' landfall on the Paria Peninsula (Venezuela) on 5 August 1498 and Spanish reconaissance of the Pacific coast in 1522. Permanent Spanish settlement was established at Santa Marta (Colombia) in 1525 and Cartagena was founded in 1533. Gonzalo Jiménez de Quesada conquered the Chibcha kingdom and founded Bogotá in 1538. Pizarro's lieutenant, Sebastián de Belalcázar, was sent north through Ecuador; he captured Quito with Diego de Almagro in 1534. Gonzalo Pizarro, Francisco's brother, took over control of Quito in 1538 and, during his exploration of the Amazon lowlands, he sent Francisco de Orellana to prospect downriver. Orellana did not return, but drifted down the Amazon, finally reaching the river's mouth in 1542, the first European to cross the continent in this way. Belalcázar pushed north, founding Pasto, Cali and Popayán (Colombia) in 1536, arriving in Bogotá in 1538. Meanwhile, wishing to secure his communications with Spain, Pizarro founded Lima, near the ocean, as his capital in 1535. The same year Diego de Almagro set out to conquer Chile. Unsuccessful, he returned to Peru, quarrelled with Pizarro, and in 1538 fought a pitched battle with Pizarro's men at the Salt Pits, near Cuzco. He was defeated and put to death. Pizarro, who had not been at the battle, was assassinated in his palace in Lima by Almagro's son three years later. In 1541, Pedro de Valdivia founded Santiago de Chile after a renewed attempt to conquer Chile. Like the Incas before them, the Spaniards were unable to master the Mapuches; Valdivia was killed in 1553 and a defensive barrier along the Río Biobío had to be built in order to protect the colony.

Since 1516 European seafarers had visited the Río de la Plata, first Juan de Solís, then Sebastian Cabot and his rival Diego García in 1527. An expedition led by Pedro de Mendoza founded Buenos Aires in 1536, but it was abandoned in 1541. Mendoza sent Juan de Ayolas up the Río Paraná to reach Peru from the east. It is not known for certain what happened to Ayolas, but his lieutenant Domingo Martínez de Irala founded Asunción on the Paraguay in 1537. This was the base from which the Spaniards relaunched their conquest of the Río de la Plata and Buenos Aires was refounded in 1580.

PRACTICALITIES

INS AND OUTS

→ BEST TIME TO VISIT PERU

Each of Peru's geographical zones has its own climate. The **coast**: summer (December-April), temperatures 25-35°C; hot and dry; these are the best months for swimming. Winter (May-November); temperature drops and it is cloudy. On the coast, climate is determined by cold seawater adjoining deserts: prevailing inshore winds pick up so little moisture over the cold Peruvian current that only May-November does it condense. The resultant blanket of cloud and sea mist extends from the south to about 200 km north of Lima. This *garúa* dampens isolated coastal zones of vegetation (called *lomas*) and they are grazed by livestock driven down from the mountains. During the *garúa* season, only the northern beaches near Tumbes are warm enough for swimming.

The **Sierra**: April-October is the dry season, hot and dry during the day, around 20-25°C, cold and dry at night, often below freezing. November-April is the wet season, dry and clear most mornings, some rainfall in the afternoon, with average temperatures of 18°C (15°C at night).

Peru's high season is June-September, which is the best time for hiking the Inca trails or trekking and climbing elsewhere in the country. At this time the days are generally clear and sunny, though nights can be very cold at high altitude. The highlands can be visited at other times of the year, though during the wettest months of November-April some roads become impassable and hiking trails can be very muddy.

The **jungle**: April-October, dry season, temperatures up to 35°C. This is the best time to visit the jungle. In the south, a cold front can pass through at night. November-April, wet season, heavy rainfall at any time, humid and hot. During the wet season, it only rains for a few hours at a time, which is not enough to spoil your trip, but enough to make some roads virtually impassable.

→ GETTING TO PERU

AIR

International flights to Peru arrive at Jorge Chávez Airport in Lima. There are a few flights a week to Cuzco from Bolivia, but no other direct flights from outside Peru.

Peak times for flights to Peru are 7 December-15 January and 10 July-10 September. If you intend travelling during those times, book as far ahead as possible. Between February and May and September and November special offers may be available. Most airlines offer discounted fares on scheduled flights through agencies who specialize in this type of fare. If you buy discounted air tickets always check the reservation with the airline concerned to make sure the flight still exists. Also remember the IATA airlines' schedules change in March and October each year. Using the internet for booking flights, hotels and other services directly can give you some good deals. But don't forget that a travel agent can find the best flights to suit your itinerary, as well as providing advice on documents, insurance, safety, routes, lodging and times of year to travel. A reputable agent will also be bonded to give you some protection if things go wrong.

From UK and Europe There are no direct flights to Lima from London. Various options are available with **Iberia**, **LAN** and **Air Europa** from Madrid, **KLM** from Amsterdam and **Air France** from Paris. Alternatively, you can fly to a US hub, then fly the airlines shown below.

From North America Miami is the main gateway to Peru, with frequent services flown by **American Airlines**, **LAN** and **TACA**. LAN also flies from New York and San Francisco. **United Airlines** fly from Newark and Houston, while **Delta** flies from Atlanta and **Spirit Airlines** from Fort Lauderdale. Daily connections can be made from almost all major North American cities. From Toronto and Vancouver, there are no direct flights or connections; fly via one of the above gateways.

From Australia and New Zealand There are no obvious connecting flights from either Australia or New Zealand to Lima. One option would be to go to Buenos Aires from Sydney (three flights a week with **Aerolíneas Argentinas**) and fly on from there (several daily flights). Alternatively, fly to San Francisco and travel down from there with **LAN**.

From Latin America There are regular flights, in many cases daily, to Peru from most South American countries: Argentina: Buenos Aires and Córdoba; Bolivia: La Paz and Santa Cruz; Brazil: Rio de Janeiro, São Paulo, Porto Alegre and Foz do Iguaçu; Chile: Santiago; Colombia: Bogotá, Cali and Medellín (via Quito); Ecuador: Guayaquil and Quito; Uruguay: Montevideo; and Venezuela: Caracas. **LAN** has the widest network, closely followed by **TACA**. From Central America there are regular flights from Mexico City (**Aeroméxico**) and

Cancún, Panama (**Copa**), San José (**LACSA**) and San Salvador. Unless stated otherwise, here again consult **LAN** or **TACA** for flights.

Airport information Jorge Chávez Airport is 16 km from the centre of Lima in the adjacent city of Callao. For arrivals or departures flight information T01-511 6055, www.lap.com.pe.

Information desks can be found in the national and international foyers. There is also a helpful desk in the international arrivals hall. It can make hotel and transport reservations. There are many smart shops, places to eat and drink and mobile phone rentals. ATMs, money changing kiosks and banking facilities can be found in many parts of arrivals and departures. Exchange rates are marginally poorer than outside. There are public telephones around the airport. Internet facilities are more expensive than in the city. Most of the terminal has free Wi-Fi. There are postal services.

Transport from the airport is provided by Remise taxis from desks outside International Arrivals and National Arrivals: **Taxi Green**, T484 4001, www.taxigreen.com.pe; **Mitsu**, T349 7722, www.mitsoo.net; and **CMV**, T422 4838, cmv@exalmar.com.pe. As a rough guide, these companies charge US$20-30 to the centre, US$22-32 to Miraflores and San Isidro, a bit more to Barranco. There are many taxi drivers offering their services outside Arrivals with similar or higher prices (more at night). To get to Miraflores by combi, take the "Callao-Ate" with a big red "S" ("La S"), the only direct link from the airport to Miraflores. Catch it outside the airport, on Avenida Faucett, US$0.50. At any time other than very late at night or early in the morning luggage won't be allowed on public buses. Do not take the cheapest, stopping buses to the centre along Avenida Faucett. They are frequently robbed. Pay more for a non-stop bus, or better still take one of the options above. Do not go to the car park exit to find a taxi outside the perimeter. Although much cheaper than those inside, they are not safe.

→ TRANSPORT IN PERU

Air Carriers serving the major cities are **Star Perú**, T01-705 9000, www.starperu.com, **LAN**, T01-213 8200, www.lan.com, **Taca**, T01-511 8222, www.taca.com, and **Peruvian Airlines**, T01-716 6000, www.peruvianairlines.pe. For destinations such as Andahuaylas, Ayacucho, Cajamarca, Jauja, Huánuco and Huaraz flights are offered by **LC Peru** T01-204 1313, www.lcperu.pe. Flights start at about US$100 one-way anywhere in the country from Lima, but prices vary greatly between airlines, with LAN being the most expensive for non-Peruvians. Prices often increase at holiday times (Semana Santa, May Day, Inti Raymi, 28-29 July, Christmas and New Year), and for elections. During these times and the northern hemisphere summer, seats can be hard to come by, so book early. Flight schedules and departure times often change and delays are common. In the rainy season cancellations occur. Flights into the mountains may well be put forward one hour if there are reports of bad weather. Flights to jungle regions are also unreliable. Always allow an extra day between national and international flights, especially in the rainy season. Internal flight prices are fixed in US dollars (but can be paid in soles) and have 18% tax added. Flights must be reconfirmed at least 24 hours in advance. You can do this online or in the town you will be leaving from. Be at the airport well ahead of your flight.

BUS

Services along the coast to the north and south as well as inland to Huancayo, Ayacucho and Huaraz are generally good, but accidents and hold-ups on buses do occur, especially at night. On long-distance journeys it is advisable to pay a bit extra and take a reliable company, but any bus can break down. All major bus companies operate modern buses with two decks on interdepartmental routes. The first deck is called *bus cama*, the second *semi cama*. Both have seats that recline, *bus cama* further than *semi cama*. These buses usually run late at night and are more expensive than ordinary buses, which tend to run earlier in the day. Many buses have toilets and show movies. Each company has a different name for its regular and *cama* or *ejecutivo* services. **Cruz del Sur** and **Ormeño** are bus lines covering most of the country. **Cruz del Sur**, generally regarded as a class above the others, accepts Visa cards and gives 10% discount to ISIC and Under26 cardholders (you may have to insist). There are many smaller but still excellent bus lines that run only to specific areas. An increasing number accept internet bookings and you may find good deals on the websites. Some bus terminals charge a usage fee of about US$0.50 which you pay at a kiosk before boarding. Many also charge for the toilet, about US$0.35 with paper and US$0.25 without. Take a blanket or warm jacket when travelling in the mountains. Where buses stop it is possible to buy food on the roadside. With the better companies you will get a receipt for your luggage, which will be locked under the bus. On local buses watch your luggage and never leave valuables on the luggage rack or floor, even when on the move. If your bus breaks down and you are transferred to another line and have to pay extra, keep your original ticket for refund from the first company.

Combis operate between most small towns on one- to three-hour journeys. This makes it possible, in many cases, just to turn up and travel within an hour or two. Combis can be minibuses of varying age and comfort, or slightly more expensive, faster but often overfilled car *colectivos*, called *autos*, or *cars*. These usually charge twice the bus fare. They leave only when full. They go almost anywhere in Peru; most firms have offices. Book one day in advance and they pick you up at your hotel or in the main plaza.

Note Prices of bus tickets are raised by 60-100%, two or three days before Semana Santa, 28 July (Independence Day – Fiestas Patrias), Christmas and special local events. Tickets are sold out two or three days in advance at this time and transport is hard to come by.

Cruz del Sur (T01-311 5050, telephone sales, www.cruzdelsur.com.pe) has its main terminal at Avenida Javier Prado 1109, La Victoria, T01-225 6163, with *Cruzero* and *Cruzero Suite* services (luxury buses) and *Imperial* service (quite comfortable buses and periodic stops for food and bathroom breaks, a cheap option with a quality company) to most parts of Peru. Another terminal is at Jirón Quilca 531, Lima centre, T01-431 5125, for *Imperial* and *Ideal* (economy) services to Arequipa, Ayacucho, Chiclayo, Cuzco, Huancayo, Huaraz, and Trujillo. There are sales offices throughout the city.

Ormeño and its affiliated bus companies depart from and arrive at Avenida Carlos Zavala 177, Lima centre (T01-427 5679); also Avenida Javier Prado Este 1059, Santa Catalina (T01-472 1710, www.grupo-ormeno.com.pe). **Ormeño** offers *Royal Class* and *Business Class* service to certain destinations. These buses are very comfortable with toilet, hostess, etc. They arrive and depart from the Javier Prado terminal, but the Carlos Zavala terminal is the best place to get information and buy any Ormeño ticket. **Cial**, República de Panamá 2469 (T01-265 8121) and Paseo de la República 646 (T01-717 8322,

www.expresocial.com), has national coverage. **Flores**, with terminals at Avenida Paseo de
le República y Avenida 28 de Julio, Avenida Paseo de la República 627 (T01-423 6069),
and Avenida 28 de Julio 1204 y J Gálvez (T01-332 1212), has departures to many parts of
the country, especially the south. Some of its services are good quality.

Other companies include: **Oltursa**, Aramburú 1160, San Isidro (T01-708 5000, www.
oltursa.pe), a reputable company offering top-end services to Nazca, Arequipa and
destinations in Northern Peru, mainly at night. **Tepsa**, Javier Prado Este 1091, La Victoria,
T01-202 3535 (www.tepsa.com.pe), also at Avenida Paseo de la República 151-A (T01-
427 5642) and Avenida Carlos Izaguirre 1400, Los Olivos (T01-386 5689; not far from the
airport), good for those short of time for a bus connection after landing in Lima). Services
to the north and the south.

Línea, Paseo de la República 959, Lima Centre (T01-424 0836, www.transporteslinea.
com.pe), also has a terminal at Avenida Carlos Izaguirre 1058, Los Olivos (see above
under Tepsa, above, T01-522 3295) and is among the best services to destinations in
the north. **Móvil**, Avenida Paseo de La República 749, Lima Centre near the national
stadium (T01-716 8000, www.moviltours.com.pe), has a 2nd terminal at Los Olivos, and
offers services to Huaraz and Chiclayo by *bus cama*, and to Chachapoyas. **Soyuz**, Avenida
México 333 (T01-205 2380, www.soyuz.com.pe) is well organized and provides services
to Ica every seven minutes. **Cromotex**, Avenida Nicolás Arriola 898, Santa Catalina,
and Avenida Paseo de La República 659 (T01-424 7575, www.cromotex.com.pe), run
services to Cuzco and to Arequipa.

HITCHHIKING

Hitchhiking is difficult. Freight traffic has to stop at the police *garitas* outside each town
and these are the best places to try (also toll points, but these are further from towns).
Drivers usually ask for money but don't always expect to get it. In mountain and jungle
areas you usually have to pay drivers of lorries, vans and even private cars; ask the driver
first how much he is going to charge, and then recheck with the locals. Private cars are
few and far between.

TAXI

Taxi prices are fixed in the mountain towns, about US$1-1.50 in the urban area. Fares are
not fixed in Lima although some drivers work for companies that do have standard fares.
Ask locals what the price should be and always set the price beforehand; expect to pay
US$3-5 in the capital. The main cities have taxis that can be hired by phone, which charge
a little more, but are reliable and safe. Many taxi drivers work for commission from hotels.
Choose your own hotel and get a driver who is willing to take you. Taxis at airports are
more expensive; seek advice about the price in advance. In some places it is cheaper to
walk out of the airport to the main road and flag down a cab. Another common form of
public transport is the mototaxi, a three-wheel motorcycle with an awning covering the
double seat behind the driver. Fares are about US$1.

TRAIN

The main railway passenger services are Cuzco to Machu Picchu, Cuzco–Juliaca–Puno
and Lima–Huancayo. Cuzco to Machu Picchu trains are run by two companies, PerúRail
(www.perurail.com) and Inca Rail (www.incarail.com). Schedules change frequently

and can be found on each company's website, as can their prices. PerúRail also runs the services from Cuzco to Puno on Lake Titicaca; trains run three to four times a week. Consult the website for exact schedules and prices. Trains from Lima to Huancayo are run by Ferrocarril Centro Andino, Avenida José Galvez Barrenechea 566, piso 5, San Isidro, Lima (T01-226 6363, www.ferrocarrilcentral.com.pe). The tourist service operates only at certain weekends, which are announced in advance (check website). The journey takes 11 hours.

MAPS

The Instituto Geográfico Nacional ① *Av Aramburú 1190, Surquillo, Lima, T01-618 9800, ext 119, www.ign.gob.pe; open Mon-Fri 0800-1730*, sells a selection of maps. Another official site is Ministerio de Transporte, Jr Zorritos 1203, Lima centre, T01-615 7800, www.mtc.gob.pe. Lima 2000's *Mapa Vial del Perú* (1:2,200,000) is probably the most correct road map available. Maps can also be obtained from South American Explorers (see page 37). The Touring y Automóvil Club del Perú ① *Av Trinidad Morán 689, Lince, Lima, T615 9315, www.touringperu.com.pe*, with offices in most provincial cities, gives news about roads and hotels (also try bus/colectivo offices). It sells three Hojas de Ruta, *North, Center* and *South*, US$1.50 each (available as pdf on website).

A good tourist map of the Callejón de Huaylas and Cordillera Huayhuash, by Felipe Díaz, is available in many shops in Huaraz, including Casa de Guías. Alpenvereinskarte Cordillera Blanca Nord 0/3a and Alpenvereinskarte Cordillera Blanca Süd 0/3b at 1:100,000 are the best maps of that region, US$24, available in Huaraz and Lima, but best bought outside Peru. Cordillera Huayhuash map, 1:50,000 (The Alpine Mapping Guild, 2nd ed, 2004) is recommended, available in Huaraz at Café Andino, US$15.

→ WHERE TO STAY IN PERU

HOTELS

All deluxe and first class hotels charge 18% in state sales tax (IGV) and 10% service charges. Foreigners should not have to pay the sales tax on hotel rooms. Neither is given in the accommodation listings, unless specified. By law all places that offer accommodation now have a plaque outside bearing the letters H (Hotel), Hs (Hostal), HR (Hotel Residencial) or P (Pensión) according to type. A hotel has 51 rooms or more, a *hostal* 50 or fewer; the categories do not describe quality or facilities. Many hotels have safe parking for motor cycles. All hotels seem to be crowded during Christmas and Easter holidays, Carnival and at the end of July; Cuzco in June is also very busy. iPeru advises that all accommodations registered with them are now listed on their website: www.peru.travel.

→ FOOD AND DRINK IN PERU

RESTAURANTS IN PERU

A normal lunch or dinner costs US$5-8, but can go up to about US$80 in a first-class restaurant, with drinks and wine. Middle and high-class restaurants may add 10% service, but not include the 18% sales tax in the bill (which foreigners do have to pay); this is not shown on the price list or menu, check in advance. Lower class restaurants charge only tax, while cheap, local restaurants charge no taxes. Lunch is the main meal and most restaurants serve one or two set lunch menus, called *menú ejecutivo* or *menú económico* (US$1.50-2.50). The set menu has the advantage of being served almost immediately and it is usually cheap. The *menú ejecutivo* costs US$2 or more for a three-course meal with

PRICE CODES

WHERE TO STAY

$$$$	over US$150	**$$$**	US$66-150
$$	US$30-65	**$**	under US$30

Price of a double room in high season, including taxes.

RESTAURANTS

$$$ over US$12	**$$** US$7-12	**$** under US$7

Price for a two-course meal for one person, excluding drinks or service charge.

a soft drink and it offers greater choice and more interesting dishes. Chinese restaurants (*chifas*) serve good food at reasonable prices.

PERUVIAN CUISINE

The best **coastal** dishes are seafood based, the most popular being *ceviche*. This is a dish of raw white fish marinated in lemon juice, onion and hot peppers. Traditionally, *ceviche* is served with corn-on-the-cob, *cancha* (toasted corn), yucca and sweet potatoes. *Tiradito* is *ceviche* without onions made with plaice. Another mouth-watering fish dish is *escabeche* – fish with onions, hot green pepper, red peppers, prawns (*langostinos*), cumin, hard-boiled eggs, olives, and sprinkled with cheese (it can also be made with chicken). For fish on its own, don't miss the excellent *corvina*, or white sea bass. You should also try *chupe de camarones*, which is a shrimp stew made with varying ingredients. Other fish dishes include *parihuela*, a popular bouillabaisse which includes *yuyo de mar*, a tangy seaweed, and *aguadito*, a thick rice and fish soup said to have rejuvenating powers. A favourite northern coastal dish is *seco de cabrito*, roasted kid (baby goat) served with the ubiquitous beans and rice, or *seco de cordero* which uses lamb instead. Also good is *aji de gallina*, a rich and spicy creamed chicken, and duck is excellent. *Humitas* are small, stuffed dumplings made with maize. The *criollo* cooking of the coast has a strong tradition and can be found throughout the country. A dish almost guaranteed to appear on every restaurant menu is *lomo saltado*, a kind of stir-fried beef with onions, vinegar, ginger, chilli, tomatoes and fried potatoes, served with rice. Other popular examples are *cau cau*, made with tripe, potatoes, peppers, and parsley and served with rice, and *anticuchos*, which are shish kebabs of beef heart with garlic, peppers, cumin seeds and vinegar. *Rocoto relleno* is spicy bell pepper stuffed with beef and vegetables, *palta rellena* is avocado filled with chicken or Russian salad, *estofado de carne* is a stew that often contains wine, and *carne en adobo* is a cut and seasoned steak. Two good dishes that use potatoes are *causa* and *carapulca*. On coastal menus *causa* is made with mashed potato wrapped around a filling, which often contains crabmeat. On other occasions, *causa* has yellow potatoes, lemons, pepper, hard-boiled eggs, olives, lettuce, sweet cooked corn, sweet cooked potato, fresh cheese, and is served with onion sauce.

The staples of **highland** cooking, corn and potatoes, come in a variety of shapes, sizes and colours. A popular potato dish is *papa a la huancaína*, which is topped with a spicy sauce made with milk and cheese. The most commonly eaten corn dishes are *choclo con queso,* corn on the cob with cheese, and *tamales,* boiled corn dumplings filled with meat and wrapped in a banana leaf. Most typical of highland food is *pachamanca*, a combination of meats (beef, lamb, pork, chicken), potatoes, sweet potatoes, corn, beans, cheese and corn humitas, all slow-cooked in the ground, dating back to Inca times.

The main ingredient in jungle cuisine is fish, especially the succulent, dolphin-sized *paiche*, which comes with the delicious *palmito*, or palm-hearts, and yucca and fried bananas. *Tocacho* is green banana, cooked and ground to a chunky paste, usually served with pork (*cecina*) and sausage (*chorizo*). *Juanes* are a jungle version of tamales, stuffed with chicken and rice.

Meat dishes are many and varied. *Ollucos con charqui* is a kind of potato with dried meat, *sancochado* is meat and all kinds of vegetables stewed together and seasoned with ground garlic and *lomo a la huancaína* is beef with egg and cheese sauce. Others include *fritos*, fried pork, usually eaten in the morning, *chicharrones*, deep fried chunks of pork ribs and chicken or fish, and *lechón*, suckling pig. A delicacy in the highlands is *cuy*, guinea pig. Very filling and good value are the many soups on offer, such as *caldos* (broths): eg *de carnero*, *verde*, or *de cabeza*, which includes a sheep's head cooked with corn and tripe. Also *yacu-chupe*, a green soup made from potato, with cheese, garlic, coriander, parsley, peppers, eggs, onions, and mint, *and sopa a la criolla* containing thin noodles, beef heart, egg, vegetables and pleasantly spiced.

Peruvian fruits are of good quality: they include bananas, the citrus fruits, pineapples, dates, avocados (*paltas*), eggfruit (*lúcuma*), custard apple (*chirimoya*) which can be as big as your head, quince, papaya, mango, guava, passion-fruit (*maracuyá*), prickly pear (*tuna*) and the soursop (*guanábana*).

DRINK

The most famous local drink is *pisco*, a clear brandy which, with egg whites and lime juice, makes the famous pisco sour. The most renowned brands come from the Ica Valley. The best wines are also from Ica, *Tabernero*, *Tacama* (especially its Selección Especial and Terroix labels), *Ocucaje* and *Santiago Queirolo* (in particular its Intipalka label). Beer is of the lager type, the best known brands being *Cusqueña* and *Arequipeña* brands (lager) and *Trujillo Malta* (porter). In Lima only *Cristal* and *Pilsen* are readily available. Other brands, including some Brazilian beers, are coming onto the market, but there is little difference between any of them. Seek out the microbreweries that are springing up, eg in Huaraz. *Chicha de jora* is a maize beer, usually home-made and not easy to come by, refreshing but strong, and *chicha morada* is a soft drink made with purple maize. The local rival to Coca Cola, the fluorescent yellow *Inca Cola*, is made from lemongrass. Peruvian coffee is good, but the best is exported and many cafés only serve coffee in liquid form or Nescafé. There are many different kinds of herb tea: the commonest are *manzanilla* (camomile) and *hierbaluisa* (lemon grass). *Mate de coca* is frequently served in the highlands to stave off the discomforts of altitude sickness.

ESSENTIALS A-Z

Accident and emergency

Emergency medical attention (Cruz Roja) T115. **Fire** T116. **Police** T105, www.pnp. gob.pe (Policía Nacional del Perú), for police emergencies nationwide. **Tourist Police**, Jr Moore 268, Magdalena, 38th block of Av Brasil, Lima, T01-460 1060/0844, daily 24 hrs, dirtur.ceopol@pnp.gob.pe. They are friendly, helpful and speak English and some German.

Electricity

220 volts AC, 60 cycles throughout the country, except Arequipa (50 cycles). Most 4- and 5-star hotels have 110 volts AC. Plugs are American flat-pin or twin flat and round pin combined.

Embassies and consulates

For all Peru embassies and consulates abroad and for all foreign embassies and consulates in Peru, see www.embassy.goabroad.com. **Note** Most businesses close for the official holidays but supermarkets and street markets may be open. Sometimes holidays that fall mid-week will be moved to the following Mon. The high season for foreign tourism in Peru is Jun-Sep while national tourism peaks at Christmas, Semana Santa and Fiestas Patrias. Prices rise and rooms and bus tickets are harder to come by.

Money ➔ *US$1 = S/2.84; 1€ = S/3.80 (Aug 2013).*

Currency The new sol (s/) is divided into 100 céntimos. Notes in circulation are: S/200, S/100, S/50, S/20 and S/10. Coins: S/5, S/2, S/1, S/0.50, S/0.20, S/0.10 and S/0.05 (being phased out). Some prices are quoted in dollars (US$) in more expensive establishments, to avoid changes in the value of the sol. You can pay in soles, however.

Festivals

Two of the major festival dates are **Carnaval**, which is held over the weekend before Ash Wed, and **Semana Santa** (Holy Week), which ends on Easter Sun. Carnival is celebrated in most of the Andes and Semana Santa throughout Peru. Another important festival is **Fiesta de la Cruz**, held on 1 May in much of the central and southern highlands and on the coast. In Cuzco, the entire month of Jun is one huge *fiesta*, culminating in **Inti Raymi**, on 24 Jun, one of Peru's prime tourist attractions. Another national festival is **Todos los Santos** (All Saints) on 1 Nov, and on 8 Dec is **Festividad de la Inmaculada Concepción**. A full list of local festivals is listed under each town. Apart from those listed above, the main holidays are: 1 Jan, New Year; 6 Jan, **Bajada de Reyes**; 1 May, Labour Day; 28-29 July, Independence (Fiestas Patrias); 7 Oct, Battle of Angamos; 24-25 Dec, Christmas.

Warning Forged US$ notes and forged soles notes and coins are in circulation. Always check your money when you change it, even in a bank (including ATMs). Hold sol notes up to the light to inspect the watermark and that the colours change according to the light. The line down the side of the bill spelling out the bill's amount should appear green, blue and pink. Fake bills are only pink and have no hologram properties. There should also be tiny pieces of thread in the paper (not glued on). In parts of the country, forged 1-, 2- and 5-sol coins are in circulation. The fakes are slightly off-colour, the surface copper can be scratched off and they tend to bear a recent date. Posters in public places explain what to look for in forged soles. See also www.bcrp.gob.pe, under **Billetes y Monedas**. Try to break down large notes whenever you can as there is a shortage of change in museums, post offices, even shops. Taxi drivers are notorious in this regard – one is simply told 'no change'. Do not accept this excuse.

Credit cards, ATMs and banks Visa (by far the most widely accepted card in Peru), MasterCard, American Express and Diners Club are all valid. There is often an 8-12% commission for all credit card charges. Bank exchange policies vary from town to town, but as a general rule the following applies (but don't be surprised if a branch has different rules): **BCP** (Mon-Fri 0900-1800, Sat 0900-1300) changes US$ cash to soles; cash advances on Visa in soles only; VíaBCP ATM with US$2 surcharge for Visa/Plus, MasterCard/Cirrus, Amex. **BBVA Continental** changes US$ cash to soles, some branches change TCs at US$12 commission; B24 ATM for Visa/Plus has US$5 charge. **Interbank** (Mon-Fri 0900-1815, Sat 0900-1230) changes US$ cash and TCs to soles, TCs to US$ cash for US$5 per transaction up to US$500; branches have **Global Net** ATMs (see below). **Scotiabank** (Mon-Fri 0915-1800, Sat 0915-1230) changes US$ cash to soles, cash advances on MasterCard; ATM for Visa, MasterCard, Maestro and Cirrus; charges US$3.50 per cheque to change TCs. There are also **Global Net** and **Red Unicard** ATMs that accept Visa, Plus and MasterCard, Maestro and Cirrus (the former makes a charge per transaction). ATMs usually have a maximum withdrawal limit of between US$140 and US$200. It is safest to use ATMs during banking hours. At night and on Sun there is more chance of the transaction going wrong, or false money being in the machine. ATMs usually give US$ if you don't request soles and their use is widespread. Availability decreases outside large towns. In smaller towns, take some cash. Businesses displaying credit card symbols, on the other hand, are less likely to take foreign cards.

All banks' exchange rates are considerably less favourable than *casas de cambio* (exchange houses). Long queues and paperwork may be involved. US$ and euros are the only currencies which should be brought into Peru from abroad (take some small bills). There are no restrictions on foreign exchange. Few banks change euros. Some banks demand to see 2 documents with your signature for changing cash. Always count your money in the presence of the cashier. A repeatedly recommended *casa de cambio* is **LAC Dolar**, Jr Camaná 779, 1 block from Plaza San Martín, p 2, T01-428 8127, also at Av La Paz 211, Miraflores, T01-242 4069. Open Mon-Sat 1000-1800, good rates, very helpful, safe, fast, reliable, 2% commission on cash and TCs, will come to your hotel if you're in a group. Another recommended *casa de cambio* is **Virgen P Socorro**, Jr Ocoña 184, T01-428 7748. Open daily 0830-2000, safe, reliable and friendly. In Lima, there are many *casas de cambio* on and around Jr Ocoña off the Plaza San Martín. In 2013 there was no real advantage in changing money on the street, but should you choose to do so, it does avoid paperwork and queuing. Use only official street changers, such as those around Parque Kennedy and down Av Larco in Miraflores (Lima). They carry ID cards and wear a green vest. Check your soles before handing over your US$ or euros, check their calculators, etc, and don't change money in crowded areas. If using their services think about taking a taxi after changing, to avoid being followed. **Moneygram**, Ocharan 260, Miraflores, T01-447 4044. Safe and reliable agency for sending and receiving money. Locations throughout Lima and the provinces. Exchanges most world currencies and TCs. Soles can be exchanged into US$ at the exchange desks at Lima airport, and you can change soles for US$ at any border. US$ can also be bought at the various borders.

Note No one, not even banks, will accept US$ bills that look 'old', damaged or torn.

Cost of travelling The average budget is US$45-60 per person a day for living fairly comfortably, including transport. Your budget will be higher the longer you stay in Lima and Cuzco and depending on how many internal flights you take. Rooms range from US$7-11 per person for the most basic *alojamiento* to US$20-40 for mid-range places, to over US$90 for more upmarket hotels (more in Lima or Cuzco). Living costs in the provinces are 20-50% below those in Lima and Cuzco. The cost of using the internet is generally US$0.60-1 per hr, but where competition is not fierce, rates vary from US$1.50 to US$4.

Students can obtain very few reductions in Peru with an international students' card, except in and around Cuzco. To be any use in Peru, it must bear the owner's photograph. An ISIC card can be obtained in Lima from **Intej**, Av San Martín 240, Barranco, T01-247 3230; also Portal de Panes 123, of 304, Cuzco, T084-256367; Santo Domingo 123, of 401, Arequipa, T054-284756; C José Sabogal 913, Cajamarca, T076-362522; Av Mariscal Castilla 3909-4089, El Tambo, 7o piso del Edificio de Administración y Gobierno de la UNCP, anexo 6056, Huancayo, T064-481081, www.intej.org.

Opening hours
Shops: 0900 or 1000-1230 and 1500 or 1600-2000. In the main cities, supermarkets do not close for lunch and Lima has some that are open 24 hrs. Some are closed on Sat and most are closed on Sun. **Banks**: see under Money, above. Outside Lima and Cuzco banks may close 1200-1500 for lunch. **Offices**: 0900-1700; most close on Sat. **Government offices**: Jan-Mar Mon-Fri 0830-1130; Apr-Dec Mon-Fri 0900-1230, 1500-1700, but these hours change frequently.

Postal services
The central Lima post office is on Jr Camaná 195 near the Plaza de Armas. Mon-Fri 0730-1900, Sat 0730-1600. Poste Restante is in the same building but is considered unreliable. In Miraflores the main post office is on Av Petit Thouars 5201 (same hours). There are many small branches around Lima and in the rest of the country, but they are less reliable. For express service: **EMS**, next to central post office in downtown Lima, T01-533 2020.

Safety
The following notes on personal safety should not hide the fact that most Peruvians are hospitable and helpful. In provincial towns, main places of interest, on daytime buses and in ordinary restaurants the visitor should be quite safe. Nevertheless, crime exists, most of which is opportunistic. If you are aware of the dangers, act confidently and use your common sense, you will lessen many of the risks.

Keep all documents secure; hide your main cash supply in different places or under your clothes. Be extra vigilant when withdrawing cash from an ATM: ensure you are not being watched; never give your card to anyone, however smart he may look or plausible he may sound as a 'bank employee' wishing to swipe your card to check for problems.

When you have all your luggage with you, be careful. From airports take official taxis or special airport buses. Take a taxi between bus/railway station and hotel. Keep your bags with you in the taxi and pay only when you and your luggage are safely out of the vehicle. Make sure the taxi has inner door handles and do not share the ride with a stranger. If possible, avoid night buses; never arrive at night; and watch your belongings whether they are stowed inside or outside the cabin. Major bus lines often issue a luggage ticket when bags are stored in the hold of the bus. You should always be vigilant in bus stations and other crowded places, such as markets.

Leave any valuables you don't need in safe-deposit in your hotel when sightseeing locally. Always keep an inventory of what you have deposited. If there is no safe, lock your bags and secure them in your room. Hostels with shared rooms should provide secure, clean lockers for guests. If you lose valuables, always report to the police and note details of the report – for insurance purposes.

Genuine police officers only have the right to see your passport (not your money, tickets or hotel room). Before handing anything over, ask why they need to see it and make sure you understand the reason. Insist on seeing identification and on going to the police station by main roads. On no account take them directly back to your lodgings. Be even more suspicious if someone seeks confirmation of his status from a passer-by.

Drugs and other substances Although certain illegal drugs are readily available, anyone carrying drugs is almost automatically assumed to be a trafficker. If arrested on any charge the wait for trial in prison can take a year and is particularly unpleasant. If you are asked by the narcotics police to go to the toilets to have your bags searched, insist on taking a witness. Drug use or purchase is punishable by up to 15 years' imprisonment.

Many places in the Amazon and in Cuzco offer experiences with Ayahuasca or San Pedro, often in ceremonies with a shaman. These are legal, but always choose a reputable tour operator or shaman. Do not go with the first person who offers you a trip. Single women should not take part. There are plenty of websites for starting your research.

In Cuzco many clubs and bars offer coupons for free entry and a free drink. The drinks are made with the cheapest, least healthy alcohol; always watch your drink being made and never leave it unattended.

Never accept food, drink, sweets or cigarettes from unknown fellow travellers on buses. They may be drugged, and you would wake up hours later without your belongings.

Insurgency Indications are that Sendero Luminoso and MRTA remain active in scattered parts of the country and to a limited degree. In the first half of 2013 there were no reports of threats to those parts of Peru of tourist interest, but it is important to be aware of the latest situation.

For up-to-date information contact the Tourist Police (see Accident and emergency, page 188), your embassy or consulate, fellow travellers, or South American Explorers (see page 37). You can also contact the Tourist Protection Bureau (Indecopi). As well as handling complaints, they will help if you have lost, or had stolen, documents.

Tax
Airport taxes US$31 on international flight departures; US$9.40 on internal flights (when making a domestic connection in Lima, you don't have to pay airport tax; contact airline personnel at baggage claim to be escorted to your departure gate). Regional airports have lower departure taxes. Both international and domestic airport taxes should be included in the price of flight tickets, not paid at the airport. 18% state tax is charged on air tickets; it is included in the price of the ticket. Note: in March 2013 the airport authorities proposed the application of the US$31 airport tax to in-transit passengers.
VAT/IGV/IVA 18%.

Telephone → *Country code+51.*
Easiest to use are the independent phone offices, *locutorios*, all over Lima and other cities. They take phone cards, which can

be bought in *locutorios*, or in the street nearby. There are payphones throughout the country. Some accept coins, some only phone cards and some take both.

The numbering system for digital phones is as follows: for Lima mobiles, add 9 before the number, for the departments of La Libertad 94, Arequipa 95, Piura 96, Lambayeque 97; for other departments, add 9 – if not already in the number – and the city code (for example, Cuzco numbers start 984). Note also that some towns are dominated by Claró, others by Movistar (the 2 main mobile companies). As it is expensive to call between the two you should check, if spending some time in one city and using a mobile, which is the best account to have.

Red Privada Movistar (RPM) and **Red Privada Claró** (RPC) are operated by the respective mobile phone companies. Mobile phone users who subscribe to these services obtain a 6-digit number in addition their 9-digit mobile phone number. Both the 6- and 9-digit numbers ring on the same physical phone. The RPM and RPC numbers can be called from anywhere in Peru without using an area code, you just dial the 6 digits, and the cost is about 20% of calling the 9-digit number. This 80% discount usually also applies when calling from *locutorios*. Many establishments including hotels, tour operators and transport companies have both RPM and RPC numbers.

Time
GMT -5.

Tipping
Restaurants: service is included in the bill, but tips can be given directly to the waiter for exceptional service. Taxi drivers: none (bargain the price down, then pay extra for good service). Cloakroom attendants and hairdressers (very high class only): US$0.50-1. Porters: US$0.50. Car wash boys: US$0.30. Car 'watch' boys: US$0.20. If going on a trek or tour, it is customary to tip the guide as well as the cook and porters.

Tourist information
Tourism promotion and information is handled by **PromPerú**, Edif Mincetur, C Uno Oeste 50, p 13 y 14, urb Córpac, San Isidro, T01-616 7400, www.promperu.gob.pe. See also www.peru.travel. PromPerú runs an information and assistance service, **i perú**, T01-574 8000 (24 hrs). Main office: Jorge Basadre 610, San Isidro, Lima, T01-421 1627, iperulima@promperu.gob.pe, Mon-Fri 0830-1830. Also a 24-hr office at Jorge Chávez Airport; and throughout the country.

There are tourist offices in most towns, either run by the municipality, or independently. Outside Peru, information can be obtained from Peruvian embassies/consulates. **Indecopi**, T224 7800 (in Lima), www.indecopi.gob.pe, is the government-run consumer protection and tourist complaint bureau. They are friendly,

professional and helpful. An excellent source of information is **South American Explorers**, in Lima (see page 37) and Cuzco (see page 52). They have information on travellers held in prison, some for up to 1 year without sentencing, and details on visiting regulations. A visit will be really appreciated!

Useful websites
www.minam.gob.pe Ministerio del Ambiente (Spanish).
www.terra.com.pe TV, entertainment and news (in Spanish).
www.livinginperu.com Informative guide in English for people living in Peru.
www.leaplocal.org Recommends good quality guides, helping communities benefit from socially responsible tourism.
www.caretas.com.pe The most widely read weekly magazine, *Caretas*.
www.peruviantimes.com
The Andean Air Mail & Peruvian Times internet news magazine.

Visas and immigration
Tourist cards No visa is necessary for citizens of EU countries, most Asian countries, North and South America, and the Caribbean, or for citizens of Andorra, Belarus, Bulgaria, Croatia, Estonia, Finland, Iceland, Israel, Liechtenstein, Lithuania, Macedonia, Moldova, Norway, Russian Federation, Serbia and Montenegro, Switzerland, Ukraine, Australia, New Zealand and South Africa. A Tourist Card (TAM – Tarjeta Andina de Migración) is free on flights arriving in Peru, or at border crossings for visits up to 183 days. The form is in duplicate, the original given up on arrival and the copy on departure. A new tourist card must be obtained for each re-entry. If your tourist card is stolen or lost, get a new one from **Migraciones**, Digemin, Av España 730, Breña, Lima, T01-417 6900/433 0731, www.digemin.gob.pe, Mon-Fri 0800-1300.

Tourist visas For citizens of countries not listed above (including Turkey), visas

cost US$32.50 or equivalent, for which you require a valid passport, a departure ticket from Peru (or a letter of guarantee from a travel agency), 2 colour passport photos, 1 application form and proof of economic solvency. Tourist visas are valid for 183 days. In the first instance, visit the Migraciones website (as above) for visa forms.

Keep ID, preferably a passport, on you at all times. You must present your passport when reserving travel tickets. To avoid having to show your passport, photocopy the important pages of your passport – including the immigration stamp, and have it legalized by a 'Notario público'. We have received no reports of travellers being asked for onward tickets at the borders at Tacna, Aguas Verdes, La Tina, Yunguyo or Desaguadero. Travellers are not asked to show an onward flight ticket at Lima airport, but you will not be able to board a plane in your home country without one.

Under Decree 1043 of Jun 2008, once in Peru tourists may not extend their tourist card or visa. It's therefore important to insist on getting the full number of days to cover your visit on arrival (it's at the discretion of the border official). If you exceed your limit, you'll pay a US$1-per-day fine.

Business visas If receiving money from Peruvian sources, visitors must have a business visa: requirements are a valid passport, 2 colour passport photos, return ticket and a letter from an employer or Chamber of Commerce stating the nature of business, length of stay and guarantee that any Peruvian taxes will be paid. The visa costs US$40 (or equivalent) and allows the holder to stay 183 days in the country. On arrival business visitors must register with the Dirección General de Contribuciones for tax purposes.

Student visas These must be requested from Migraciones (address above) once you are in Peru. In addition to completing the general visa form you must have proof of adequate funds, affiliation to a Peruvian body, a letter of consent from parents or tutors if you are a minor. The cost is US$40. Full details are on the Digemin website (in Spanish).

If you wish to change a tourist visa into another type of visa (business, student, resident, etc), you may do so without leaving Peru. Visit Migraciones and obtain the relevant forms.

Weights and measures
Metric.

INDEX

NOTES

NOTES

NOTES

CREDITS

Footprint credits
Editor: Felicity Laughton
Production and layout: Emma Bryers
Maps: Kevin Feeney
Cover: Pepi Bluck

Publisher: Patrick Dawson
Advertising: Elizabeth Taylor
Sales and marketing: Kirsty Holmes

Footprint DREAM TRIP Peru
1st edition
© Footprint Handbooks Ltd
September 2013

ISBN: 978 1 907263 73 6
CIP DATA: A catalogue record for this book
is available from the British Library

® Footprint Handbooks and the Footprint
mark are a registered trademark of
Footprint Handbooks Ltd

Published by Footprint
6 Riverside Court
Lower Bristol Road
Bath BA2 3DZ, UK
T +44 (0)1225 469141
F +44 (0)1225 469461
footprinttravelguides.com

Printed in Spain by GraphyCems

Photography credits
Front cover: Markus Friedrich/Age Fotostock.com
Back cover: Mariusz S. Jurgielewicz/Shutterstock.
com; naD photos/Shutterstock.com; Joel Shawn/
Shutterstock.com
Front cover flap: Joel Shawn/Shutterstock.com;
Ralf Broskvar/Shutterstock.com;
Rafał Cichawa/Shutterstock.com;
Ksenia Ragozina/Shutterstock.com
Colour pages: Photo Chris/Dreamstime.com p1; Harald
Toepfer/Shutterstock.com p2; Jacek Kadaj/Shutterstock.
com p2; Pavalache Stelian/Dreamstime.com p3; Rafael
Martin-Gaitero/Shutterstock.com p3; Christopher Kolaczan/
Shutterstock.com p4; Gary Yim/Shutterstock.com p6;
Wideweb/Shutterstock.com p6; Anton Ivanov/Shutterstock.
com p7; Vilaine Crevette/Dreamstime.com p7; Alexander
Ryabintsev/Shutterstock.com p8; Joel Shawn/Shutterstock.
com p9; Chris Howey/Shutterstock.com p9; tr3gin/
Shutterstock.com p9; worldswildlifewonders/Shutterstock.
com p10; agap/Shutterstock.com p10; Shootsphoto/
Dreamstime.com p10; MP cz/Shutterstock.com p11;
Biosphot/SuperStock.com p11; Toni Salado/Shutterstock.
com p12; Gary Yim/Shutterstock.com p14; Pablo Hidalgo/
Shutterstock.com p15; Paul Clarke/Shutterstock.com
p15; Yaromir/Shutterstock.com p15; Jarno Gonzalez
Zarraonandia/Shutterstock.com p16; Jarous/Shutterstock.
com p16; tr3gin/Shutterstock.com p17; Curioso/
Shutterstock.com p17; Tomaz Kunst/Shutterstock.com
p18; njaj/Shutterstock.com p19; Chris Howey/Shutterstock.
com p19; Rechitan Sorin/Shutterstock.com p20; Itay.G/
Shutterstock.com p21; Jaroslava V/Shutterstock.com p21;
Michael Zysman/Shutterstock.com p21; Michael Zysman/
Shutterstock.com p22; Christopher Howey/Dreamstime.
com p22; Luis Carlos Torres/Shutterstock.com p23; R. Gino
Santa Maria/Shutterstock.com p23; ShutteHUGHES Herv/
Hemis.fr/SuperStock.com p23; Rechitan Sorin/Shutterstock.
com p25; /Shutterstock.com p26; Juan Jose Gabaldon
Alarcon/Dreamstime.com p27; Yolka/Shutterstock.com
p27; Dirk Ercken/Shutterstock.com p28; Lukasz Janyst/
Shutterstock.com p28; Eric Gevaert/Shutterstock.com p29;
Dr. Morley Read/Shutterstock.com p29; Rafal Cichawa/
Shutterstock.com p30; Joan Egert/Dreamstime.com p30;
Juan Manuel Borrero/SuperStock.com p31; Jarno Gonzalez
Zarraonandia/Shutterstock.com p32.